CHESS
FOR EVERYONE

KNACK

CHESS FOR EVERYONE

A Step-by-Step Guide to Rules, Moves, & Winning Strategies

Al Lawrence

Photographs by Stephen Gorman and Eli Burakian

Guilford, Connecticut
An imprint of Globe Pequot Press

Editorial Director: Cynthia Hughes
Editor: Katie Benoit
Project Editor: Tracee Williams
Cover Design: Paul Beatrice, Bret Kerr
Interior Design: Paul Beatrice
Layout: Kevin Mak
Diagrams by Al Lawrence
Front cover photos by Stephen Gorman and Eli Burakian; and Courtesy of Sam Frentress/St. Louis Chess Club and Scholastic Center; © Losevsky Pavel | shutterstock; and © blueking | shutterstock.
Back cover photo by Stephen Gorman and Eli Burakian.
Interior photos by Stephen Gorman and Eli Burakian with the exception of page viii (left): © Viktor1 | shutterstock; page viii (right): Courtesy of Al Lawrence; page ix (left): © AVAVA | shutterstock; page ix (right): © Sergey Lavrentev | shutterstock; page x (left): © Stepanov | shutterstock; page xi: © blueking | shutterstock; page xii (right): Courtesy of crossgenerationchess.com; page 1 (left): Courtesy of crossgenerationchess.com; page 1 (right): © Zsolt Nyulaszi | shutterstock; page 2 (right): © Monkey Business Images | shutterstock; page 3 (left): Courtesy of Al Lawrence; page 3 (right): Courtesy of crossgenerationchess.com; page 4 (left): © ben44 | shutterstock; page 4 (right): © Alex Kosev | shutterstock; page 5 (left): Courtesy of Al Lawrence; page 5 (right): Courtesy of Sam Frentress/St. Louis Chess Club and Scholastic Center; page 6 (left): Courtesy of Al Lawrence; page 7 (left): Izaokas Sapiro | shutterstock; page 7 (right): Courtesy of Al Lawrence; page 8 (right): Courtesy of Frank Brady; page 9 (left): Courtesy of Al Lawrence; page 9 (right): Courtesy of Al Lawrence: page 10 (right): Courtesy of Al Lawrence; page 11 (left): Courtesy of crossgenerationchess.com; page 11 (right): © Orange Line Media | shutterstock; page 229: © nhtg | shutterstock; page 230: Courtesy of Al Lawrence; Page 231: Courtesy of Sam Frentress/St. Louis Chess Club and Scholastic Center.

Library of Congress Cataloging-in-Publication Data
Lawrence, Al.
 Knack chess for everyone : a step-by-step guide to rules, moves & winning strategies / Al Lawrence ; photographs by Stephen Gorman and Eli Burakian.
  p. cm.
 ISBN 978-1-59921-510-5
 1. Chess. I. Title.
 GV1449.5.L38 2010
 794.1'2--dc22

                              2009048392

Printed in China

10 9 8 7 6 5 4 3 2 1

The information in this book is true and complete to the best of our knowledge. All recommendations are made without guarantee on the part of the author or Globe Pequot Press. The author and Globe Pequot Press disclaim any liability in connection with the use of this information.

This book is dedicated to Gary Colvin, with the wish that chess brings everyone such a lifelong friend.

Acknowledgments

My thanks to three-time U.S. Chess Champion Lev Alburt for his bottomless chess knowledge and willingness to share it, and for his hours carefully looking over the manuscript of this book to make it accurate and helpful. My thanks also to Ed Scimia for his contributions to the text.

Thanks to Renée Yarzig of www.crossgenerationchess.com for so many great photos of people enjoying chess.

And thanks to Katie Benoit and Tracee Williams at Globe Pequot Press, whose patience and professionalism turned the manuscript into a book.

CONTENTS

INTRODUCTION

by Ed Scimia
About.com Guide to Chess

My chess journey started very early in life. I can't remember when I first learned chess, but I can recall the excitement I had playing the game as a young child. Every game was another opportunity to test a new idea. Seeing my opponent fall into an opening trap that I'd just read about in a book made me feel like a grandmaster (the all-stars of chess), and every simple tactic was thrilling. I could beat my friends, and I even won more games than I lost against my father. That important fact alone was enough to make me assume I had mastered chess!

Somewhere around third grade, I started playing chess as part of a program at school. It suddenly became apparent that there was a lot more to learn about this game than I thought! We received weekly lessons from a master who

showed us what real chess looked like. I quickly found out that one-move tricks and traps wouldn't work against serious opponents, who would see them coming and defend appropriately. Deeper strategies and more tactics were required. The beautiful complexities of chess started to become apparent to me. Our class looked at games by some of the greatest names in chess: Paul Morphy, Bobby Fischer, Garry Kasparov, and many more. I tried (unsuccessfully) to model my play after their brilliancies. Along with my classmates, I traveled to chess tournaments and competed against scholastic players from across the country.

Despite everything I learned from my first teacher, I did not turn out to be a chess prodigy. When my family moved and my new school didn't have a chess program, I no longer participated in tournaments or took lessons. But my love for the game was already deeply ingrained, and nothing could stop me from playing. I read the few chess books I had over

and over again and gave lessons to my overmatched friends so that they'd keep playing with me.

My chess journey continued when I rejoined the chess community in college. I started playing in tournaments again, this time against other adult players. I was a much stronger player now, but so were my opponents. I was amazed at the depth of their play and the level of understanding they showed. These tournament players had memorized every opening line, thought dozens of moves ahead, and never fell into traps. At least, that's how it seemed to me at the time! In reality, they were just a little further along the same journey I was on. They made mistakes, but they were just more subtle than mine, and I needed to better understand chess before I could beat these tournament players. This is a realization that every chess player comes to many times—that there are always players who are just a little bit better who will push you to improve. I joined my local chess club,

analyzed my play with stronger players, and slowly saw my tournament results improve.

It was then that I tried playing in my first major chess tournament—the World Open in Philadelphia, one of the largest open tournaments. It was thrilling to be there. While famous grandmasters battled it out on the top boards, I competed in a section for lower-rated players. I had worked hard to prepare for the tournament, and expected to do well, but I never thought I'd do as well as I did. After three days and nine games, I finished first in my section without losing a single game. Winning such a prestigious event gave me a sense of accomplishment that I'll never forget.

Since then, I've continued to compete in tournaments and play at local chess clubs, steadily improving my play. I even managed to win my section at the Connecticut State Championships one year, notching another unforgettable milestone on my chess journey. There is still so much to discover

problem never fails to bring a smile to my face. I've also become a tournament director and organizer. These duties, helping others to enjoy the world of competitive chess, come with their own sets of rewards and challenges.

Chess can be much more than a game, and your chess adventure may take you in another direction entirely. For some chess enthusiasts, the game is a form of artistic expression, either through imaginative play or the composition of chess puzzles. Others especially appreciate the endless variety of imaginative and artistic sets and boards, collecting them for their beauty. Of course, gaining a better understanding of chess will also help you better comprehend the games played by the world's elite players, allowing you to follow chess as a spectator sport.

No matter where or how far your personal chess journey takes you, the information in this book will prepare you for your journey. If you're a complete beginner, you can use this book to learn the basics of chess and start playing. If you already know the rules but want to improve your play, this book will teach you all the chess concepts needed to

about chess, and the more I learn, the more it becomes clear that there's even more I can work on to improve my play. There are still those players who seem just barely beyond my grasp—to say nothing of the world of grandmasters.

But chess isn't just about competitive play, and my journey has taken me in many different directions. I teach chess to children, a deeply rewarding experience in its own right. Chess offers a number of benefits to children, and the excitement a young girl or boy gets from solving a difficult

understand advanced play. You'll learn about tactics like forks and pins that can be used to win material, as well as long-term strategic concepts like pawn structure and proper piece placement. Many of the most popular opening systems are explained in this book, allowing you to pick variations you enjoy and start each game with confidence. Endgames and checkmates are covered so that you'll know how to finish off your opponents. Each key concept is fully explained using visual aids designed to reinforce the information presented. You can also use this book to learn more about the world of chess culture and how to get more involved in the chess community.

I hope this book will prove to be the beginning of your rewarding chess journey. Chess is one of the few games or sports that place people of all ages on equal footing, allowing schoolchildren to play against senior citizens without either player holding back. And certainly chess provides lifelong benefits as well. Children who play chess show improved academic achievement, higher test scores, and better problem-solving skills. Later in life, chess can prove even more beneficial; studies suggest that adults who play chess regularly are significantly less likely to develop Alzheimer's disease.

Most of all, chess is simply great fun. Millions of people around the world enjoy playing every day, and most of them will be eager to help you begin your own chess journey. In fact, chess may well be the world's greatest game, as well as one of the most challenging hobbies you'll ever participate in. I hope that your chess journey proves to be as rewarding and enjoyable as mine has been.

Good luck and good chess!

FUN FOR ALL AGES

Nearly anyone of any age can learn and enjoy chess—and compete with anyone else!

In contrast to many sports or hobbies, chess is a lifetime activity that can be enjoyed by elementary school children and senior citizens. Not only that, but players of different ages, genders, and backgrounds can all participate together without anyone feeling the need to hold back. With no physical or athletic requirements for playing, chess is truly a game for all ages.

People of any age can pick up chess quickly. Before you know it, young beginners can start defeating adult opponents. When kids decide to play competitive chess, they often start in scholastic events in which only children can play, but they aren't restricted from participating in open events as well. In chess tournaments around the world, adults of all ages play

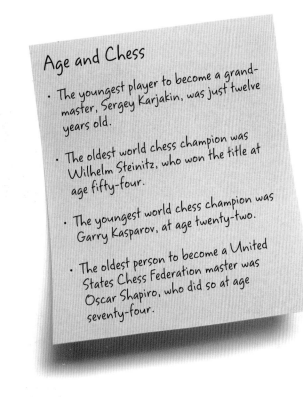

Age and Chess

- The youngest player to become a grand-master, Sergey Karjakin, was just twelve years old.

- The oldest world chess champion was Wilhelm Steinitz, who won the title at age fifty-four.

- The youngest world chess champion was Garry Kasparov, at age twenty-two.

- The oldest person to become a United States Chess Federation master was Oscar Shapiro, who did so at age seventy-four.

A Game for All Ages

- Chess can be enjoyed by nearly anyone of any age.

- With no physical requirements to play, it's common for young children to play with adults of all ages on even footing.

- While there are some tournaments just for children or seniors, there are also open tournaments, in which players of all ages play together.

- Young children can quickly become good enough to defeat most adults, and strong players keep playing well late in life.

alongside children. Age isn't used as a division between sections of serious tournaments, but rather the skill level of the competitors. If you're good enough to compete against the other players, you will never be too young or too old!

And age isn't the only barrier overcome by chess. Men and women regularly compete against each other (although tournaments just for girls and women do exist), and players of different backgrounds often find common ground on the chessboard. You can never judge the skill of chess players by looking—you need to play them!

ZOOM

Even world-class chess players range from very young to very old. Most top players become grandmasters as teenagers. As of 2009, the youngest player to become a grandmaster was Sergey Karjakin, of the Ukraine, who accomplished the feat at the age of only twelve years, seven months. At age seventy-five, Viktor Korchnoi won the 2006 World Senior Open Chess Championship.

Anyone Can Play

- Chess is played in nearly every country in the world.

- Players from different backgrounds often socialize and play together at chess clubs and tournaments.

- The history of chess spans a number of different cultures, with influences coming from Asia, Europe, the Middle East, and Africa.

- Nobody can make judgments about your chess based on your age or physical appearance—only on how you play.

Men and Women in Chess

- Men and women can play on equal footing, and most tournaments are open to all competitors.

- The top female chess player of all time, Judit Polgar, has competed for the world chess championship and was once ranked among the top ten players in the world.

- In addition to open competition, there are exclusive tournaments and titles for women.

- Some team tournaments offer prizes for teams made from a combination of male and female competitors.

BENEFITS OF CHESS
Playing chess has been shown to benefit minds of all ages!

The benefits of playing chess can last a lifetime. Many studies show that playing chess can keep the mind sharp no matter what your age. In recent years, a growing body of scientific evidence has reinforced what anecdotes have suggested all along: Chess is good for your brain.

Many studies have shown that schoolchildren benefit greatly from chess. Not only do young chess players show improved test scores, but they also develop critical-thinking skills, problem-solving abilities, social skills, and self-confidence. While chess is sometimes seen as an enrichment tool for gifted children, these benefits are just as apparent in students of any level. Chess isn't just for "smart kids," but rather chess can help make kids smarter! Chess is used in many countries as a part of the public school curriculum, and because it is inexpensive, chess is also a popular choice for programs designed for at-risk youth. Kids not only reap great benefits

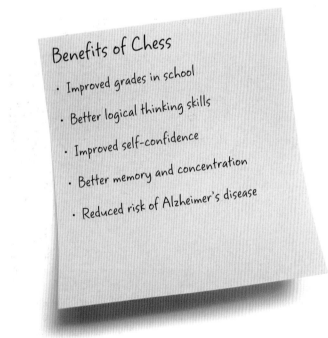

Benefits of Chess

- Improved grades in school
- Better logical thinking skills
- Improved self-confidence
- Better memory and concentration
- Reduced risk of Alzheimer's disease

Benefits for Adults

- Adults who play chess regularly appear less likely to develop Alzheimer's disease later in life.

- Playing chess can help keep the mind sharp by using analysis and evaluation skills.

- Studying chess helps develop memory and pattern-recognition skills.

- Chess can also be a social activity for adults. Chess clubs are a great way to meet local players who may become lifelong friends.

from playing chess, but they stick with it because the game is fun and challenging. Chess is the only one-on-one sport of the mind!

Chess can also improve the lives of adults and seniors. The game exercises the mind, keeping skills like memory, visualization, and concentration sharp. Studies suggest that people who play chess or take part in other mentally stimulating activities throughout their lives are significantly less likely to develop Alzheimer's disease later in life. It's also been noted by many chess commentators that Alzheimer's disease seems to be very rare among dedicated chess players. If having fun playing chess can help promote better mental health for a lifetime, who wouldn't want to learn the game!

Benefits for Children

- Children who learn chess have shown improvement in academic testing in several studies.

- Chess is a great way to improve problem-solving and critical-thinking skills.

- Children who play chess show improved self-confidence and self-esteem.

- Chess classes and clubs provide a safe social environment for children to make friends and allow boys and girls to play together at any age.

Chess in Schools

- Chess is part of the public-school curriculum in nearly thirty nations around the world.

- Many school districts in the United States offer chess as an enrichment activity, either as part of the school day or in after-school programs.

- Scholastic tournaments allow individuals and school teams to compete for local, state, and national honors.

- Since chess is inexpensive, it has become a popular addition to programs aimed at low-income and at-risk children.

MAKE FRIENDS ANYWHERE

Chess can bring you lifelong friends around the country and even around the world

Chess can be a very rewarding social activity. That may be surprising—after all, there are usually only two people playing a game, and since most of the action takes place while the players are in thought, there's very little talking or interaction. But while a tournament game might not be conducive to socializing while you play, becoming a part of the worldwide community of chess players is a great way to meet new people and make friends. And during casual play, friends talk and even joke. (Of course, both players have to agree on these ground rules!) No matter where you are, nearly anywhere in the world, you'll be able to find fellow chess players looking for a game. From serious tournament competition down to

Make Friends Anywhere

- Chess is played all over the world by hundreds of millions of people—you can find an opponent almost anywhere.

- Cafés and parks are popular locations to find casual chess games.

- There are thousands of local chess clubs that welcome visitors.

- Even if you don't speak the local language, you can communicate with the language of chess.

Chess on the Go

- Since chess is not a game that requires movement or large equipment, it can be played nearly anywhere.

- Small travel sets allow you to take chess with you wherever you go so that you'll always be ready when someone wants to play.

- Magnetic travel sets make it possible to play even on airplanes or mass transit.

- Wherever you are in the world, a PC will give you instant access to a human chess partner anytime you want one, sometimes someone living on another side of the world!

games in a local park or coffeehouse, chess is everywhere.

While it's hard to pinpoint exactly how many people play chess, it's estimated that hundreds of millions know at least the rules, with several million playing competitively on some level. The rules of chess can serve as a common language, breaking down barriers between cultures and nations. Even if you can't speak a word of the local language, you can be sure that a player sitting down at a chessboard in a café is looking for an opponent, and that when you sit across from them, they'll know you want to play.

Chess clubs can be a great venue for making new friends who play the game. As the backbone of the chess community, clubs organize tournaments, encourage members to play and learn together, and even organize social events that go beyond chess activities. Like any sport or hobby, chess can be the first step in meeting new people who share common interests and establishing friendships or relationships that last a lifetime.

An International Game

- Chess is popular in nearly every country.

- Former world chess champion Boris Spassky of Russia is shown in the photo above. Other world champs have hailed from many different nations, including Germany, Cuba, the United States, and India.

- Chess tournaments and festivals are held in major cities in many countries and attract players from around the world to play and socialize together.

- The Chess Olympiad, held every two years, attracts the top teams from more than one hundred nations.

The Popularity of Chess

- Photo above: Players gather outside the St. Louis Chess Club on the city's Central West End. It's estimated that hundreds of millions of people know the rules of chess.

- FIDE, the World Chess Federation, has 158 member nations.

- Chess has been recognized as a sport by the International Olympic Committee.

- In the United States, over 80,000 players of all ages are members of the United States Chess Federation (USCF).

CONNECT WITH CHESS CULTURE

Chess has had an impact on everything from the arts to computer science to advertising and sports

Chess is much more than just a game between two players. Away from the board, chess has made a profound impact on our culture. You'll find chess everywhere you look in the arts, and the game is often used to create metaphors in sports and politics. Chess carries connotations of intelligence and strategy. If a character on your favorite television show plays chess, you can be sure she won't be easily fooled!

Chess also has a culture all its own. There have been countless books written about chess, from instructional texts to important historical works and narratives on tournaments and players. Other chess material is published in magazines, newspaper columns, and Web sites, all of which are devoted

Chess in Culture

- Today, chess culture can be found everywhere: on television, in the movies, even at fairs, where experts—like your author, shown above—take on all comers.

- Chess has a long history of being a part of culture; it is often used to represent intelligence or strategic brilliance.

- Chess is often used as a metaphor: a football game is like a chess match, and a political battle with no progress is a stalemate.

Chess Publications

- There are hundreds of magazines devoted to the game of chess.

- Many chess magazines are available for free as a part of membership in a state or national chess federation.

- Most major newspapers have a weekly chess column. These often contain a recent game and one or more problems to solve.

- There are also thousands of blogs and Web sites that cover the chess world.

to different facets of chess: its history, player personalities, the latest tournaments, opening theory, middle game principles, endgame methods, other chess instruction—and lots more.

Chess provides a number of different avenues for enjoyment other than simply playing the game. Many people enjoy the aesthetic qualities of chess. There is an endless number of beautiful boards and sets available to collect and display. Some fans use the game as a creative outlet by composing chess problems, and there's no shortage of players willing to try solving them.

Tournament play is a big part of chess culture, encompassing everything from local scholastic events for children to the world chess championship. There are people who play important roles in chess that have nothing to do with winning titles: tournament organizers and directors, for instance, or chess instructors, who teach others how to improve their play. No matter what interests you about chess, there's a place in the game's culture for you.

Chess Books

- If you'd like to add to your book collection, chess will give you countless options.

- Along with popular instructional chess books, there are also historical works, tournament reports, and examinations of chess culture.

- If you like collecting antique books, there are classic works of chess literature spanning several centuries.

- Not sure which books are right for you? Many chess publications include book reviews as a regular feature.

Cultural Events

- Chess lovers often take part in cultural events that bring the game to a wider audience.

- One popular activity is the live chess game, where each piece is represented by an actual person who moves around the board.

- In a simultaneous exhibition, a grandmaster or other strong player competes against dozens (or even hundreds!) of players at the same time. Above, former women's world champ Susan Polgar takes on a crowd of players at the World Chess Hall of Fame in Miami.

RICH HISTORY

The fascinating history of chess stems from an ancient Indian war game

The history of chess stretches back more than 1,500 years. While nobody is entirely sure when or where chess was first played, the most likely theory seems to be that the game developed between the third and sixth centuries in India, as *Chaturanga*, a name that refers to the four divisions of an army represented on the board. Although the game is clearly an ancestor of modern chess, historians are not sure exactly how it was played. By the year 1000, the game had become quite popular in Persia under a new name: *Shatranj*. While the game still differed greatly from chess as we know it today, any modern player would recognize the similarity. Several of the pieces—namely the rooks, knights, and king—moved

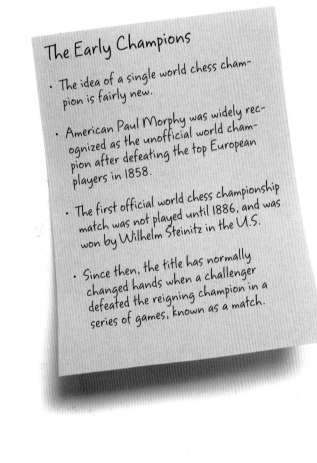

The Early Champions

- The idea of a single world chess champion is fairly new.

- American Paul Morphy was widely recognized as the unofficial world champion after defeating the top European players in 1858.

- The first official world chess championship match was not played until 1886, and was won by Wilhelm Steinitz in the U.S.

- Since then, the title has normally changed hands when a challenger defeated the reigning champion in a series of games, known as a match.

Twentieth-Century Chess

- In the mid-twentieth century, chess was dominated by the Soviet Union, which produced seven out of the eight world champions from 1948 until the fall of the U.S.S.R. in 1991.

- The lone exception was American Bobby Fischer, shown above as a young man, who won the world chess championship in 1972.

- In 1997 Deep Blue became the first computer program to defeat a world chess champion in a match.

- Today, the top computer programs are often used to analyze difficult positions.

exactly as they do today.

By the year 1500, the rules of chess were essentially what they are today, and the game was popular throughout Europe. Famous players began to emerge: Ruy Lopez in sixteenth-century Spain, Gioachino Greco in Italy a half century later, François-André Philidor in eighteenth-century France.

The first official world championship match took place in the United States in 1886, when Wilhelm Steinitz defeated Johannes Zukertort to claim the title. Since then, the title has changed hands fourteen times. As of 2009, Viswanathan Anand of India reigns as world champion. Each champion has learned from his predecessors, as have the millions of amateur players who study games from centuries ago as intently as those played today.

Today, computers analyze positions at lightning speed, and tournament reports are available instantly on the Internet— yet chess is still essentially the same game that has been played for hundreds of years. We can all learn lessons from the rich history of chess, a history still being written today.

Chess Today

- Today, the world chess champion is Viswanathan Anand, the first world chess champ from India. Pictured above, Alexandra Kosteniuk, who lives in Miami, is the current women's world champion.

- Many of today's top players are young stars, such as Norway's Magnus Carlsen, who is just eighteen.

- The Internet has been a great asset for chess, providing instant coverage of elite tournaments and allowing you to play opponents around the world without leaving home!

Learning from the Past

- By examining the games of Paul Morphy and others, Wilhelm Steinitz (pictured above), world champ from 1886 to 1894, formulated the first thorough explanation of good chess play.

- Over the past thousand years, millions of chess games have been recorded and preserved for later generations.

- These games can be found in books and huge computer databases.

- Studying games of the past is a critical part of chess study for players who want to improve their game.

9

INEXPENSIVE, EASY TO LEARN

An initial investment of a few dollars gives you thousands of hours of fun

Getting started in chess doesn't take a big investment of time or money. In fact, compared to most hobbies or sports, the cost of getting started is very, very low. You can get a chess set and board that will give you thousands of hours of enjoyment for just a few dollars.

Learning how to play chess is easier than you might think,

given the game's cerebral reputation. It's true that it takes most of us time and effort to become a very strong player. On the other hand, the rules of the game are fairly simple, and with the help of someone who already knows how to play, you can start playing your first real game in under an hour. And a player who reads a good book on the game can

What You Need to Play Chess

- A board—vinyl or wooden boards are most popular.

- Pieces—plastic sets are inexpensive and durable, while wood sets go well with wooden boards.

- That's it! Chess requires very little equipment, making it an inexpensive hobby.

Chessboards and Sets

- All kinds of decorative sets are available and are fun to look at, like this Muppets chess set, above. But they are not good to play a serious game with.

- Staunton (the design shown in this book) pieces are standard in the chess world. Weighted pieces are

especially good because they won't get knocked over when your hand brushes against them.

- Vinyl roll-up boards, like the ones shown in chapter six, are durable, inexpensive, and portable. They are the most common boards used by tournament players.

10

quickly learn to beat the vast majority of chess players who know only the moves and few other techniques.

A good plastic set and a vinyl roll-up board are durable enough to last for decades and are the same equipment used by serious tournament players. Of course, you can buy very expensive sets as well, but they aren't required, and no one plays better based on the cost of his or her chess set! If you plan on playing in tournaments, you will probably also want to purchase a chess clock—really two clocks in the same housing that keep track of the time each player has used for the game.

YELLOW LIGHT

While you can get a good chess set for only a few dollars, there are some sets to avoid. Many toy stores sell chess sets containing cheap, hollow plastic pieces that tip over too easily and red-and-black checkerboards. Avoid these if possible. Sets of heavier, more durable plastic pieces and vinyl boards with white and green squares can be found for the same price (or cheaper) from any vendor of chess equipment. (See "Resources.")

Learning to Play

- It's easiest to learn chess with the help of someone who already knows how to play.

- Another way to learn is with someone else who is also new to chess. You can learn and test ideas together at your own pace.

- Chess is a great game for families. Children can often play as well as or better than adults.

- You won't need to purchase a chess clock unless you plan to play in tournaments or try "speed chess," games that give the players only a few minutes apiece.

Learning the Basics

- While the strategies and tactics of chess are complex, learning how to play step-by-step, as we do in this book, is easy and painless.

- The basic rules of chess can be learned in under an hour.

- Even children, sometimes as young as age four, are capable of learning and playing chess.

- Once you understand how each piece moves and the object of the game, you're ready to start playing!

THE CHESSBOARD

Know the battlefield so that you can effectively deploy your army!

All you need to play chess is a board and pieces. Sometimes people call this combination a "chess set," but to an experienced chess player, this phrase means only the chessmen, not including the board. So before you order or buy a chess set and expect it to include a board, be careful to make sure of what you're getting!

All chessboards are made up of thirty-two light squares and thirty-two dark squares. This convention of "checkering" the

board with light and dark squares is a European tradition that dates back to about 1000 A.D. The squares of the board are seldom a stark white and black, but they could be. Wood boards are often made up of a combination of squares stained light and dark. The roll-up boards used in official competitions are most frequently beige and dark green, because this combination of colors is easy to look at for the hours a tournament game sometimes requires.

Light on Right

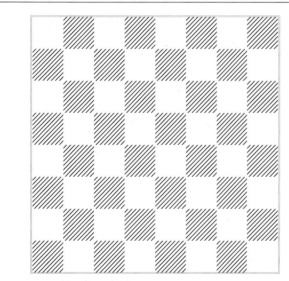

- Chessboards must be set up with a light square on the right-hand corner square of each player.

- The chessboard has sixty-four squares, eight on a side. Boards can be rigid or they can fold to carry and store.

- The squares alternate between light and dark.

- Tournament boards have squares between two and two and a half inches wide. But all kinds of sizes are used in casual play, as long as the pieces aren't too big for the board, crowding the squares.

Files, Ranks, and Diagonals

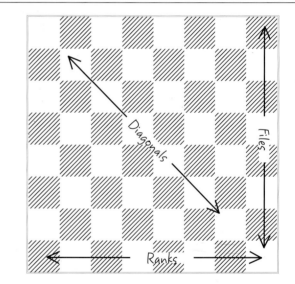

- The chessboard is divided into *files*, *ranks*, and *diagonals*.

- *Files* are the rows of eight squares that run vertically up and down the board.

- *Ranks* are rows of eight squares that run horizontally across the board.

- *Diagonals* are squares linked only by their corners. Each diagonal is made up of all light or all dark squares. Diagonals vary in length from two to eight squares.

Even red-and-black cardboard American "checkerboards," found in many inexpensive game sets, can be used to play chess in a pinch. In that case, the red squares should be used as the light squares. If two players each have acceptable sets and boards and don't agree on which one to use, the player of the black pieces has the choice.

The very first thing to learn about playing chess is that you need to turn the board so that there is a light-color square on the right-hand corner of each player as he or she faces the board. This convention goes back to the Middle Ages. Setting it up this way is the only official way to play. The advantages of this rule will become clear as you learn more about playing the game. Look carefully, and you'll be able to spot many mistakes made in movies, television shows, and print advertisements—where the board is improperly set up with a dark square on the right!

Border Numbers and Letters

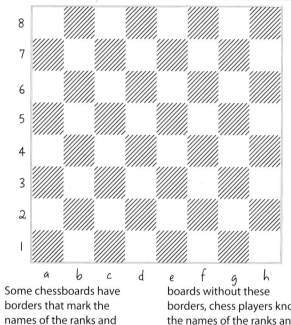

- Some chessboards have borders that mark the names of the ranks and files. These borders can run along all four sides of the chessboard or just two, as shown in the diagram above.

- Even when playing on boards without these borders, chess players know the names of the ranks and files.

- These names of the ranks and files never change and are the same on every chessboard, wherever it is used in the world.

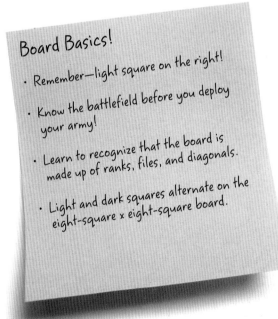

Board Basics!

- Remember—light square on the right!

- Know the battlefield before you deploy your army!

- Learn to recognize that the board is made up of ranks, files, and diagonals.

- Light and dark squares alternate on the eight-square x eight-square board.

FILES, RANKS, & ADDRESSES
The chessboard is like a map on which every square has its own address

Being able to see that the board can be divided into files, ranks, and diagonals is an important skill in playing chess. Chess players analyze game positions to understand them better and to find the right moves. The word "analyze" means to break something down into its component parts to see how they work together. Sometimes you can better see

what's happening in a game if you visualize the board in its parts—diagonals, ranks, and files.

Chess players study the important diagonals to see which pieces exert force along these lines. Players look along the ranks and files for the same reason. Doing so helps players see through the confusion in positions with a lot of pieces

Files Go Up and Down

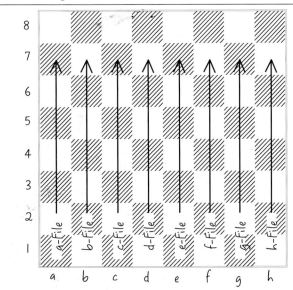

Ranks Go Left and Right

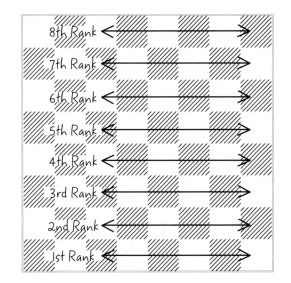

- Each file is a straight row of squares running up and down the chessboard between the players.

- Each file is identified by a letter, from "a" to "h."

- The file to White's far-left is the a-file. The file to White's far-right is the h-file.

- The file to Black's far-left is the h-file. The file to Black's far-right is the a-file.

- Each rank is a straight row of squares running to the left and right of the players.

- Each rank is identified by a number, from 1 to 8.

- The board is set up so that the first rank is closest to the player with the white pieces.

- The rank immediately in front of the player of the black pieces is the eighth rank.

on the board. Ranks and files are important in another way as well. By understanding how chess players name these horizontal and vertical rows of squares, you can find any individual square on the board. Then, once you learn the pieces, it will be only a short step to learn to "read and write" chess. It's fun being able to write down any chess move—or even a whole game—so that a player thousands of miles away can "see" it!

ZOOM

Take a look at the diagram at right. This is the way you will see the board printed in newspapers, magazines, and many books. You'll get used to these diagrams quickly.

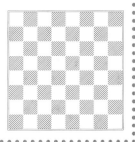

Square Addresses

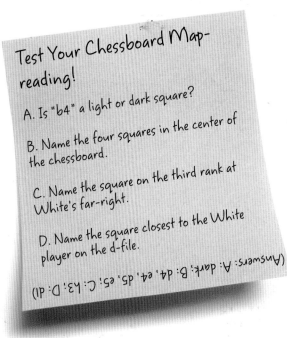

- Every square on the chessboard has a unique name or "address."

- A square is named after the file and the rank that intersect, or cross, on that square.

- The square closest to White, at his far left, is "a1." The square closest to White, at his far right, is "h1."

- The square closest to Black, at his far left, is "h8." The square closest to Black, at his far right, is "a8."

Test Your Chessboard Map-reading!

A. Is "b4" a light or dark square?

B. Name the four squares in the center of the chessboard.

C. Name the square on the third rank at White's far-right.

D. Name the square closest to the White player on the d-file.

(Answers: A: dark; B: d4, e4, d5, e5; C: h3; D: d1)

15

KINGS OF THE BOARD

To begin a game, the pieces are set up exactly the same way each time

All traditional chess games begin from exactly the same position, the starting set-up. To begin a chess game, each player sets up an army of sixteen chessmen in a prescribed way on the first two rows immediately in front of the player. Each piece is placed in the center of the proper square. The lighter-color chess army is always called "White," and the darker army is always called "Black," no matter what the actual colors of the armies are. If you are playing a number of games, take turns playing White and Black. If you are playing only one game, you can toss a coin to decide who takes White.

Once all the pieces are set up, White always moves first. White makes one move, and then Black makes one move.

Six Types of Chessmen

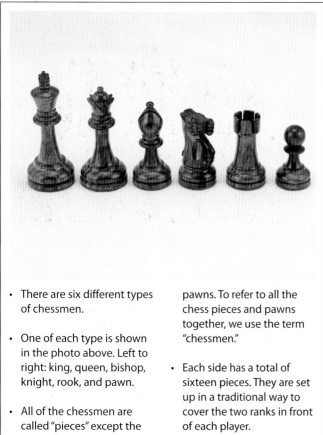

- There are six different types of chessmen.

- One of each type is shown in the photo above. Left to right: king, queen, bishop, knight, rook, and pawn.

- All of the chessmen are called "pieces" except the pawns. To refer to all the chess pieces and pawns together, we use the term "chessmen."

- Each side has a total of sixteen pieces. They are set up in a traditional way to cover the two ranks in front of each player.

Values of the Chessmen

♚ = Infinite Value

♛ = 9 points

♜ = 5 points

♝ = 3 points

♞ = 3 points

♟ = 1 point

- Not all the chessmen are equally valuable, but chessmen of the same type are of equal value. Memorize the chart above.

- The total value of pieces remaining on the board does not determine who wins, but it indicates whether one side has a lead in material, which usually makes winning easier.

- Before exchanging one of your pieces with one of your opponent's, be careful to note the value of each piece. For example, trading a knight for a bishop is generally an even trade.

The players continue in this fashion, taking turns making one move at a time. If a player makes an illegal move, it must be taken back immediately—and if it's legal to do so, he must move the same piece.

A player is not forced to capture an enemy man. A player is never forced to make any move—unless it's the only legal move available. When capturing another man, a player does not "jump" over his opponent's man, but replaces it with the capturing chessman on the same square, removing the captured man.

The diagram at right shows how the kings are represented on a board in many books, magazines, and newspapers. Very quickly you'll get used to reading such diagrams.

The Kings

- Each side has only one king. It's the most important piece, as its name suggests, but certainly not the most powerful.

- Chess players write the king as "K."

- The king is the tallest piece, often featuring a cross at its top.

- It's impossible to assign a number value to the king, because it cannot be captured or exchanged, and if placed in checkmate, the game is over. The side with the checkmated king loses. So protect your king!

Kings off Color

- To begin the game, the white king is placed on the e1-square, and the black king is placed on the e8-square.

- Notice that the kings are placed "off color." That means that if your board is set up correctly (with a light square on the right), the white king is on a dark square, while the black king sits on a light-color square.

- Our "king" is the translation of the Persian word "*shah*."

THE MAJOR PIECES

Queens and rooks are the major pieces, more valuable than the rest, save the king

The queens and rooks are the heavy artillery of the chessboard. Unlike the other pieces, a single queen or rook can force checkmate—the winning goal of the game—when there are no other chessmen except the kings on the board. This ability becomes a critical distinction when planning how to win a chess game! When you are left with just a knight or a bishop and your king against only the opponent's king, you can't force checkmate, so you can't win.

Players are often confused about the "touch-move" rule in chess. The official rules of chess state that if a player who is on move touches any of his own chessmen, he must move it (if moving it is legal), even if the move is a terrible blunder.

The Queens

- Each side starts with one queen. (Some sets come with an extra queen for each side, but only one is used at the beginning of the game.) It's the most powerful piece, nearly twice as powerful as the rook.

- Chess players write the queen as "Q."

- The queen is the second-tallest piece. She is often topped with the shape of a crown.

- The queen used to be one of the weakest pieces, but in the late fifteenth century, she was given her special powers to speed up the game.

Queens on Color

Queenside   Kingside

- To begin the game, the white queen is placed on the d1-square; the black queen is placed on the d8-square.

- The queens are placed "on color." The white queen stands on a light square, while the black queen stands on a dark square.

- The left and right halves of the board are named after the two most important pieces. The "kingside" is the half of the board including the king—made up of the e-, f-, g-, and h-files. The "queenside" includes the d-, c-, b-, and a-files.

Likewise, if a player touches one of his opponent's men, he must capture it, if possible, no matter how bad the consequences. You may decide in your practice games with your friends to be able to take back moves. But avoid getting in the habit of touching pieces before you move them, or "hovering" your hand over a piece while you're thinking about moving it. The rules of chess say doing so is a distraction to your opponent. Keep your hands down while you're thinking about your game. Chess is played chiefly with your mind, not your hands!

The diagram at right shows how the queens and rooks are represented on a board as printed in many books, magazines, and newspapers.

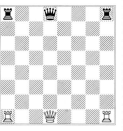

The Rooks

- Each side starts with two rooks. The rook is the second most powerful piece. Two rooks are generally worth a bit more than a queen.

- Chess players write the rook as "R."

- The rook often has a crenellated or notched top, like the tops of turrets on a castle. In fact, the name "rook" comes to us from the Italian "*rocco*," meaning tower—a misunderstanding of the Persian name "*rukh*," which really meant "chariot." It's easy to think of this fast-moving and powerful piece as a rampaging war chariot!

The Rooks Stand on the Corners

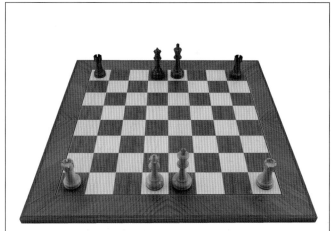

- To begin the game, a rook is placed at each side of each army. The white rooks begin on a-1 and h-1. The black rooks start out on a-8 and h-8.

- You'll see that a rook, together with the king, is part of the only chess move that involves moving two pieces at once, "castling."

- Many non-players call the rook a "castle," perhaps partly in a reference to its special moving power, but "castle" is not the correct name for the piece.

THE MINOR PIECES
The bishops and knights are the minor pieces, approximately equal in value

The bishop and the knight each have unique qualities that add to the wonderful challenge and beauty of chess. The bishops, because they move and capture only diagonally along either the light squares or dark squares, are each limited to thirty-two squares—only half the board. Indeed, the bishop is the *only* chess piece (remember, "pieces" excludes pawns) that cannot legally reach every square on the board. On the plus side, the bishop is fast-moving, capable of zipping from one side of the board to the other along vacant diagonals.

The knight is the only piece that can jump over other chessmen. It can jump over men in its own army as well as enemy

The Bishops

- Each side starts with two bishops, one at the side of the king and one at the side of the queen.

- Chess players write the bishop as "B."

- The bishop has the most "pointy" top of any piece, and often has an angled slot cut in its top to simulate the miter, a religious headgear worn by bishops and abbots.

- A bishop starts out on a light or dark square and can never cross over to the other color squares.

The Bishops Go next to the King and Queen

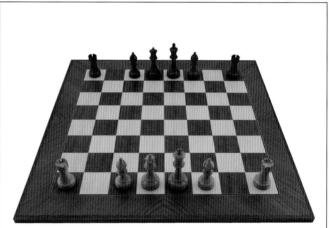

- In the beginning of the game, White's bishops are placed on c1 and f1. Black's bishops are placed on c8 and f8.

- A bishop starting on the queenside (on the c-file) is sometimes called the "queen's bishop." A bishop starting on the f-file can be called the "king's bishop."

- The bishops are especially powerful in pairs, since two bishops together can cover all the squares on the chessboard, and neither duplicates the force of the other.

pieces. That makes it the only piece that can move before any pawn is moved out of the way. Jumping over a piece, however, does not capture it. Like all other chessmen, when capturing, the knight lands on the captured man and takes its place on the square.

The knight is a short-range piece, requiring four moves to travel from one side of an empty board to the other. (The bishop can cross the board in just one or two moves, depending on its starting position.)

ZOOM

The diagram at right shows how the bishops and knights are represented on a board when depicted in books, magazines, and newspapers.

The Knights

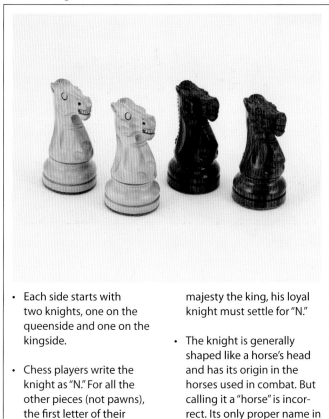

- Each side starts with two knights, one on the queenside and one on the kingside.

- Chess players write the knight as "N." For all the other pieces (not pawns), the first letter of their name is used. But since "K" is already claimed by his

majesty the king, his loyal knight must settle for "N."

- The knight is generally shaped like a horse's head and has its origin in the horses used in combat. But calling it a "horse" is incorrect. Its only proper name in English is the "knight."

Knights Go between the Rook and Bishop

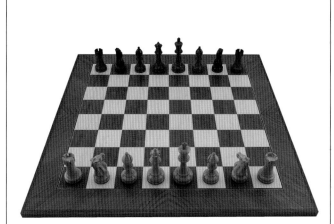

- The white knights are set up on b1 and g1. The black knights are set up on b8 and g8.

- A knight starting on the queenside, on the b-file, is sometimes called the "queen's knight." The knight beginning on the kingside, on the g-file, can be called

the "king's knight."

- The knight moves like no other piece. Its movement resembles an "L," and it can leap over any other chessman.

- Unlike the bishops, the knights are generally not more powerful in pairs.

FOOT SOLDIERS OF CHESS
The lowly pawn has been called the "soul of chess"

Because the pawn can capture any of the enemy men, it's always a dangerous threat—since any piece he exchanges himself for is more valuable than he is! And, like the infantry in a real battle, there are more pawns than any other type of chess soldier.

Since the earliest form of chess, an ancient Indian war game called *Chaturanga,* the pawns have represented the humble foot soldiers, marching out in front of the more royal

members of the chess army. Pawns are often first to clash with the enemy—and first to be exchanged or sacrificed in early skirmishes.

The modest pawn has a unique ability that adds much to modern chess, and one that no other piece enjoys—even the king and queen. The pawn can be promoted. Like a low-ranking soldier in a real war, the pawn can distinguish himself by advancing through enemy lines to the very base camp of

The Pawns

- Each side starts with eight pawns. They fill the second rank in front of each player. Each pawn in a set is interchangeable with its brothers of the same color.

- Chess players call a pawn by the file it stands on—for

example, the pawn in front of the king is an e-pawn. The pawns in front of the rooks are a-pawns and h-pawns, and so on.

- The pawn is always the shortest piece, reflecting its humble rank.

The Pawns Go in front of the Pieces

- Two other ways the pawn is unique: It's the only chessman that cannot capture in the same way that it moves. Additionally, it's the only man that can't go backward—like an infantryman with orders never to retreat!

- Even though the pawn is worth only one point on

the chart of relative values, there are a lot of them, so they are a force to be reckoned with.

- Because pawns cannot go backward, you must be very careful when moving them, since you won't get a chance to correct a mistake!

the enemy, the opposite side of the chessboard. There, he is exchanged for a knight, bishop, rook, or queen of the same color by his general. Normally, of course, the pawn is promoted to a queen, the most powerful piece. Later, we'll see how this is done.

The pawn, like the real infantryman it's modeled after, is strongest when he stands side-by-side in a phalanx with his comrades. But the rules of chess require one move at a time, so a pawn must step out alone in front of his comrades before they can catch up.

The way the pawns are deployed greatly determines the character and planning of a chess game. So advance your slow-moving but important foot soldiers with a plan in mind!

Setup Completed

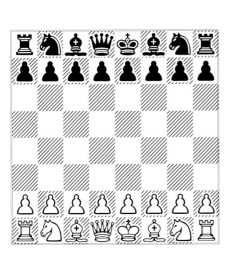

- The diagram above shows the way that a fully set-up position looks in magazines and newspapers.

- Rather than a full representation of each piece, notice that a diagram uses a figure to represent each chessman on the board.

- Sometimes you'll see these same piece- and pawn-figures used to represent the chessmen off the board—instead of the system of using "K," "Q," "R," "B," "N," and the name of the file for a pawn.

Like Pieces Face Each Other

- Remember, set up properly, the types of pieces face each other from across the board. The enemy rooks face each other, the queens face each other, and so forth. The queen is always on her same color—white queen on light square, black queen on dark square. The king is on his opposite color. And a light square is in the far right-hand corner of both players!

THE QUEEN MOVE

The fast-moving first lady is the most powerful piece on the chessboard

Standing regally on the center of an empty board, the queen attacks twenty-seven squares. She's a dominating presence—the superhero of chess. But even the queen can't reach every square on the board in one move.

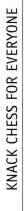

Possible Queen Moves

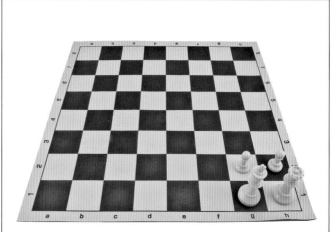

A "Smothered" Queen

- Think back to the files, ranks, and diagonals of the chessboard. The queen can move in a straight line along any of these three. The "Xs" mark the squares she can move to on the board above.

- She can move up and down the file she stands on;

- She can move back and forth along the rank she's on;

- She can move along any of the diagonals that intersect the square she's on.

- The queen can't jump over pieces, whether members of her own army or the enemy's.

- Like all the other pieces and pawns, she can't capture her own men.

- So how many moves can the white queen on the board in the photo above make? [Answer: None!] It's important to realize that even the most powerful piece can be turned into a weakling if placed poorly. Good chess players plan to give their pieces *mobility*. Compare this queen to the mobile queen in the center of the board.

24

Reading and Writing the Queen Move

If the queen on the diagram at right moved to the starred square, the move would be written "Qd5-g8," indicating the piece abbreviation ("Q"), the square it's on (d5), the move or "to" symbol (-), and the square it lands on (g8). Out loud, we'd read this: "Queen on d5 to g8." There's another simpler way to write the same move—"Qg8," giving the piece abbreviation and the square it's moving to.

Queen Captures

- The queen captures in the same directions she moves. In the photo above, the black queen can capture any of six enemy pieces, as marked by the arrows.

- She captures by landing on the square of the enemy piece and removing it from the square.

- Chess players write a capture with an "x" rather than the "-" (to) symbol. If the queen captured the knight in the picture above, we'd write it " ... Qe5xe6." The three dots in front of the move indicate that it was a move by Black.

Queen Exchange Values

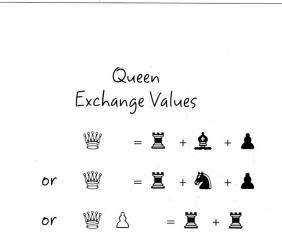

- Trading your pieces and pawns for your opponent's pieces and pawns is a normal process during a game. But you need to make sure the value of the piece you swap is at least equal to the piece your opponent trades.

- The queen is your most powerful piece, so you want to be careful how you trade her.

- Compare the piece values you've learned with the exchange values above. For example, a queen (9) and a pawn (1) add up to a value of 10. So do a rook (5) plus another rook (5).

25

THE ROOK MOVE
The rook moves straight ahead, backward, and side-to-side

From any square of an empty board, a rook attacks fourteen squares. So you can already see why it's about one-half as valuable as the mighty queen. But the rook is no weakling. If you were choosing teammates from a group of volunteers, the rook would be your second choice.

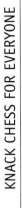
Possible Rook Moves

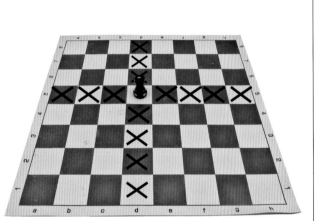

A Restricted Rook

- The rook moves on the files and ranks, but not on the diagonals. The "Xs" mark the squares it can move to on the board above.

- It can move up and down the file it stands on, like an elevator going up and down its shaft.

- It can move from side-to-side along the rank it's on.

- The rook can't jump over pieces, whether members of his own army or the enemy's.

- Like all the other pieces and pawns, he cannot capture a man in his own army.

- So how many moves can the black rook on the board in the photo above make? [Answer: Just one. He can move to g8.] Compare this trapped rook's mobility to his free range of movement when he's in the center of the board.

Reading and Writing the Rook Move

If the rook on the diagram at right moved to the starred square, the move would be written "Re5-a5," indicating the piece abbreviation ("R"), the square it's on (e5), the move or "to" symbol (-), and the square it lands on (a5). Out loud, we'd read like this: "Rook on e5 to a5." There's another simpler way to write the same move—"Ra5," giving only the piece abbreviation and the square it's moving to.

Rook Captures

- The rook captures in the same direction it moves.

- The rook captures by landing on the square of the enemy piece and removing it from that square.

- In the position above, the black rook can capture any one of three white men, as marked by the arrows. These captures are not necessarily good moves, but show the possibilities.

- If the black rook captured the white pawn on its right in the picture above, we'd write the move "... Re5xa5."

Rook Exchange Values

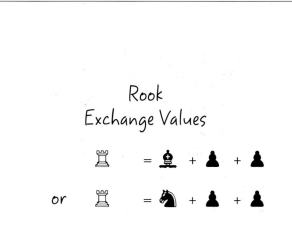

- Because the rook is worth more than any other chessman except the queen, be careful when swapping a rook for enemy material. Chess players have a special term for getting only a minor piece—knight or bishop—for a rook. We call it "losing the Exchange." (Notice the capital "E.")

- On the other hand, if you manage to trade a bishop or knight for one of your opponent's rooks, you "win the Exchange."

- The chart above shows what you can exchange for a rook without getting behind in material.

MOVING & CAPTURING

THE BISHOP MOVE

Each bishop moves only along the diagonals and is limited to the light or dark squares

From the center of an empty board, a bishop attacks thirteen squares. But there are thirty-two squares it can never move to or attack! Each of your bishops is limited forever to the color of the square it begins on. Two bishops can cover the whole board. But a lone bishop is cut off from 50 percent of the action!

Possible Bishop Moves

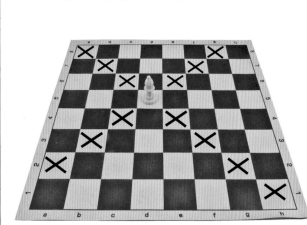

- The bishop moves only along the diagonals. The "Xs" mark the squares it can move to on the board above.

- It can move backward and forward.

- Notice that the diagonals, unlike the files and ranks, are of varying length. The two longest diagonals go through the center of the board and connect the corner squares. The bishop in the photo above stands on one of these "long diagonals," the h1-a8 diagonal.

"Bad Bishop" vs. "Good Bishop"

- Like the queen and the rook, the bishop can't jump over pieces, whether members of its own army or the enemy's. And no chessman can capture one of its own.

- Look at the white bishop on the light square, b3. It's blocked in by its own

pawns and has no moves. Chess players call a bishop like this a "bad bishop." It lacks mobility.

- On the other hand, White's bishop on the dark square, e5, is unblocked. It's a "good bishop" and enjoys great mobility.

Reading and Writing the Bishop Move

If the bishop on the diagram at right moved to the starred square, the move would be written "Bg2-a8," indicating the piece abbreviation ("B"), the square it's on (g2), the move or "to" symbol (-), and the square it lands on (a8). Out loud, we'd read it like this: "Bishop on g2 to a8." There's another simpler way to write the same move—"Ba8," giving only the piece abbreviation and the square it has moved to.

Bishop Captures

- The bishop captures in the same directions it moves, by landing on the enemy piece or pawn and removing it from the square.

- In the position above, the black bishop on e5 can capture any one of three white men, as marked by the arrows.

- If the black bishop captured the white bishop in the picture above, we'd write the move "... Be5xg3." Or, in short form, just "... Bxg3."

Bishop Exchange Values

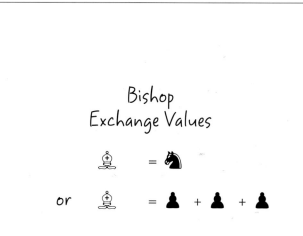

- Trading a bishop for another bishop or a knight is generally an equal exchange.

- Keep in mind, however, that, all other things being equal, you should try to keep your pair of bishops intact, since two bishops are worth more than twice the value of just one.

- Compare the piece values you've learned with the exchange values above. For example, one bishop (3 points) is roughly equal to three pawns (1 point each). As we will see, these exchange values are only a rough guide.

MOVING & CAPTURING

29

THE KNIGHT MOVE

The unique knight can leap over other men and change directions while it's moving

More than any other piece, the knight's mobility is increased when it is *centralized*, moved toward the center of the board. On the first rank, it has only two to four moves, depending on how far from the corner of the board it is. On the second rank, it has four to six. But in the center, or near it, it attacks eight squares.

The knight makes up for its short range by being the only chessman that can leap—and it can leap over friend and foe alike.

Possible Knight Moves

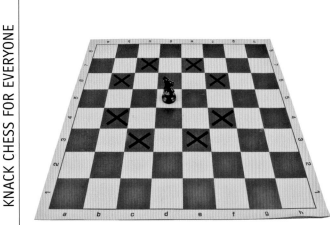

- You can think of the knight's move as a capital "L." The knight takes two steps straight and then one to the side.

- Or you can think of the knight as taking one step along the rank or file and another step along the diagonal, moving away

- from the original square.

- The "Xs" mark the squares the knight on the board above can move to.

- The knight is the only piece that must change the color of the square it lands on every time it moves. Practice moving it and see.

"A Knight on the Rim Is Dim"

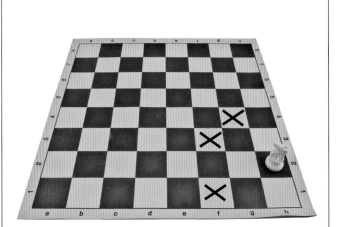

- Since the knight can leap over other pieces, it's difficult to block. But when it's near the edge of the board, it loses much of its power.

- The white knight above on h2 has only three moves.

- Can you put the knight on a square that has even fewer moves? [Answer: When on any of the corner squares (a8, h8, h1, or a1), the knight has only two moves.]

Knight Captures

- Like the rest of the pieces, the knight can capture any enemy piece that it can land on with its normal move. The captured piece is removed, and the knight takes its place on the square.

- In the position above, the black knight on e5 can capture any one of six white men as marked by the arrows.

- If the black knight captured the white bishop on c4 in the picture above, we'd write the move "... Ne5xc4." Or, in short form, just "... Nxc4."

Knight Exchange Values

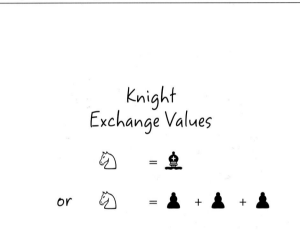

- Trading a knight for another knight or a bishop is generally an equal exchange.

- Swapping a knight for three pawns gives you material equality, but you need to make sure the pawns can't quickly advance to promote.

- There is no special advantage to preserving your pair of knights. So, exchanging one of your knights for one of your opponent's two bishops is often a good strategic idea.

MOVING & CAPTURING

THE PAWN MOVE

The seemingly simple pawn is the only piece to capture differently than it moves

The pawn is humble, yet it has unique characteristics not shared by any other chessman, both in its limitations and its possibilities. The pawn can move only straight ahead and can never move backward. With one exception, it can step ahead only one square at a time.

On the other hand, it is the only piece that captures in a different direction than it moves. In a special case, as we'll see later, it can capture another pawn and land on a square the enemy infantryman didn't even occupy!

Possible Pawn Moves

- The pawn moves one step at a time, straight ahead.

- On its very first move, each pawn has the one-time *option* of moving two squares forward. In other words, only on its initial move, the pawn can move one or two squares forward.

- The pawn can't leap over other chessmen, so if it is blocked in its straight-ahead march, it can't move—unless a capture on the diagonal is possible.

- The "Xs" on the board above mark the squares each pawn can move to.

Locked Pawns

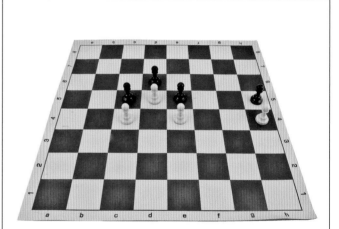

- The lowly pawn can't leap. So when it butts heads with an enemy pawn on the same file, and there's nothing to capture diagonally, the two pawns are at a standstill, like two bulls with their horns locked.

- None of the pawns on the board above can move.

They can only stand and wait for the rest of their armies to extricate them.

- For their part, the pieces have to maneuver carefully around a locked-pawn formation, and often the knights have an advantage over the bishops because of their jumping ability.

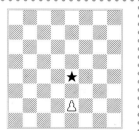

Pawn Captures

- The pawn captures diagonally on the squares immediately to its left and right. Think of how a Roman soldier holding a shield in front of him had to strike to the side of that shield.

- On the board above, the possible pawn captures are marked with red arrows.

- Capturing is an optional move. No capture is ever mandatory in chess unless it's the only legal move. For example, any of the pawns above could move forward rather than capturing.

Remember!
- The pawn is the only chessman that captures differently than it moves. This means that it guards another pawn on the diagonal, not when the two pawns are side-to-side. In this diagram, White's d3-pawn protects its colleague, while neither of Black's pawns are protected.

33

THE KING MOVE

This move now seems simple—it's like the queen's, only one square at a time

The king is the most important piece, but hardly the most powerful. His majesty's is probably the simplest move to remember. He can move in any direction he wishes, as befits a royal leader, but he can only step one square at a time. After all, you wouldn't expect a king to hurry!

The king is the only piece that can't be captured or traded.

So it does not have an exchange value. The king is so important that it can't be given a value, except to say that his value is infinite! But this privilege and value has its *noblesse oblige*— a royal obligation not to move onto any square on which it could be captured. Likewise, he must immediately move off of any square on which he has been attacked.

Possible King Moves

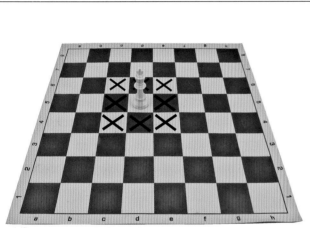

The Safe King

- The "Xs" on the board above mark the squares the king can move to.

- Although we've shown the king in the center of the board, it is generally too dangerous to bring your king to the middle until the very end of the game, when most pieces have been

exchanged.

- In fact, some chess teachers say that the king has no fighting value—or even has a negative value, since it requires troops to guard him—until most of the pieces come off, when the king is given a value of three points.

- Until most of the pieces are exchanged and come off the board, the mobility of the king is not an important factor. The "X" on h1 on the board above shows the only available move for the white king.

- In the beginning and the middle of the game, the

king should stay safely out of the action, in the corner of the board, tucked securely behind three of his unmoved kingside pawns.

- Notice that the king above has castled (we'll show you this special move in a bit) into this protected position.

Reading and Writing the King Move
If the king on the diagram at right moved to the starred square, the move would be written "Kh3-h4," indicating the piece (K), the square the king is moving from (h3), the move or "to" symbol (-), and the square the king lands on (h4). Out loud, we'd say this move "king on h3 to h4." The short form is "Kh4," indicating the piece and square it has moved to.

Kings Must Avoid Check

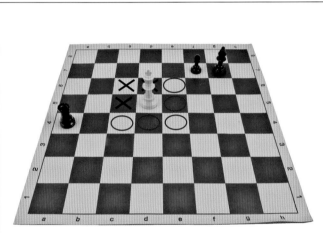

King Captures

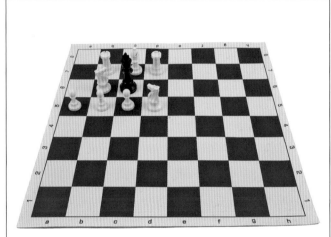

- The "'Xs" on the board above mark the squares that the white king can move to.

- The king can't move onto a square controlled by an enemy piece or pawn. The red circles mark the squares that he should be able to move to but can't, because an enemy piece controls them.

- The king can never be captured. If it is threatened (placed in check), it must escape check on the very next move.

- The king can capture any unprotected piece on a square the king can move to. It can't capture a piece if doing so puts the king in check.

- What pieces and pawns can the black king capture? (The position is very unrealistic. It's only useful for this exercise.) [ANSWER: The king can capture the rook on b7, the pawn on b5, and the pawn on c5. The other white men are guarded, so the king cannot capture them because he would be moving into check.]

CASTLING

Castling is the only move that allows moving two friendly pieces at the same time

The standard way to whisk his majesty out of the center of the action is to *castle*. The king moves out of the center toward the corner, and the rook moves out of the corner toward the center.

Chess is an ancient pastime that evolved over centuries to a more and more exciting game. The same switch of king and rook once took two moves, one with the king and the next one with the rook. Castling also serves to balance attack and defense. There were many regional variations on the early versions of castling. But sometime in the first half of the 1600s, the modern way of castling became widely accepted. Now a player who doesn't know how to castle is essentially

Kingside Castling: Before

Kingside Castling: After

- Kingside castling, the most common form of the move, takes place in nearly every game between experienced players.

- On the board above, White is ready to castle kingside.

- But White cannot castle in the diagram below, because of rule number one, above.

- The photo above shows the position after White has castled kingside. We write the move "0-0."

- White COULD NOT HAVE CASTLED in the diagram to the right, because of rule number two, above.

doomed to defeat.

Although a king can castle kingside (switching sides with his king's rook) or queenside (switching with his queen's rook), a majority of master games see both players castling kingside. Generally, a player is ready to castle kingside sooner. And often the king is safer on the kingside, since, upon completing castling, he is in position to protect all three pawns that form his front guard.

Here's the general castling rule: The king is moved two squares along the first rank toward the rook, which lands on the final square the king has crossed. Like a lot of definitions, this one becomes clear after you study some examples.

1. The king or rook involved cannot have previously moved during the game, even if they have moved back to their original squares.

2. There can be no chessmen of either color between the king and the rook.

3. The king cannot pass over a square controlled by an enemy piece, and he can't castle into check.

4. The king cannot castle while he is attacked (in check).

Queenside Castling: Before

- Queenside castling is less common, but not all that unusual.

- In the diagram above, Black is ready to castle queenside.

- Black CANNOT CASTLE in the diagram to the right, because of rule number three, above.

Queenside Castling: After

- The photo above shows the position after Black has castled queenside. We write the move "... 0-0-0."

- Black CANNOT CASTLE in the diagram to the right, because of rule number four, above. In fact, he has to move his king out of check and can then never castle, because of rule number one, above.

PAWN PROMOTION

The lowly pawn can earn a promotion to any friendly piece except his king

The foot soldier of chess begins the game on the second rank and is often thrust out into the dangerous fray because he is of modest value.

But a pawn that survives to make it all the way down the board to the enemy's back rank must be "promoted," exchanged for any other piece except the king.

The laws of chess permit the pawn to become any piece except a king and enjoy full privileges of the new piece. It can't remain a pawn. A promoted pawn can even produce duplicates of those pieces already on the board. Normally, of course, a player promotes his pawn to a queen, the most powerful piece. But, depending on the position on the board,

Almost a Queen

- On the board above, the pawn is about to step onto its enemy's back rank, a major event in any game. New power is being created. (Remember that in books and magazines, White normally moves "up" the board.)

- This pawn, on reaching the enemy's back rank, must be promoted to a piece. The player promoting, in this case White, can choose *any* piece to add to his army.

- Of course, it generally doesn't help to promote a pawn that can be immediately captured.

Birth of a Queen

- On the board above, the pawn has reached its *queening square*, and—as part of the same, single move—has been promoted to a queen.

- This move is written f7-f8=Q or, in the shorter form, f8=Q.

- Many games are won or

lost because either White or Black promotes a pawn to the powerful queen, gaining an overpowering material advantage.

- Promotion gives players a chance to replenish their depleted armies and adds many fascinating ploys and strategies to the game.

there can be reasons to choose a different piece instead—to *underpromote*.

The knight is—very rarely—chosen for promotion instead of the queen. The diagram to the right shows a position where it makes sense to promote to a knight. This move would be written e7-e8=N+ (The "+" indicates check.) White wins.

The new knight checks the black king and wins the black queen. Promoting to a queen would only have reached a materially even and probably drawn game.

It's not all that unusual for a game to see two queens of the same color at the same time. (But you'll never see a legal game that has more than one king of each color.) And, technically, a player, through pawn promotion, can have several of each piece—multiple queens, bishops, knights, and rooks.

Capturing to Promote

- The board above shows a black pawn about to reach his *queening square*.

- The diagram to the right shows another way for a pawn to get to the back rank, by capturing. The black pawn can capture the white rook to reach f1 and

queen. This move would be written e2xf1=Q.

Underpromotion

- The player promoting the pawn decides what new piece to choose. He does this by immediately removing his promoted pawn and substituting the proper piece. On the board above, he's chosen to underpromote to a knight.

- Sometimes the player

promoting a pawn already has a queen on the board and there is no extra queen available.

- In such cases, it's perfectly acceptable to use one of the already exchanged rooks and turn it upside down on the square to use it as the queen.

EN PASSANT

The pawn is the only chessman that can capture by moving to an empty square

The French phrase *en passant* means simply "in passing." This special rule is the final one to evolve in the rules governing pawns in modern chess. Reviewing the three major enhancements of the pawn's powers over time can help us understand the logic for "*en passant*." First, the pawn was rewarded with the power to be promoted. Next, as we know, the pawn

was given the right on its very first move to step forward two squares, not just one. But this option by itself would give the pawn power to stride past an enemy pawn that stands ready to capture it. This made the game less logical. So the refinement of "in passing" was finally added.

The requirements for using the rule are strict. For example,

En Passant *Setup*

En Passant *Capture*

- The white pawn on the board above exercises its right to move two squares forward on his first move, going from f2 to f4.

- Because the enemy black pawn has already advanced to the fourth rank on the adjacent e-file, the black pawn is in the required

position to perform the *en passant* capture.

- Notice that if the white pawn had instead moved ahead only one square to f3, Black's pawn could have captured the enemy pawn in the normal way.

- If the player of the black pieces decides to capture *en passant*, he moves his pawn to f3 and removes White's pawn.

- From Black's point of view, you can think of this process as pushing White's

pawn back one square to f3, and then capturing it in the normal way. Some chess coaches teach their students to use this two-step procedure until they are comfortable with the *en passant* move.

when a black pawn stands on the fourth rank, and an as-yet-unmoved white pawn exercises its right to push forward two squares, the black pawn may take the white pawn as if it had moved forward only one step. But if Black doesn't capture a pawn in this way on its first opportunity, he gives up the right to take that same pawn *en passant* for the rest of the game.

The same rules apply on the other side of the board as well. There a black pawn can't exercise its ability to move forward two squares on its first move without allowing capture by an adjacent white pawn on the fifth rank.

Chessmen are never forced to capture unless there is no other legal move, and this general rule applies to *en passant*. The pawn presented with the opportunity to employ the *en passant* rule is never forced to capture, unless it's the only legal move available.

Result of En Passant

- Having completed the *en passant* capture, Black's pawn winds up on f3.

- An *en passant* capture occurs in approximately 10 percent of games between experienced players. Many occasional players miss the opportunity to capture an advancing enemy pawn simply because they don't know the rule!

- This move would be written "e4xf3 ep." The letters "ep." are an abbreviation for *en passant*. This move could also be written as "exf3 ep." As usual, the written move indicates the square the chessman lands on.

Reviewing En Passant

- *En Passant* is an *option* to capture an enemy *pawn* that has just exercised its first-move opportunity to step forward two squares.

- To capture *en passant*, a white pawn must be on the fifth rank. (The diagram above shows a white pawn in position to capture *en passant* if the black pawn advances two squares.)

- The capturing pawn must be on a file adjacent to the enemy pawn.

- To capture, push back the enemy pawn one square; then take it normally.

CHECK

Check is the only threat that can't be ignored—a king must get out of check immediately

A *check* is any move that attacks the king. A king that is being attacked is said to be *in check*. Chess players also use it as a verb—as in, Black's bishop checks the white king.

Being in check takes the highest priority. The rules of chess demand that you get out of check immediately. Indeed, as we'll see, if you can't get out of check in one move, you lose! You can think of check as being a strong electric shock to the king, one that can be lethal if applied for more than a moment.

There are three ways to get out of check:
1. Move your king;
2. Capture the checking piece;
3. Interpose (block with) one of your own pieces.

Check on the File

- The black king above on e8 is placed in check by White's rook on e1, the whole length of the chessboard away.

- A king is put in check by any move that threatens to capture him.

- A king can never really be captured because he must immediately escape check or his side loses.

- The black king above can get out of check by using method number one above: moving his king—to any one of four squares, f8, f7, d7, or d8. He can't move to e7—he would still be in check from the rook.

Check on the Diagonal

- On the board above, the white king is being checked by the black bishop.

- The side giving check may quietly say "check." It is also perfectly correct not to say check. But a player should never slam down a piece and say "check" threateningly, as we see in the movies. Such behavior is very unsportsmanlike. Besides, giving check is often not a winning move, and sometimes it's not even a good one!

- In your early games with friends, we recommend you say "check" as a courtesy.

42

Sometimes more than one of these methods is available to the one in check. In that case, the defender has his or her choice of ways to get out of check. The only commandment is: Get your king out of check at once!

There's an important corollary to this commandment: A king may not move into check. In other words, it cannot move onto any square controlled by an enemy chessman. This makes it impossible, for example, for the two kings to stand on adjacent squares, since they would be putting each other in check.

Check by Queen and Knight

- On the divided board above, the white king is being checked by the black queen, and the black king is being checked by the white knight.

- To get out of check, the black king can move to any of the five squares it could normally move to.

- The white king must get off the first rank, to f2, g2, or h2.

- Checking moves are written as any other move, except at the very end, a "+" is written to indicate the move was check. Alternatively, the check can be written as "ch."

Checks by a Pawn

- The pawn, since it captures differently than it moves, also checks differently than it moves. Check, after all, is the threat of capture.

- The board pictured above is divided because a game following the rules of chess could not have a position in which both kings were in check at the same time.

- The white king on e4 is placed in check by the black pawn on f5. The black king on b6 is being checked by the white pawn on c5.

CHECKMATE!

The object of the game of chess is to checkmate your opponent's king

The most dreaded word in chess comes to us from the Persian *shah*, meaning king, and *mat*, meaning helpless or defeated. In checkmate, the king is in check and can't legally get out of check. The player of the checkmated king loses.

The elegant fact that checkmate alone determines the winner, not the total material count of piece and pawn values of each army, injects much of the magic into chess. Few board games or sports allow this kind of drastic come-from-behind drama, in which material and every other kind of advantage can be sacrificed as long as checkmate results.

Perhaps boxing is the closest modern analogy, since a fighter can lose every round—including all but ten seconds

Rook Checkmates

- A player is checkmated when he cannot legally get his king out of check.

- The board above shows a basic mating pattern. The rook on a8 checks the black king along the eighth rank. The rook on b7 prevents the king from moving off his back rank.

- Practice the two-rook mate with a friend, starting with the position below.

Checkmate by the Queen

- The position above shows a basic checkmate by the queen. Notice that the queen here needs support, in this case from the black pawn. Otherwise, the white king could simply capture the queen.

- A move that checkmates is written like any other move, except that the "#" sign is written at the end of the move, or simply the word "checkmate," or, for short, "mate."

- Keep in mind that a major piece—a queen or rook—can force checkmate with only the help of its king, against a lone enemy king.

of the final round—only to knock out his opponent to win. Another parallel—there are accounts of ancient battles in which one army was being routed until it captured or killed the opposing leader to win the day. Chess, after all, is based on ancient war strategies.

Most decisive games of chess do not, however, actually end in checkmate, because the losing player sees that "mate," as it's often called for short, cannot be avoided and so *resigns*. This is equivalent to giving up. (Chess experts do not like to be checkmated.) On a master level, losing a piece (this means losing a piece without receiving material in exchange for it) is reason to resign. This is because players of great skill can trade down the rest of the pieces until the advantage of one piece is so significant that either checkmate, or pawn promotion followed by checkmate, is inevitable.

Until you reach an advanced skill level, you should play your games with friends until completion—one player wins by checkmate or neither player can force checkmate, making it a draw.

Smothered Mate

- The photo above illustrates the fact that checkmate can sometimes overcome brute material force. The material count on the board favors Black seven to three, but Black is checkmated.

- The photo also shows a very beautiful concept that only the knight, because of its unique leaping ability, can deliver: the *smothered checkmate*, in which a knight delivers checkmate unaided.

- Because Black's king is boxed in by his own army, doesn't have a single move, and Black can't capture the knight—it's checkmate.

Mate in the Opening

- All the checkmates we've looked at so far are simplified positions with few pieces on the board. But the position above shows that checkmates can happen even in the very early stages of the game, if someone makes a very bad mistake.

- The white queen stands on f7, giving check. She's supported by her bishop on c4, so the black king can't capture her (he'd be moving into check), and he can't move away—and none of his other pieces defend the square.

STALEMATE—A DRAW!

Sometimes a player has no legal moves but his king is not in check

If the player on move has no legal moves and his king is not in check, the game ends immediately in a stalemate. Stalemate normally takes place late in the game, with only a few pieces on the board. Otherwise, there would be many available legal moves.

Stale is from a Middle English word that meant "imitation." This seems appropriate, since stalemate is an unsatisfactory imitation of checkmate.

Stalemate ends the game as a draw. Don't be confused by the way the word "stalemate" is sometimes used outside of chess—to indicate a kind of temporary standoff. In chess, stalemate is final. It ends the game, just as checkmate does, but with a different result.

Queen Stalemate

King and Pawn Stalemate

- If you're way ahead in material, you should be able to win by forcing your opponent into checkmate. But you must be careful to avoid accidentally stalemating your opponent.

- Your opponent may be hoping that you aren't paying close attention, taking the win for granted. He could try to "swindle" you into a stalemate.

- The position above shows how easy it is to stalemate, even for a lone queen. Black's king can't move, but isn't in check. Game over, draw.

- The position above shows a frequently occurring stalemate. Black is a pawn ahead and is trying to force his pawn to the first rank to promote it to a queen so that he can then checkmate White.

- It's White's move. But White is not in check, and he can't make a move that doesn't put him in check. White has saved the draw.

- Now assume it's Black's move and practice with a friend. You'll find that Black can promote his pawn.

Checkmate or Stalemate?

- In the position above, White has an overpower-ing material advantage. His queen and bishop add up to twelve points. Black has only a lone pawn, for a single point.

- But the evaluation of the position depends on whose move it is.

- If it's White's move, he wins, mating Black in one move—1. Qb6-c7, check-mate or even 1. Ba 2-e6.

- If it's Black's move, it's a draw by stalemate. He's not in check and has no legal moves.

Special Chess Symbols

Chess players write or type the following special symbols at the end of a move as shorthand:

- # Checkmate
- ! A good move
- !! A very good move
- ? A weak move
- ?? A blunder
- !? An interesting or provocative move, often risky
- ?! A dubious or doubtful move
- +- White is winning
- -+ Black is winning
- + - White has a clear advantage
- - + Black has a clear advantage
- + = White has a slight advantage
- = + Black has a slight advantage
- = Chances are equal

UP, DOWN, LEFT, & RIGHT

Before going on, let's make sure you're comfortable moving the pieces—starting with the rook

Moving the rook is like driving a car on a perfectly laid out grid of streets. You can go forward, backward, left, and right. There are no one-way, diagonal, or curving roads to navigate.

Follow the directions below each of the photos to earn your driver's permit. Spoiler alert: We confirm the solution in the last bullet-point.

Special Note: Remember, a real game position is illegal without both the White and Black kings being on the board. But often in this book, we leave one or both kings off the board to focus on the main point you should learn.

The Old One-Two

- A rook can get to any square on an open board in one or two moves.

- Get the white rook from h1 to b7 in two moves.

- The trick is to make only one "turn."

- ANSWER: The white rook can go forward to the seventh rank and turn left to b7, with 1. Rh1-h7 and 2. Rh7-b7. Or it can go left to the b-file and then up the board to b7, playing 1. Rh1-b1 and 2. Rb1-b7.

Move and Check

- Find two different Black moves that give check.

- Notice how the rook can zoom across an open board, from one corner to another, to threaten the enemy at a very long distance.

- ANSWER: The black rook can check the white king on the first rank by moving straight ahead to a1 with 1. ... Ra8-a1+. Or it can slide sideways to h8 to threaten the white king with 1. ... Ra8-h8+.

Numbering Moves

You already know how to "read and write" the moves of chess. Now add to that knowledge by understanding that chess players number each pair of White and Black moves. For example, it's common for a game to begin 1. e2-e4 e7-e5.

The move on the left was White's first; the one on the right was Black's. (When we're solving a puzzle, it's also okay to number the first move we find "1," even though it's obvious there were moves already played.)

Rook Mate in One

Checkmate, Not Stalemate!

- Find the Black move that checkmates White.

- We've seen how two rooks can checkmate. The rook on a2 traps the white king on the first rank.

- Chess players love puzzles that challenge them to find checkmates, because it is very important for players to stay alert to checkmate themes and possibilities. You'll see puzzles challenging you to find "mate in two" and "mate in three." The puzzle above is a "mate in one" problem.

- ANSWER: Simply 1. ... Rb8-b1 checkmates White.

- Find two different solutions. First find the White move that checkmates. Then find the White move that stalemates.

- You've already seen that sometimes would-be defenders, deployed incorrectly, just get in the way of the king's escape.

- If you're playing to win and there are only a few pieces remaining on the board, you must look very carefully before making your move—to avoid stalemate.

- ANSWERS: The mate in one is 1. Rh1-h8#. The stalemate is 1. Bg5-f4.

BISHOP PRACTICE

It moves at an angle to the rook's straight lines, but its reach is also long

The bishop's slanted moves cut across the up-and-down, left-and-right of the rook. Both the rook and bishop can zoom completely across an empty board. But, as we've seen, the bishop is restricted by a special limitation no other piece has. The rules of chess limit each bishop to the color squares it begins the game on. So, in your first games, checking the result of your bishop move to make sure it stayed "on-color" is a useful safeguard.

On an empty board, a bishop can reach any square of the color it stands on in two moves. But remember, that's only half, thirty-two, of the sixty-four total (light and dark) squares on the board.

Take the Pawn

- Move each bishop twice in a row to capture its enemy pawn.

- ANSWER: White plays 1. Bf1-g2 and 2. Bg2xBb7. Or he can play 1. Bf1-a6 and 2. Ba6xb7, but in a real game, with the players taking turns, moving 1. Bf1-a6 would allow 1. ... bxa6.

- ANSWER: Black plays 1. ... Bf8-g7 and 2. ... Bg7xd4. Another way is 1. ... Bf8-c5 and 2. ... Bc5xd4. Again, in a real game, the bishop would surely be captured by White with 2. d4xc5.

Capture without Recapture

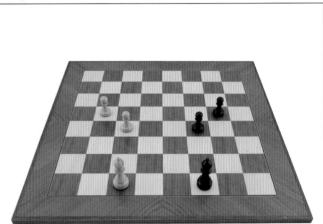

- Which bishop can take the enemy pawn without being recaptured?

- In a real game, you wouldn't want to trade your bishop (worth three points) for the pawn (worth only one point).

- Remember, in books and magazines, white pawns move "up" the board, black pawns "down."

- ANSWER: Black's bishop wins a pawn with 1. ... Bf1xc4. If White plays 1. Bc1xf4, then 1. ... gxf4, and Black has won a bishop for a pawn—a net gain of two points.

Practice moving the bishop by answering the challenges given below each photo.

The Advantage of the Bishop Pair
In a game with open files and diagonals, having the "bishop pair" can be a threatening advantage. An opponent has the "bishop pair" when he still has both his long-range bishops so that they can cover both color squares, while his opponent has one bishop and a knight, or two knights. Both sides may have other pieces as well.

Bishop Mate in One

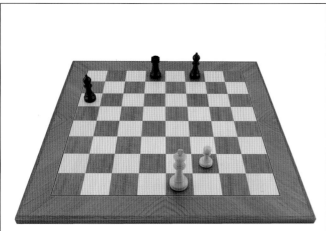

- Make one move with a bishop to checkmate White.

- You already have some key hints here. Let's find another that makes this puzzle very easy. You know that checkmate means we need to put the king in check. Since the white king stands on a black square,

you must move the dark-square bishop.

- Even though easy to find, the mating move still seems a bit surprising—that's part of what keeps chess forever interesting!

- ANSWER: Black mates with 1. ... Bf8-b4 checkmate.

Stalemates Galore

- Find a mate in one and then find at least three stalemates.

- This is a good position to remember. With two bishops and a king, you can force mate against a lone king. But be careful to avoid stalemate.

- White's winning move is 1. Bc1-b2 checkmate. Any other move with White's dark-square bishop leaves Black in stalemate. Any move up and down the a2-g8 diagonal also leaves Black in stalemate (except, of course, 1. Bg8, when Black's king would capture the bishop and assure a draw).

QUEEN PRACTICE

The queen radiates power, making her both a dangerous enemy and an important ally to safeguard

In every chess game, no matter how long or how short, how straightforward or how complicated, the queens are an important part of the landscape. Even a single lost pawn can lead to defeat, so it's easy to see that the queen, worth nine pawns, is truly the crown jewel in a chess player's arsenal.

Practice moving the queen by answering the challenges given below each photo. As usual, the answers are confirmed in the last bullet-point.

Farther Away Before Capturing

- The queen can capture the pawn in two moves in a number of ways. But find the one way in which her first move takes her farther away from the pawn.

- ANSWER: First move like a rook, moving farther away from the pawn: 1. Qd1-a1, then like a bishop: 2. Qa1xg7.

Queen Mate in One

- Find the move by the white queen that mates Black.

- Notice that a rook could not perform this mate in one. It can check on e8, but the king would escape to f7.

- The solution illustrates the importance of the queen's multifunctional move—her combination of rook and bishop powers.

- ANSWER: White mates with the simple 1. Qe2-e8 checkmate. Her "rook" power checks the black king along the eighth rank, while her "bishop" power seals off the f7 square.

Don't Bring Your Queen Out Too Early

Your queen is your most valuable piece. Like heavy artillery in a modern battle, she should be kept out of harm's way until she can take up a position to exert her immense power without being trapped by chessmen of lesser value. Even if she is not captured, your opponent can attack your queen in the center of the board with pieces, developing his army while chasing her.

Avoid the Stalemate

- Find the black queen move that stalemates the white king. Then find the queen move that checkmates White.

- White's king is trapped on the h-file by Black's queen on g8. But the king is unobstructed by other chessmen, so the queen needs support from the bishop to swoop down for the checkmate.

- ANSWER: If Black is careless, he would score only a draw by stalemating White with 1. ... Qg8-g3 or 1. ... Qg8-a2. Mate is much to be preferred: 1. ... Qg8-g1 checkmate.

The Queen in a Battery

- Find the white move that checkmates, as well as a move Black could make to prevent the mate.

- The battery is another important chess concept, lining up two or more of your long-range pieces—any pieces other than the knight or king.

- ANSWER: 1. Qe4xh7 checkmate. Black's king can't capture the queen because the bishop backs her up. If Black could move first, he'd prevent immediate mate with 1. ... g7-g6 or 1. ... f7-f5.

KNIGHT PRACTICE

Some beginners find the knight move tricky, but a bit of practice will make it come naturally

Many great master games have featured elegant and unexpected play with chess's most surprising piece, the knight. The leaping antics of the knight can seem mysterious or even hard to remember at first, but the horseman adds poetry and surprise to the royal game.

Practice moving the knight by answering the challenges given below each photo. The answers are given in the last bullet-point.

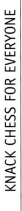
How Many Knight Moves?

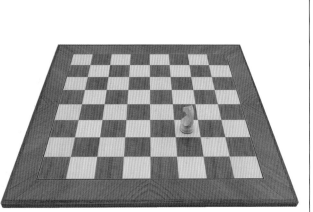

- How many moves does it take the white knight on f3 to get to a8?

- Here's a trick: A knight requires an even number of moves to get to the same-color square it starts on and an odd number to reach a square of the opposite color.

- ANSWER: It takes four moves. One route: Nf3-d4-b5-c7-a8. (This is a shorthand notation to show a piece's multi-move plan or path.) Other routes are no faster.

Hoppin' Mad

- White moves: Take all of Black's men in ten straight knight moves in a row.

- This is easy practice. Just find the first capture and then you'll see there's only one legal capture possible on each move.

- This drill can make you comfortable with the knight move. Take it a step further and set up the pieces in a different way that works.

- ANSWER: Nf3xg5xe6xc7x a8xb6xa4xc3xd1xf2xh1.

The Joy of Leaping

The knight is a short-range piece. Unlike the bishop, it cannot zoom across an open diagonal from corner to corner. But it is generally considered about the same value as the bishop. Why? It has a power unique to only its fellow horsemen—it can leap! It leaps over both enemy men and its own men. So it is very hard to block in or corral! Combine this with the fact that when it moves, it always switches square-color, and you have a very surprising minor piece!

Find a Path

- A bit harder: Move the black knight three times in a row to capture the white bishop.

- Because of its ability to jump over either friend or foe, the knight is much harder to box in than any other chess piece. But it still can't land on a square occupied by one of its own men. So you'll have to find a path through the black army around the knight.

- Create your own puzzles like this for more practice.

- ANSWER: Nf6-e8-d6-c4.

Two-Knight Mate

- Make the move that check-mates Black. Watch out for stalemates.

- Normally, the two knights can't force checkmate against a lone king. But when the opposing king is already in the corner, some-times the knights can hop themselves to a checkmate.

- When the enemy king is in the corner, you must be particularly careful about allowing a stalemate.

- ANSWER: 1. Ne5-f7 check-mate! Any other move by the knight on e5 leaves Black's king in stalemate.

KING PRACTICE

Kept in safety most of the game, his majesty is an important player in the endgame

The king is a bit of a split personality in his role during a long game. At first he hides behind his lowly pawns, as the resources of his entire army can be drawn on to defend their leader.

But when the armies are depleted through exchanges, the king walks slowly but importantly out into the action, attacking enemy pawns and even pieces, and even "shepherding" one of his own pawns to its queening square.

Practice moving the king by answering the challenges given below each photo. The final bullet-point gives you the answers.

Goalkeeping

- Take the black king as the goalkeeper and have a friend take White. Can you keep White's king from getting to the eighth rank? Take turns moving. Have White move first. Then try it with Black moving first.

- When the kings face each other in this way, the one "on move" has to give ground. A king can't move into check.

- When White moves first, Black can keep him off the eighth. But when Black must move first, White scores.

King in the Middle

- Which pieces can the white king legally capture?

- In the middle of a group of enemy pieces is not where a king wants to be, but this position is just for practice. Here he's in check by the black bishop and must capture something to get out of check.

- ANSWER: He can capture the black knight on f6 or the black bishop on f4. The black knight on d4 is protected by the rook on d6, which is protected by the bishop on f4.

The First Rule of Good Chess Play

Good chess players always look after their king. You can give up any other chessman and may still win the game. But when your king is in the hands of the enemy, you lose! You should ask yourself at every move, "Is my king safe?" Indeed, your king should remain safely in a corner of the board, sheltered by unmoved pawns until the battlefield is clear of so much danger. Then he may move in to help.

Castling

- Castle queenside for White. Castle kingside for Black.

- ANSWER: Make sure your board now looks like this:

Who Can Castle?

- Can both sides legally castle?

- Remember, there are restrictions on the right to castle. Assume that neither king nor rook has moved.

- Both sides above have an enemy piece controlling one of the squares between the king and the rook.

- ANSWER: Black can legally castle queenside because the white bishop strikes at the b8 square, which the black king does not pass over. The white king cannot castle, since the black bishop controls g1. The white king can't castle through or into check.

MOVE PRACTICE

PAWN PRACTICE

Never move a pawn unless you're sure you're comfortable with its new location

Sound and carefully planned pawn play is the hallmark of an experienced player. Too many beginners will make a hasty pawn push because they're not sure what else to move. Actually, if you are unsure of what to do, moving a pawn should be your last choice, since a pawn can't ever get back to where it came from.

The first step in pawn play is to see all the possible pawn moves at a glance. Practice will make this second nature.

Practice moving the pawn by answering the challenges given below each photo. As usual, the answers are provided in the last bullet-point.

Race to Promote

- How many moves will each pawn need to make to get promoted to a queen?

- All the pawns need to reach the first rank.

- ANSWER: All the pawns reach the first rank in the same number of moves. The pawn on the sixth rank can reach the first rank in five moves. But so can the pawns on the seventh rank, exercising their option to move two squares on the first move. All the pawns would hit the fifth rank on their first move.

Faster to Move or Capture?

- Does the white pawn queen faster by moving straight ahead or by capturing the six black pieces?

- This is a very unrealistic arrangement, just for practice!

- The pawn queens faster—in five moves—by moving straight ahead. It takes the pawn six moves to capture by Black's chessmen one square at a time. It's not the fact that it's moving diagonally, as opposed to straight ahead, that slows White's pawn down. It's the first-move option of two moves that makes the difference!

Power to the Peons!

The pawn is a lowly front-line fighter. In fact, he's the only chessman that doesn't have the title of "piece." But there are many more pawns than any other type of chessman. And we've seen that he has some special moves. He moves straight ahead and captures diagonally. He can forge ahead two squares on his first move. He can even use the *en passant* to take an enemy pawn trying to use this two-move option to avoid him! But most of all, the pawn who gets to the other side of the board safely can become a queen!

How to Queen?

More Tricks

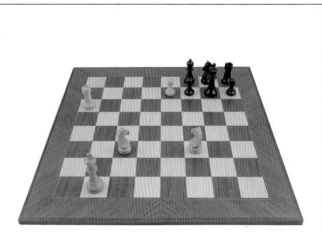

- White and Black take turns moving, as in a real game. White moves first. How does he queen a pawn?

- This requires creativity, but is very practical knowledge. Try different moves.

- White pushes either of his pawns. If the black pawn captures it, the other pawn moves to queen. If the black pawn doesn't capture, then the first pawn just keeps moving. Notice that, because White's pawns are advanced, his pawn queens before Black's. That's important in a real game!

- What is White's best move?

- White is a pawn down, but his pawn has advanced all the way to the seventh rank, and can even capture Black's bishop. So White can win in a number of ways. Your task is to find the fastest win.

- Notice that the white rook on a6 cuts the king off, and his own pieces box him in. A single check is mate.

- ANSWER: e7-e8=N checkmates Black. No other single move does.

DON'T PLAY GIVEAWAY!
The first level of improvement: Make sure your pieces can't be captured for free

There is an infrequently played variation of chess called "giveaway chess." In this game, each player tries to get his opponent to capture all of his pieces. It's a bad habit to get into. Truthfully, we can't recommend it as practice. In fact, you should try hard every move not to let your opponent take your pieces for "free."

When you move, be careful! Emphasizing the positive is important whenever you're learning a new skill. But there's no way around this important lesson. We have to put it in the negative. Be careful! Don't give away your chessmen!

Almost all games involving a beginner are won or lost because one player makes a move that immediately loses material.

Is It Free?

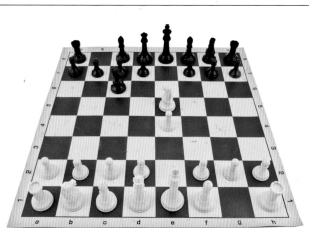

Mate Threat

- White has just played 3. Nf3xe5. Punish him.

- Look at the difference between the photo above and the diagram at right

- Notice the difference in the location of Black's knight in this diagram compared to the photo.

- In the photo above, Black's pawn on e5 was not *en prise*. It was defended by Black's knight on c6. So 3. ... Nc6xe5 wins Black a knight for a pawn.

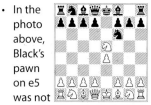

- Black has just played 3. ... Qh4, threatening mate. Can you refute his attempt to end the game with this early attack?

- Black threatens 4. ... Qh4xf2 checkmate.

- Frequently, early attacks are not properly prepared.

To be successful, an attack normally requires overwhelming force on a weak point. Chess is a fair and logical game!

- ANSWER: Just by paying close attention, White can, instead of losing immediately, gain an material advantage with 4. Nf3xh4.

Before you move, visualize (mentally "see") the piece or pawn you are thinking about moving on its new square. Carefully check the files, ranks, and diagonals that come together on that square.

Do any enemy chessmen attack your chessman? Remember that queens, bishops, and rooks can be at an opposite corner of the board and still threaten your man. If you're moving a piece (rather than a pawn), first carefully confirm that the new square is not attacked by an enemy pawn's capturing move. You don't want to lose a piece for a pawn!

Blunder or Brilliancy?

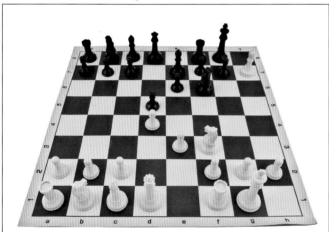

- White has just played 5. Bd3xh7+. Is this a blunder or a brilliancy?

- This move sometimes signals the beginning of a successful attack. But conditions have to be right, and the attack well planned.

- Answer: It's a blunder! Black should grab the bishop with either 5. ... Kg8xh7 or 5. ... Nf6xh7, and enjoy a winning advantage of a piece for a pawn. White has no effective follow-up.

Worst Move on the Board

- Often, the worst move on the board is a pawn move. In the position above, Black plays the terrible blunder 1. ... e7-e5??. What's wrong with it and what should he have moved?

- 1. ... e7-e5 loses either to 2. d5xe6 ep. or even to 2. d5-d6, since White's pawn queens first. Instead of losing, Black could win with 1. ... Kh3-g3 (or g4), strolling over to capture the white pawn, who cannot advance without being captured.

WHAT DOES HE THREATEN?

Always look at your opponent's last move as if it was a serious threat—it probably is

Caution number one stressed the importance of looking carefully before you make a move, to make sure you aren't putting a piece on a square where it can immediately be taken for free. Caution number two emphasizes the importance of studying each move your opponent makes.

Paying attention to your opponent's moves is mandatory in chess. Imagine playing one-on-one basketball without watching your opponent. Or think of trying to get a hit in a baseball game without watching the pitcher throw the ball. In chess, carefully studying your opponent's last move is very much like "keeping your eye on the ball" in sports. There is no chance for success without it.

Two-Piece Attack

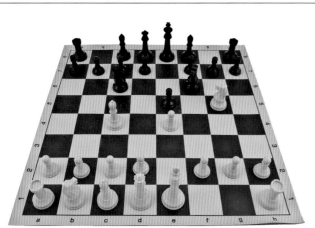

- The game began 1. e2-e4 e7-e5 2. Ng1-f3 Nb8-c6 3. Bf1-c4 Ng8-f6 4. Nf3-g5. What does White threaten?

- This kind of attack is typical in the king-pawn openings.

- In fact, this specific sequence of moves is a modern opening line in the

Two Knights Defense.

- Answer: White threatens Black's traditional pre-castling weak point, f7. It's defended once but attacked twice. Here Black frequently plays 4. ... d7-d5! and after 5. e4xd5, 5. ... Nc6-a5. A complex game follows.

Double Trouble

- White has just played 1. Qe3-e4. What are his threats? Can Black defend?

- A move that threatens two important squares at once can be decisive.

- Answer: Make sure you see the checkmate threatened on h7! At the same time, Black's rook is threatened. Black has no move that defends both, so this time there is no adequate defense. Black can play ... g7-g6, blocking the mate, but will lose his rook to 2. Qe4xa8+.

In a real game, no flashing lights go off when a move is especially dangerous, and your opponent will certainly not tell you. Don't count on studying your opponent's face. Poker players have nothing on experienced chess players when it comes to hiding their intentions. Besides, in chess, the move is what it is, regardless of what the players feel about it. The game rewards objective truths and the game is on the board.

Study each of the positions below and solve the challenge given in the first bullet below each photo.

ZOOM

The photos of the board in each box often pick up where the last move of the previous box left off. But when the photo doesn't continue from the previous box, we insert the symbol "*(D)*" after the move that reaches the position of the photo above it. You'll see this same system in many books and newspapers. The "D" stands for "diagram."

Almost Promoted

- White has just played 1. d6-d7. Who should win?

- A pawn this advanced is always dangerous. It's inviting to push it, especially when you can attack two pieces, the black rook and knight. No matter which one Black moves, White will capture the other. So what is Black's best?

- Answer: Black can ignore White's pawn and play the game-ending 1. ... Re8-e1 checkmate. White committed the sin, mortal in this case, of not noticing his opponent's threat!

Remember the Six Basic Move Cautions!

1. Don't leave your men en prise.

2. Ask yourself, "What is my opponent threatening?"

3. Look before you move!

4. Don't trade for less.

5. Count attackers and defenders.

6. Keep your king safe!

LOOK BEFORE YOU MOVE
Chess rewards players who are careful with every move they make

This move caution is closely related to Caution Number One, "Don't Play Giveaway," but here the lesson can be more subtle. In these examples, one player is not simply giving away material by leaving it *en prise*.

The main idea is the same, however. Be careful! Mentally picture your intended move on its new square. Check files, ranks, and diagonals—and not just the ones close to your man—that intersect the new square. See what forces are

being applied to the square by your opponent. Don't step into a trap!

Study each of the positions below as if you are the player about to move. Answer the question in the first bullet.

Backward and Far Away

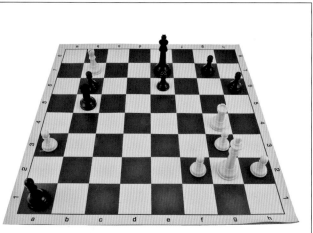

- It's your move as White. Should you grab that black pawn on g7 with check?

- This puzzle illustrates one of the most frequent simple missteps in chess. Even veteran players fall victim. If you'll remember this lesson, you'll save yourself many lost pieces.

- Did you see the black bishop on a1? It's a long way off. And for some psychological reason, a backward bishop move is the hardest for a human to see. It makes White's taking on g7 a blunder!

Capture the Queen?

- It's White's move. The black queen is a juicy target in the crosshairs of the white bishop. Should White play 1. Bd3xg6?

- Even when something very tempting appears on the board, don't just snap off a move. Look very carefully at the consequences.

- Answer: Grabbing the queen loses immediately. If White's bishop moves to take the enemy queen, it opens the d-file for Black's rook to play 1. ... Rd7-d1 checkmate!

Look a Gift Horse in the Mouth

That's an old expression meaning that it is bad manners to look for faults (like old teeth) in a gift. But it shouldn't apply to chess! When your opponent appears to be giving you something for free, perhaps he has made a terrible mistake—what chess players call a *blunder*. Of course you want to win material when you can. But look carefully before capturing. He could be setting a trap!

Capture the Rook?

- Decide if White should play 1. Bb3xf7.

- Okay, this one's a more complicated challenge. Analyze. Think to yourself, what can Black do if I move my bishop—is it performing an important function where it is now? Be especially alert to mating threats against you.

- Answer: Notice that the bishop on b3 also reinforces d1. Why is that important? If the bishop moves away, Black can play 1. ... Rc8-c1+!. What happens then? (See the diagram in the next box.)

Let's look at what happens after 1. ... Rc8-c1+!.

- Answer: White can't play 2. Kh2 because the black bishop controls that square. So White must give away both of his rooks, temporarily blocking check. When Black takes the second rook, it's checkmate.

- Bonus Points! In the original position in the photo at left, why is 1. Re2xe5 the best move?

ANSWER: It gives White's King a flight square on h2.

65

DON'T GET SHORTCHANGED!

When you trade pieces or pawns, make sure you get your money's worth

A fairly simple idea is at the heart of winning chess. When you capture an enemy chessman, you don't "win" it if your man can be recaptured. Suppose you capture an enemy bishop with your bishop, but your opponent recaptures it with a pawn. That's an even swap. You haven't won anything.

But beginners sometimes talk of "winning" a queen or "winning" a rook when they've really traded for it. The art of the trade is a big part of winning chess. The first thing you should learn about this skill is how to add up the material value of a trade. This is where those "Exchange Value" tables we studied become important.

We'll see how the value of a piece and even a pawn is not

Bishop Sacrifice

- How good a move is White's 4. Bc4xf7+ here? Is it a sound sacrifice?

- A sacrifice is an intentional giving up of material to gain some other advantage. A sacrifice is different from a blunder—if it works!

- White's move is a blunder. After 4. ... Ke8xf7, White has traded a bishop for a pawn. Yes, he's made Black's king move, removing Black's ability to castle. But White has no clear way to follow up the attack. 4. 0-0 would have been a good move.

Bishop for Knight

- Is 4. Bxc6 a good move for White?

- The possibility of trading minor pieces (knights and bishops) for each other happens very frequently.

- Many openings, ways to start a game, have been deeply analyzed and given

names. This pattern is one of the most important. It's called the Ruy Lopez.

- This exchange is a fair trade. After Black plays 4. ... d7xc6, material is equal. Black's pawns are some-what less effective, but he has the bishop pair as compensation.

absolute—that certain pieces are better in certain kinds of positions. And, in different stages of the game, different chessmen grow in value. We've already noticed this about the king.

As you're used to doing by now, study each of the positions below as if you are the player about to move. Answer the question in the first bullet below each photo.

Doubled Rooks

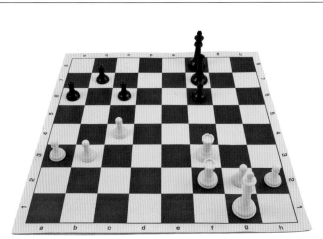

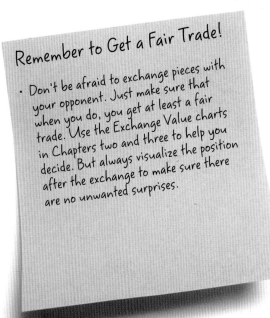

Remember to Get a Fair Trade!

- Don't be afraid to exchange pieces with your opponent. Just make sure that when you do, you get at least a fair trade. Use the Exchange Value charts in Chapters two and three to help you decide. But always visualize the position after the exchange to make sure there are no unwanted surprises.

- Would White's 1. Rf3xf6 be a good move?

- Rooks on the same files or ranks are doubled rooks. They are a powerful form of the battery. The rook in front is guarded by the one in back.

- ANSWER: 1. Rf3xf6 is a perfect way to mop up. It immediately takes a pawn and forces Black to take only a rook for his queen. The queen can't move away because she would then expose her king to check. Ten points to five.

COUNT ATTACKERS & DEFENDERS

Simple arithmetic helps you determine whether an attacker has enough force to capture a man

When you're up against an experienced opponent, you won't often get a chance to snap up his pieces *en prise*. The contest is more subtle. His pieces may stand on squares attacked by your pieces. But his pieces will be defended.

The process of attacking an opponent's vulnerable or immobilized piece with more and more of your own men can be described as *piling on*. Your opponent will keep finding ways to defend, and you will look for ways to add force. How can you tell when you have enough pressure on an enemy chessman to capture it? It sounds complicated, but really it's just a matter of counting.

Let's switch perspectives. You want to move one of your

Count to Two

- White to move: Predict his next two moves.

- Count attackers and defenders. How many times is the knight on e4 defended? How many times is it attacked?

- The knight is protected only once, by the black pawn on

d5. White attacks the knight twice, by White's king and bishop.

- ANSWER: White plays 1. Bg2xe4. After Black's 1. ... d5xe4, White wins a pawn with 2. Kd3xe4. He will force his pawn to the eighth rank, upgrading it to a queen, and checkmate Black.

Count Again

- White to move: What's his best?

- White targets the f7 square in Black's camp. It's good to get lots of practice evaluating attacks on this square, which is Black's Achilles' heel before he castles. (Once Black castles kingside, h7 is the pressure point most

often attacked by White to get at Black's king.)

- ANSWER: The attackers-versus-defenders count is two to one in White's favor. He should play 1. Bc4xf7+, then 2. Bf7xe8, taking the more-valuable rook with his bishop. He should win easily.

68

pieces to what you think is a better square for it. But that square is attacked by other enemy pieces. If you're willing to allow your piece to be exchanged for the enemy attacker, count. Simply count the number of attackers. If, after moving to the new square, your piece has as many defenders supporting it as there are attackers, your enemy won't win your piece for nothing.

Besides counting, you have to check to compare the value of the pieces that would be exchanged if wholesale trades begin on the square. Apply the principle of not getting

shortchanged. For example, if your rook would be defended by your pawn but attacked by a knight, you certainly don't want to play into that exchange.

In general, the attacker needs a plus-one advantage in the court!

Study each of the positions below as if you are the player about to move. Answer the question in the first bullet below each photo.

Breaking Open the Center

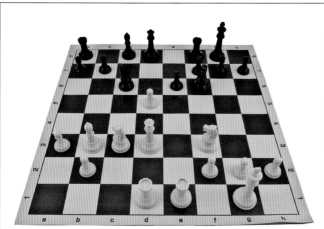

- White just played 1. d4-d5. Good or bad move?

- White's rooks on d1 and e1 are ready to put powerful pressure on the middle files. Black's queenside pieces are still on their original squares.

- ANSWER: It's a very good move. White's d-pawn is defended four times (find all the defenders), but attacked only three times. After 1. ... e6xd5 2. Nc3xd5 Nf6xd5 3. Bb3xd5, White gets his pawn back and ripped open the center so that all of his pieces bear down on Black's position.

Can White Capture?

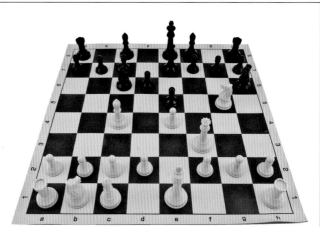

- Here's another threat to f7. White to move: Can he capture on f7 and come out ahead?

- First, count the number of times White attacks f7. Then count how many times Black defends the pawn.

- White attacks f7 with N(g5), B(c4), and Q(f3). Black defends f7 with K(e8), Q(e7), and N(h6). It's three to three.

- ANSWER: White shouldn't capture on f7. He would lose a piece. His attack is premature.

KEEP YOUR KING SAFE

Whatever stage of the game you're in, looking after your king's safety is your highest priority

We've seen that checkmate is the knockout of chess. Regardless of how many points you may be ahead, if you're checkmated, the game is over. Whether it's the early rounds or the last moments of the fight, checkmate threats can spring up quickly. Overlook one, even if you're ahead a queen, and you'll be the loser.

So one of the Six Basic Move Cautions is to keep a constant lookout for your king's safety.

Chess players need constantly to improve their skill of *assessing a position*, of making a judgment about which side has the better game in a position and why. In making such a judgment, chess players of course look at *sample lines*, what

Shattered Pawns

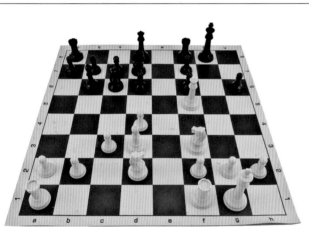

Breathing Room

- It's Black's move. If it were White's, he'd checkmate Black in one move.

- The pawns in front of Black's king are shattered. They can't lock arms to protect each other or their monarch. None of the black pieces are guarding their king.

- White's king is protected by unbroken pawns and a knight on f3 and a rook on f1.

- White's king is much safer. In fact, White wins this position easily. Practice by finding the best moves you can for each side.

- You've seen how the rook can checkmate a king on the back rank, hemmed in by his own pawns.

- Here the positions of the two decimated armies are very similar. But Black's king has an escape square from the back rank—a7. So he is in no danger of a back-rank mate.

- Black's king is safer. In fact, if it's White's move (it better be, or Black will checkmate him in two moves, beginning with 1. ... Rf7-Rf1#), he should immediately push a pawn to give his king breathing room. Then the game would be dead even.

moves each player might make. But unless there is a clear, forcing line that wins, making a judgment goes beyond looking at possible moves. It includes looking at the positions of the pieces. Are they effective and mobile? Are the pawns weak or strong? You'll learn many factors to aid your judgment. But a critical, basic point to assess is king safety.

Study each of the positions in the photos below to answer the important question: "Which king is safer?"

Kingside Safety
Although castling on either side is possible, most often a well-placed king is castled kingside behind three healthy pawns sheltering it, with a knight on f3 (or, for Black, on f6).

Harassed in the Center

- You can see at a glance that Black's king is in a very unsafe position. He's trapped near the center of the board, harassed by White's army. White's king is safe in the corner.

- This position illustrates why the king should stay protected in the corner of the board until most of the power players are traded off.

- If it's White's move, he mates immediately with either 1. Ra4-c4# or 1. Bb2-a3#. Even if it's Black's move, White mates in no more than three moves.

Tight Corridor

- Chances are you could see right away that Black's king is less safe than White's—showing you've learned a lot about chess already.

- In this case, it's critical who is on move. If it's White's move, he mates Black with 1. Rd2-h2#.

- But if it's Black's move, he can play 1. ... Rg8-f8, giving his king a square on the back rank. The game would then be balanced. Can you see how White could then win the g6-pawn?

71

PINNING & PILING ON

Tactics are 99 percent of chess—the pin is one of the most common tactics

This chapter alone, if you study it carefully, will make you a dangerous over-the-board opponent. What you learn here will win you many chess games.

Tactics are the short-term goals of chess. Long-term planning in chess is called *strategy*. Strategy could be compared to the generals at headquarters standing over maps and charts, determining the grand battle plans and deployments for the entire war. Tactics, on the other hand, are the actions of the patrols, or even individual soldiers, engaging in hand-to-hand combat with the enemy. We'll study ten common types of tactics.

The *pin* is one of the two most-employed tactics. In fact, a

Frequent Pin

- This basic pin is often seen in the opening moves of a game, when White moves his dark-squared bishop from c1 to g5, pinning Black's knight against his queen.

- At least temporarily, Black's knight is immobilized.

- This is a relative pin. Although the black knight can legally move, he can't relocate without permitting White to take off the most powerful player in the Black army. Then, even if the position allowed Black to recapture the bishop, the trade of queen for bishop would leave Black lost.

Absolute Pin

- Black's rook on e8 controls the e-file, pinning White's queen to her king. The rook is supported by his fellow rook on a8. (The black rooks are doubled on the eighth rank.)

- It's illegal for the queen to move away from the file because doing so would put her king in check. This pin is absolute.

- Because White has no less-valuable men to block the e-file or capture the rook on e8, this pin wins a queen for a rook.

game without a pin is an extreme rarity. The pin normally involves three chessmen, the pinning piece and two enemy men, all three lined up along a file, rank, or diagonal. The pinning piece attacks an enemy piece that can't move without exposing a vulnerable piece (usually a more valuable one) behind it. The enemy piece in front is thus pinned to his square.

Queens, rooks, and bishops can pin. Bishops are the most frequent pinners. Their first move from the back rank may even be to initiate a pin.

Technically, there are two kinds of pins, *absolute pins* and *relative pins*. Most pins are relative. That means that if a player wanted to move his piece, even though it is pinned, it would be legal to do so. An absolute pin is a pin against the king. Since it's illegal to make a move that puts your king in check, a piece pinned against its king cannot be moved to expose its king.

Piling on is a technique sometimes used to take advantage of a pin. The player who has pinned an enemy piece keeps adding attackers against the immobilized enemy man, hoping to add more attackers than his opponent can find defenders.

Piling On

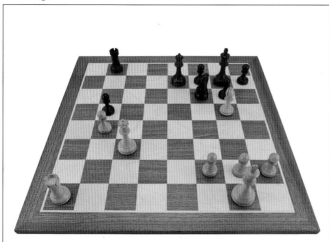

- There are *two* pins against the knight. White's bishop on g5 holds the black knight in a relative pin. The white queen pins the knight absolutely.

- The pinned knight is attacked twice and defended twice. Do you see a good move for White?

- 1. Ra1-a6! piles on a third time. Black can't deploy a third defender. So the knight will fall. If Black could move first, he could play 1. ... h7-h6 and, after 2. Bg5-h4, follow up with 2. ... g6-g5, with a close-to-even game.

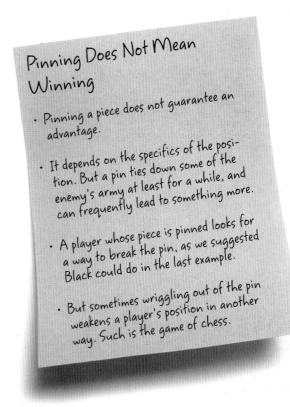

Pinning Does Not Mean Winning

- Pinning a piece does not guarantee an advantage.

- It depends on the specifics of the position. But a pin ties down some of the enemy's army at least for a while, and can frequently lead to something more.

- A player whose piece is pinned looks for a way to break the pin, as we suggested Black could do in the last example.

- But sometimes wriggling out of the pin weakens a player's position in another way. Such is the game of chess.

DOUBLE ATTACK

Together with the pin, the double attack is the most commonly occurring of the "Tough Ten"

The *double attack* is the simplest of the Ten Tough Tactics to understand. It occurs when any chessman moves to make two separate threats at the same time. Such a double attack has another common name—the *fork*. (Another type of double attack, by two different pieces, happens due to a *discovered attack*.)

All chessmen are capable of double attack. But the most common double attacks are performed by queens and knights. (Chess players generally prefer the word "fork" when the knight or the pawn is involved in a double attack.) Double attacks can happen at any time in the game—after only a few moves, when the board is crowded with pieces, or late

Knight and Bishop Forks

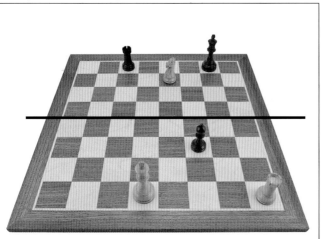

- The Black side of this divided board illustrates a common winning knight fork. Black's king is in check and his rook is attacked. Black must take time to move his king. Then the white knight will capture the rook.

- The White side of the divided board shows a typical double attack by the black bishop. It checks the king and at the same time makes an attack on the rook. White's king must move, and his rook will fall.

Battery and Double Attack

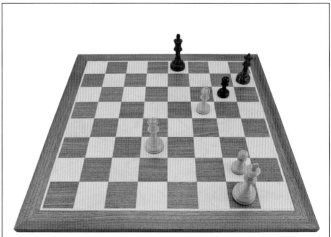

- This position features a white queen-bishop battery (the lineup on d3 and f5).

- White to move will play 1. Bf5xg6+, winning the black queen with a killing double attack by the bishop.

- Black to move would simply capture the bishop with 1. ... g6xf5 and get an approximately even game.

in battle, when only a few pieces remain.

You'll have more chances to fork with your knights than with your bishop, in part because the knight's move is surprising. Watch out for your opponent's knights!

Double attacks frequently take players by surprise. Keep your defensive eyes open for possible double attacks against your own men.

Look for double attacks against your opponent's men. If you do, you'll often hear a phrase that's music to a chess player's ears, at least when it comes from an opponent: "I didn't see that!"

Separated and Unsupported

- It's Black's move. Does he have a winning double attack?

- Notice that White's two pieces, his rook on c2 and his knight on g6, are widely separated and unprotected, making them vulnerable to a double attack.

- Black plays 1. ... Bb7-e4! and wins one of White's pieces. Notice that the white rook can't scoot safely to c6 to guard the knight, because c6 is covered by Black's effective bishop.

Double Attack on the Rank

- When enemy pieces stand on the same rank or file and are unprotected, look to your heavy artillery! Here White wins with 1. Rb2-b5!.

- At right, study the double attack by the pawn.

- Black wins one of the pieces for a pawn. Such pawn forks are very common. Enemy pawns can be dangerous to your pieces' health!

SKEWER & BACK-RANK MATE

The skewer and the back-rank mate are two more deadly tactics that make you a winner

The *skewer* is very similar to the pin, but can be more immediately devastating. Like the pin, it involves three pieces—an attacker and two enemy pieces—all lined up on a diagonal, rank, or file. Unlike the pin, however, in the case of a skewer, the more valuable piece is in front of the less valuable piece. So when the more valuable piece runs away, its colleague is exposed to direct attack.

You've already seen the effects of a *back-rank checkmate*. A rook or queen gives check along the back rank against an enemy king hemmed in on the rank by his own men. Ironically, usually he's blocked in by the three pawns posted as his front guard. This devastating theme crops up in many games

Skewered Knight

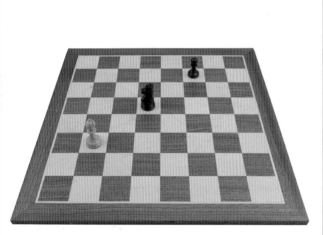

- This is a simple, classic example of the tactic of the skewer. The white bishop on b3 attacks the black knight, which is undefended and has to move. When it does, White's bishop will snap up the pawn.

- A pin immobilizes the pinned piece. The power of the skewer is that it immediately chases away the enemy piece in front and captures the piece it was shielding.

Skewer the King

- It's White's move. Find the move that skewers Black's pieces.

- Notice that Black's king and queen stand on the same diagonal, and that his queen is unprotected.

- White plays 1. Qd3-a3+!. The black king must move off the diagonal, and White will capture the black queen, leaving him with an easy win.

on all levels, but is very frequently an unwelcome surprise in the games of beginners.

So the lesson is clear. Guard your back rank! Keep enough protection on your first rank, or make sure your king has an escape square to run to. (See Zoom at right.)

ZOOM

Escape Squares
To prevent a sudden back-rank mate against you, give your king an escape square, as in the diagram at right. The black king is in check but can escape to h7.

Back-Rank Mate

- Here's the classic back-rank mate position.

- The lone rook checkmates the enemy king, who is restricted by his own pawns.

- Countless games have been lost because the losing side simply overlooked the power of the back-rank mate theme.

- Note well that if Black had pushed any of its pawns on his previous move, he would have given his king some breathing room, avoiding mate.

A More Complicated Challenge

- This position, with White to move, combines the ideas of batteries, counting attackers and defenders, and back-rank mating threats.

- Black's king is in the corner and can't move off the eighth rank. But his back rank is defended.

- Count the attackers and defenders on d8. Include the white queen who "x-rays" d8 through the black queen on c7.

- Play over this winning line on your own board: 1. Rd3-d8+! Rb8xd8 2. Rd2xd8+ Qc7xd8 3. Qa5xd8 checkmate!

DISCOVERED CHECKS & ATTACKS
A discovered attack starts an explosive two-move combination against your opponent

There is only a small but intensifying difference between a *discovered attack* and a *discovered check*. A discovered check is a two-move *combination*, a sequence of moves that forces your opponent down a path to your advantage.

When you launch a discovered attack, you move one of your pieces with a powerful threat that must be answered.

But in moving that piece, you uncover another of your pieces lurking behind it. So it's your second move that does the damage. It's a bit like getting to make two moves in a row.

If the first move delivers a check, your opponent has no choice but to deal with it, allowing you to do your worst to him with your second move.

Basic Discovery

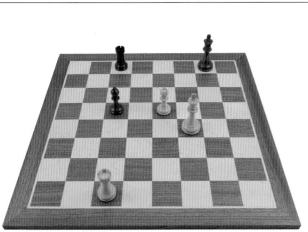

- Here's a simple illustration of a discovered attack. It's Black to play. Can you find it?

- Black plays 1. ... Bc5-e3+!. White's king must move— his best is to capture the offending bishop.

- Black then moves the rook his bishop uncovered: 2. ...

Rc8xRc1. He's won the rook for a bishop.

- Recall that chess players have a special term for getting a rook for the less valuable bishop (or knight): *Winning the Exchange*. (Notice the capital "E." With a lower case "e," "exchange" simply means a trade.)

Discovered Attack with the Knight

- Here's a discovered attack using the knight as the first piece to move. This can be particularly surprising to an opponent. Can you find the move?

- 1. Ne4-g5+!. Even though Black would love to move his queen out of harm's

way, he loses her because the check forces Black to move his king or capture the knight, which is pro- tected, with his queen.

- Then White follows up with 2. Re1xe7, winning a whole queen.

Looking Behind Your Opponent's Pieces
Don't just study the enemy pieces closest to your king or other men. Also look carefully behind them to see if there is a potential discovered attack lurking in the background. Is there a long-range piece like a queen, rook, or bishop behind one of his pieces? If so, study what it would attack if the piece in front of it suddenly moved. Anticipate and avoid discovered attacks! Study the examples below.

Discovered Attack with the Bishop

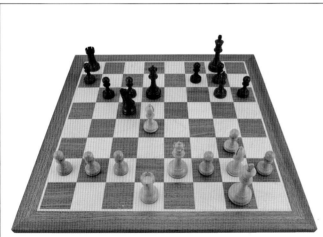

Discovered Check!

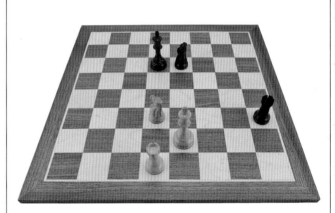

- This is a realistic game position. Material is equal. But White has a discovered attack on the queen.

- 1. Bd4xg7! uncovers White's supported rook against the black queen on d6. If

White's first move had been check, he would have won the queen. But Black gets a chance to move her. Then White moves his bishop back out of danger, having won a small but important pawn.

- This one shows you that complications can crop up in even simple-looking positions.

- 1. Nd3-f4+: discovers check and attacks the black rook. But Black blocks the check with his own check!: 1. ... Ne6-d4+. After 2. Rd1xd4+, Black can double attack

with his king: 2. ... Kd6-e5. But White plays 3. Ra4, protecting his knight. The resulting position, however, is a draw! If Black had lost his rook, he would have lost the game. After 1. Nd2-f2+, 1. ... Ne6-d4+ comes to the same result.

UNDERMINING

This surprise tactic removes the protection from an apparently well-protected piece

The word "undermine" comes from the days of ancient battles when one army would literally dig under the enemy military positions (and sometimes even under enemy tunnels) to collapse them.

In chess, *undermining* is a name for a group of themes used to remove the guard from an enemy piece. Undermining can do this in several ways. An undermining move may decoy an enemy piece to a particular square it's vulnerable on. Or an undermining move can deflect an enemy piece from a square it's safe on.

All in all, undermining is one of the most interesting, subtle, and devastating tactics. And it's always a very unpleasant

First to Move, First to Undermine

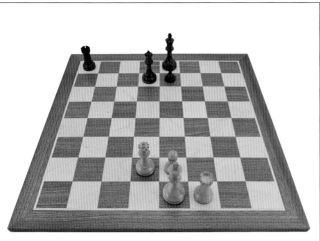

- Material is perfectly even. At first glance, Black's king looks a bit safer than White's. If it's Black's move, he can undermine the support of White's queen simply with 1. ... Ra8-a1+! 2. Ke2-f2 (2. Qd2-d1 is not any better). Now White's queen is *en prise*: 2. ... Qd7xd2.

- Black won with a simple two-move combination.

- But the truly beautiful undermining belongs to White here. If White moves first, he plays 1. Rf1-f8+!!. (Surprise!) Black has only 1. ... Ke8xf8, and then White wins the queen, 2. Qd2xd7.

Undermining in the Opening

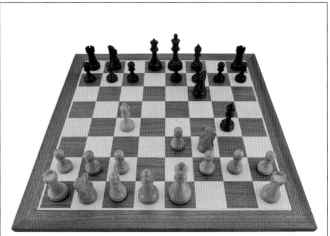

- It's White's move. He has an opportunity that can sometimes crop up in the opening before Black has castled. This undermining move is simple, but often overlooked, even by experienced players. Can you see White's undermining move?

- Remember Black's weak point before he has castled: 1. Bc4xf7+!. Black's King must capture the bishop. When he does, he moves away from guarding his queen. White then wins with 2. Qd1xd8.

surprise to your opponent.

As always, examples are clearer than words. Let's look at some illustrations of undermining.

Not So Safe

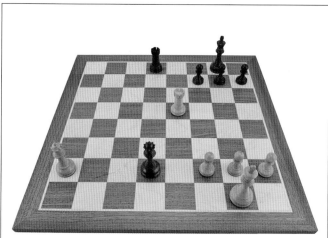

- Black has a powerful queen-rook battery lined up on the d-file. He even threatens 1. ... Qd2-d1, with mate in one. Black's queen is attacked by White's but is supported by her rook on d8.

- It's White's move. He has an undermining blow that

gets to the real truth of the position.

- 1. Qxd2!, and Black must recapture or be down a whole queen. But on 2. ... Rd8xd2, White mates in one with 2. Re5-e8.

Decoy

- This is a beautiful example of the undermining theme of decoy. Let's do some preliminary analysis. Black can check White's king with 1. ... Qg8-a2+ in an attempt to skewer the queen, but doesn't accomplish anything because White can move his king to d3, still guarding his queen. Do you

see a preparatory undermining move?

- 1. ... Rf8-f2!!. White's queen must take the rook. But now she stands one square farther away from her king. After 2. Qe2xf2, 2. ... Qg8-a2+! wins the white queen.

DOUBLE-CHECK & IN-BETWEEN MOVE

While the double-check is the game-shattering nuclear warhead of chess, the in-between move is subtle

The double-check is a form of the discovered check you've already studied. But what makes the double-check particularly explosive is that the piece that uncovers the check on the enemy king also gives check, putting the enemy king in check from two different attackers at the same time. When recording a move that gives double-check, we write "++" at

the end. Double-check drastically limits the king's options of getting out of check. He can't capture both checking pieces at once and can't block them both at once. He *must* move his king. Then the attacker gets a virtually free move!

In-between moves are the surprising disappointment of chess. The Germans have an alarming-sounding word that

Basic Double-Check

- White will play 1. Nc3-d5++. The knight on d5 checks the king and uncovers another check from the rook on c2.

- To the right, we've added some defenders to highlight the special power of the double-check.

- Although his pieces control the squares, Black can't take either white piece because Black would still be in check. Black's king must move, and the queen falls.

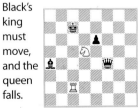

Double-Check Checklist

- Double-check requires the king to move.

- Don't fall into a double-check!

- Every chessman except the king can move to give double-check.

- Trivia: Sometimes a pawn capture allows a pawn move to give double-check.

- Black has just played 1. .... g7-g5. White gives double-check with 2. h5xg6 ep.++.

82

Americans sometimes use for this idea—*Zwischenzug* (TSV ISH-un-tsook). Your opponent makes a threat or captures one of your pieces, thinking that you have only one reply, favorable to him. But his high hopes are dashed when you play a different move that crosses up his plan.

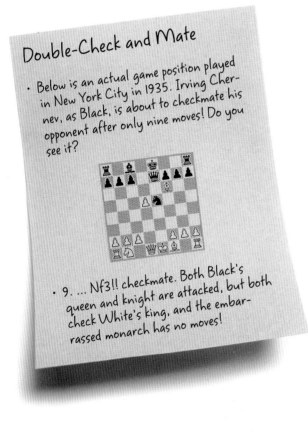

Double-Check and Mate

- Below is an actual game position played in New York City in 1935. Irving Chernev, as Black, is about to checkmate his opponent after only nine moves! Do you see it?

- 9. ... Nf3!! checkmate. Both Black's queen and knight are attacked, but both check White's king, and the embarrassed monarch has no moves!

Which In-Between Move?

- Black has just played 1. ... Ne4-g5, attacking the white rook on f3. This move also discovers an attack from Black's queen on g6 on White's queen.

- Black's plan does look superficially appealing. He sees that if White moves his queen, or even plays 2.

Qc2xg6, Black will plan his own in-between move, 2. ... Ng5xf3+. After White moves his king, Black could then recapture on g6.

- But White plays the simple *Zwischenzug* 2. Qc2-c8+, and after Black blocks the check with 2. ... Bg7-f8, takes the knight on g5.

83

THREE STAGES OF A GAME

In the first stage of the game, control the center, develop your pieces, and castle

There are three stages to a complete chess game: *opening*, *middle game*, and *endgame* (sometimes called the *ending*). To play chess well, it's important to recognize what phase of the game we're in because we should be guided by different principles in each stage of the game when we're looking for good moves. Not every game makes it through all three phases, but equally matched opponents generally do.

The *opening* is the initial stage of the game. It begins with White's first move, and the first player enjoys an initiative in a well-played opening. It's more difficult to pinpoint when the opening phase ends, but in general, the opening is over when the pieces of the two armies are off the back rank and

Stage 1: Opening

- You can recognize that the players are still in the *opening* in the photo above. Each player has developed two minor pieces, and has played one center pawn out two squares, opening diagonals for their king-bishops and queens.

- This opening is called the Ruy Lopez.

- White's bishop was originally developed to b5 and chased to a4 by Black's pawn move ... a7-a6. This bishop indirectly influences the center by attacking Black's knight on c6, which in turn directly controls the center.

Stage 2: Middle Game

- This is a *middle game* position from the same game. Both sides have developed all their minor pieces. (Black has relocated his dark-square bishop to activate his rook.

- Black's king rook and White's king rook have been developed to the e-file.

- Our example is a famous game—Bobby Fischer–Boris Spassky, Reykjavik, Iceland, 1972. It's the tenth game of the world championship match won by Fischer.

deployed for the coming battle.

Then the opening transitions into the *middle game*, the most complicated part of the game. In this phase, both sides formulate long-term strategies. The possibilities of forced combinations dominate the middle game. Such short-term plans are called *tactics*.

The middle game transitions into the *endgame* when most of the pieces have been exchanged off. Most endgames revolve around the possibilities of *promoting* the pawns that remain on the board.

Stage 3: Endgame

- Above is an *endgame* position from the same game. There are only a few pieces left on the board. Although here each side has only two pawns, an endgame can have many pawns.

- Notice that White has two obvious advantages. He has the advantage of the

Exchange (rook for minor piece—in this case rook for bishop). Additionally, White's two pawns are *united* (next to each other, so one can protect another) while Black's pawns are *isolated* (separated from neighboring pawns).

Tactics in the Endgame

- Above is a later *endgame* position that could have happened in the game.

- Notice that White *pins* the black bishop against the black rook. Tactics abound in all phases of the game, including the endgame.

- Do you see how White, on move, can immediately take advantage of this pin? He wins the bishop with the pawn push 58. g4-g5!. Spassky resigned a few moves earlier because he saw his position was hopeless.

IDEAL SETUPS & DISASTERS
The opening sets the stage for the rest of the battle

The opening is a crucially important part of the game. We'll see that checkmate can be delivered in as few as two moves—very bad moves for the losing side. But the importance of the opening goes beyond avoiding immediate disaster. The opening is the initial staging of your chessmen for the fight to come—and an army that is badly positioned for a coming battle is lost before the first skirmish.

At the very beginning of the game, there are twenty possible moves. After that the choices quickly multiply. The renowned mathematician and father of the digital age, Claude Shannon, calculated that the number of possible moves in a chess game exceeds the number of atoms in the universe! So it's an understatement to point out that there are a lot of choices to be made in chess. The good news is that just a few important principles can guide us to making good moves in the opening.

Ideal Opening Position

- Think of the position above as an ideal development for White if he were allowed to make ten moves in a row without crossing the center line onto the fifth rank.

- White has developed all of his pieces and has castled. Notice that his knights are on f3 and c3—in what is normally the best positions for them, where they bear on the center.

- White has limited himself to two pawn moves—putting pawns on e4 and d4, occupying the center.

Fool's Mate

- White has played the opening disastrously. The game went: **1. f2-f3? e7-e5 2. g2-g4?? Qd8-h4#.**

- This is the shortest checkmate possible in chess—requiring only two moves. It is known as "fool's mate" because White has played like a fool!

- This theme of checkmating on the short diagonal to the king diagonal can occur against either side; for example: 1. e2-e4 g7-g5 2. Nb1-c3 f7-f5 3. Qd1-h5#.

- Tip: Don't move your f-pawn too early!

Although it's useful to know both the Fool's Mate and Scholar's Mate below, you should *not* think your task in the opening is to win the game. That idea would lead to reckless, over-pressing play that would boomerang against a good opponent. Instead, you should play developing moves that put you in a sound position for the game to come. The great Hungarian champion and theoretician Lajos Portisch wrote: "Your only task in the opening is to reach a playable middle game."

Scholar's Mate

- Another famous opening disaster, a four-move checkmate called "scholar's mate": **1. e2-e4 e7-e5 2. Qd1-h5 Nb8-c6 3. Bf1-c4 Bf8-c5** (or 3. ... Ng8-f6) **4. Qh5xf7#.**

- Black could have prevented the mate with 3. ... g7-g6!.

If White then plays 4. Qh5-f3, Black blocks the mate while developing with 4. ... Ng8-f6. Later, Black can play ... Bf8-g7. When a bishop is developed in this way on b2, g2, b7, or g7, we say it is *fianchettoed*, from Italian, meaning "played on the side."

Bad Defense

- Many games begin: **1. e2-e4 e7-e5 2. Ng1-f3.** These good moves control the center and aid development. But now Black has to decide how to defend his e-pawn. A good move would be 2. ... Nb8-c6, defending and developing at the same time.

- In the panel above, Black has played **2. ... f7-f6?** to defend the e-pawn. But he gets an unpleasant surprise after **3. Nf3xe5!.** If 3. ... f6xe5, then White has 4. Qd1-h5+ g7-g6 5. Qh5xe5+, double attacking Black's king and the black rook on h8. Black's busted.

CONTROL THE CENTER

In the opening, move one or two center pawns and play to control the center!

The center of the chessboard is the high ground. As any student of military strategy will tell you, if you control the high ground, you control the battlefield. That's why "Centralizing" is the first of our "CDC" principles of the opening.

Although there are at least two basic schools of chess about how to influence the center, each recognizes the importance of the center. The Classical School—championed by Siegbert Tarrasch and William Steinitz, and based on the lessons learned from Paul Morphy's play—taught that the center is best controlled by being occupied, normally with pawns. In fact, a broad pawn center of two or more pawns on the fourth rank is often called a "classical center." But, beginning in

The Small Center

The Expanded Center

- The box in the board above shows the four squares that constitute the *small center*: e4, e5, d4, and d5. These squares are the "high ground" of the chessboard—the prime territory to control in a battle.

- Every piece except the rook has more moves in the center than on the edge of the board.

- Sound opening moves should fight for the center. Make opening moves that gain control of this area.

- The box in the board above shows the sixteen squares of the *expanded center*.

- The squares around the small center can be attacked or supported

easily from squares surrounding it. The battle for the center is not over until all the squares in the expanded center are taken into account.

the 1920s, the Hypermodern School—led notably by Richard Reti and Aaron Nimzovich—preached that the center could be counterattacked and controlled from the wings. The hypermoderns delighted in permitting their opponents to build up an impressive classical center and then undermining it.

Most modern masters incorporate ideas from both schools. And most, if given a choice, would enjoy establishing a well-protected, two-pawn classical center. We'll take a look at the major openings, including the hypermodern favorites, in the next four chapters, but for now we'll say that it's much easier to play with a center than without it. And without a stake in the center, you can be quickly overrun.

Centralizing incorporates moving a center pawn, or two at most, and developing your pieces so that they influence the center. But centralizing also often involves developing a piece to a square that threatens or immobilizes an enemy piece influencing the center. Frequently this process makes use of the *pin*.

Opening Pawn Moves

- In the opening, each side should make only one or two pawn moves, and these should control or occupy the center.

- The opening shown above is the first two moves of the French Defense, a sound way to open the game, used on the highest levels.

White, with the advantage of the first move, has put two pawns in the small center. Black challenges White's control of the center by counterattacking it with a supported center pawn.

Hypermodern Openings

- In the 1920s, some young masters began to challenge the idea of occupying the center, developing the alternative strategy of attacking their opponents' central pawns from the flanks.

- The opening shown above is called the Modern Defense. Its idea is to attack White's broad pawn center—the pawns on e4 and d4—from the flanks. Note the black pawn on d6, within the expanded center.

DEVELOP YOUR PIECES

In the opening, get your pieces off the back rank and develop them toward the center

Think of the pieces in their beginning positions as soldiers in their barracks. To get them ready for operations, your first job is to get them out of their bunks and into an effective array for the coming fight. That's what chess players mean by *development*.

Keep these ten tips for good opening play in mind:

1. Develop your knights and bishops first.

2. Develop at least one knight before moving a bishop. 95 percent of the time your king knight belongs on f3 (if you're White) or f6 (if you're Black).

3. Move a piece once to a good square; don't waste time moving it twice.

4. Develop with a threat whenever possible—you will gain

Four Knights

French Defense

- This is a position in the Four Knights Opening, so-called for the obvious reason that all four knights are brought out before any other pieces: 1. e2-e4 e7-e5 2. Ng1-f3 Nb8-c6 3. Nb1-c3 Ng8-f6 4. Bf1-b5 Bf8-b4.

- It's an opening that nowadays has a dull reputation—

"drawish" is the word used by chess players. But it's a sound opening that follows the principles of CDC: all the moves influence the Center, three pieces are Developed in four moves, and both players are ready to castle.

- This is a position from the French Defense. The subvariations of openings also have names—this is the Classical Variation of the French Defense, Steinitz Variation: 1. e2-e4 e7-e6 2. d2-d4 (White has set up the *broad center*) 2. ... d7-d5 (the defining move of the French—Black counterat-

tacks the center immediately) 3. Nb1-c3 Ng8-f6 4. Bc1-g5 Bf8-e7 5. e4-e5 Nf6-d7 6. Bg5xe7 Qd8xe7 7. f2-f4.

- The moves (including the trades) all have to do with developing and controlling the center.

time as your opponent defends.

5. Look carefully at every one of your opponent's moves to understand what it does.

6. Always keep your king safe.

7. Look for ways to keep your opponent's king in the center.

8. If you can effectively parry a threat by developing a piece, you'll gain time.

9. Break or contest pins as soon as possible.

10. Don't take the b-pawn with your queen.

Remember, these are generally good rules for the opening phase of the game. If there's a good reason to violate any of them, then go ahead. But double-check your reasoning, because these rules are most often good advice!

All of the openings below have been used thousands of times in tournament play. All follow the principles of Centralizing, Developing, and Castling. All begin with either 1. d2-d4 or 1. e2-e4. We recommend that as White you start your games with one of these two moves. They occupy and control center squares and open diagonals to enable developing other pieces.

Queen's Gambit

- A "gambit" is the offer of a pawn in the opening for an advantage. The Queen's Gambit is not a true gambit.

- After eight moves by White (and seven by Black) both sides have developed many of their pieces, are fighting for the center, and are ready to castle.

- This position comes from the Ragosin Variation of the Queen's Gambit Declined. We'll take a look at openings and their names later.

King's Indian Defense

- White has advanced a broad three-pawn phalanx in the center, developed three minor pieces and castled—all in seven moves: 1. d2-d4 Ng8-f6 2. c2-c4 g7-g6 3. Nb1-c3 Bf8-g7 4. e2-e4 d7-d6 5. Ng1-f3 0-0 6. Bf1-e2 e7-e5 7. 0-0.

- Black has developed his kingside in a fianchetto formation and castled. He has counterpunched in the center with 6. ... e7-e5. On his seventh move, he can play 7. ... Nb8-d7, developing another piece.

CASTLE EARLY

Castle, usually kingside, to bring your king to safety and your rook into the game

You've seen a number of positions in which Black has paid attention to the principle of castling early. In the four photos below, let's look at a game that illustrates the dangers of ignoring this advice. This game was played more than 140 years ago in London by Wilhelm Steinitz, an Austrian who, twenty-three years later, became the first official world champion and an American citizen.

The contest was an exhibition game, and many think it was an "odds" game—a game in which a handicap is given to one player. Such a handicap can be the first move (an advantage), a pawn (most often the f-pawn), a piece, or even the queen. When the odds are a piece, the odds-giver removes

Queen-Bishop Fork

- With his knight on a5, Black forks White's queen on b3 and dangerous bishop on c4. He plans for White to move his queen, allowing Black to take the bishop, and after White recaptures, Black can castle.

- But in doing this, Black has placed his knight offsides and left his king on the open e-file.

- White has an in-between move in mind that is very unpleasant for Black.

Walking the Plank

- **11. Rf1-e1+ Bc8-e6** (11. ... Ke8-d7 loses quickly. Black blocks the check. He'll lose a bishop, but White's queen is still under attack.) **12. d5xe6 Na5xb3** (Black takes a queen, but his king begins a dangerous walk.)

- **13. e6xf7+ Ke8-d7** (now Black will never castle) **14. Bc4-e6+ Kd7-c6** (D) **15. Nf3-e5+** (White is in no hurry to recapture on b3.) **15. ... Kc6-b5 16. Be6-c4+** (Black's king is forced to the edge of the board.) **16. ... Kb5-a5.**

the piece from its home square before the start of the game. In the case of the game below, one version of the story says that Steinitz started without his queen's rook. You'll see that he didn't need it!

If you're replaying the game on your own board, take off the white rook on a1 to give yourself a feel for how this would have looked and felt. Starting a rook down is a serious handicap!

This game took place before Wilhelm moved to the United States and became William. He was young and still a player who largely followed the Romantic School—whose followers

valued attack above all else. Defense was sometimes actually criticized as a sign of cowardly play! Well, that attitude may be the best when playing a rook down—after all, you can't let the game go to an ending!

Steinitz played White. We pick up Steinitz-Rock, London, 1853 after the moves:

1. e2-e4 e7-e5 2. Ng1-f3 Nb8-c6 3. Bf1-c4 Bf8-c5 4. b2-b4 Bc5xb4 5. c2-c3 Bb4-a5 6. d2-d4 e5xd4 7. 0–0 Ng8-f6 8. Bc1-a3 Ba5-b6 9. Qd1-b3 d7-d5 10. e4xd5 Nc6-a5. (See "Queen-Bishop Fork," far left.)

Checkmate on the Edge

- 16. ... Kb5-a4 comes to the same end: 17. a2xb3+ Ka4-a5 18. Ba3-b4#.

- Now White checkmates Black in two moves, ending on a humorous note: **17. Ba3-b4+ Ka5-a4 18. a2xb3#.** White recaptures the knight that took his queen, giving checkmate!

The Final Position

- Black's king has been forced to walk from his original square on e8 to the a-file, where it is checkmated by White's minor pieces and a pawn.

- Notice that, with or without White's queen rook, the game and the result would be the same.

- Lesson: Castle early! The middle of the board is no place for your king in the opening or middle game!

OPENING TRAPS & TRICKS
Sound principles will normally get you safely through the opening, but beware traps

Hundreds of different traps have been discovered—most during actual play—in the popular openings. Scores of books have been written on this specific subject, collecting opening traps and tricks. A number of these traps have claimed as victims some of the best players in the world.

It's important to know that there are ways to go wrong and lose in the opening. And it's important to know the likely-to-happen traps in the openings you play. But don't fixate on learning hundreds of opening traps that you may never use.

In the following chapters we'll recommend some openings for you to begin your games with. We'll show you some of the traps your opponent can fall into and tricks that you should

Noah's Ark Trap

- The position above is the end of the famous Noah's Ark Trap in the Ruy Lopez. Black snaps the trap shut on White's bishop with **11. ... c5-c4,** hemming in and winning the bishop. This trap has claimed many victims.

- It happens after the moves **1. e2-e4 e7-e5 2. Ng1-f3 Nb8-c6 3. Bf1-b5 a7-a6 4. Bb5-a4 d7-d6 5. d2-d4 b7-b5 6. Ba4-b3 Nc6xd4 7. Nf3xd4 e5xd4 8. Qd1xd4? c7-c5! 9. Qd4-d5 Bc8-e6! 10. Qd5-c6+ Be6-d7 11. Qc6-d5,** when we have the position above.

Pawn Fork

- In this position, after **1. e2-e4 e7-e5 2. Nb1-c3 Ng8-f6 3. Bf1-c4 Nb8-c6 4. Ng1-f3,** Black can play a number of good moves, for example, 4. ... Bf8-c5 or 4. ... Bf8-e7. He can also play the surprising **4. ... Nf6xe4.** But how can he dare to do this, since White's knight on c3 guards White's e-pawn?

- If **5. Nc3xe4,** then Black has the pawn fork **5. ... d7-d5!.** Whatever White does, Black recovers the piece with an approximately equal game.

avoid. Then we'll take a brief look at all the other popular openings. Whether you stick with the openings we recommend or you see others you think you'll like better, keep playing the same openings for a while. You'll learn the thematic play and traps in the opening for both sides.

Below we give a sampling of opening traps to show you the idea.

Pinning and Winning

- White can make good use of two pins (one along the d-file and one along the a2-g8 diagonal): **12. Nd4xe6! f7xe6** (if 12. ... Qd7xe6 Re1xe4!) **13. Re1xe4!.**

- In both variations above, Black can't recapture his knight on e4 without exposing his queen.

- The game began as another Ruy Lopez: **1. e2-e4 e7-e5 2. Ng1-f3 Nb8-c6 3. Bf1-b5 a7-a6 4. Bb5-a4 Ng8-f6 5. 0-0 Nf6xe4 6. d2-d4 b7-b5 7. Ba4-b3 d7-d5 8. d4xe5 Bc8-e6 9. c2-c3 Bf8-e7 10. Rf1-e1 0-00 11. Nf3-d4 Qd8-d7?.**

Smothered Queen

- Here White has **13. Nc3xd5!**. After **13. ... c6xd5,** White follows up with **14. Bf4-c7,** smothering the queen.

- Black's best is then 14. ... Nd7-c5, but White quashes Black's hopes with 15. Rc1xc5. Whatever Black does, he will be behind in material.

- The game began: **1. Ng1-f3 d7-d5 2. c2-c4 e7-e6 3. d2-d4 Ng8-f6 4. Bc1-g5 Nb8-d7 5. e2-e3 Bf8-e7 6, Nb1-c3 0–0 7. Ra1-c1 c7-c6 8. Bf1-d3 a7-a6 9. c4xd5 e6xd5 10. 0-0 Rf8-e8 11. Qd1-b3 h7-h6 12. Bg5-f4 Nf6-h5.**

OPENING WITH 1. e4
You need to have an opening plan in mind to begin a game

Every chess player needs to have a plan of how to open a game with White. You should not waste the opportunity to have the initiative. For hundreds of years, one of two first moves has been the choice of the world's best players: 1. e2-e4 or 1. d2-d4. These two moves are equally good.

In general, the first move 1. e2-e4 leads to *open* positions. Open positions offer available files and diagonals for the pieces to attack, control, and defend squares through the center of the board. In general, the first move 1. d2-d4 leads to *closed* positions. Closed positions contain locked pawn formations that block the files and diagonals that pass through the center of the board.

We recommend that you play 1. e2-e4 until you learn the possibilities of the open games, where tactics abound. Later, you may want to experiment with 1. d2-d4 to see how you like closed positions, which normally put off the major battle

Scotch Gambit

- **3. ... e5xd4**

- **4. Bf1-c4** (Instead, 4. Nf3xd4 would make it a Scotch Game—which we'll see in Chapter 22.)

- **4. ... Bf8-b4+** (We'll look at other choices later.)
  5. c2-c3 d4xc3 6. b2xc3 Bb4-a5 (Traps abound

when White has this much initiative! Other reasonable-looking bishop moves lose immediately: If 6. ... Bb5-e7, then 7. Qd1-d5 threatens mate. Then if 6. ... Ng8-h6, 7. Bc1xh6!; and if 6. ... Bb5-c5, then 7..Bc4-f7+! Ke8xf7 8. Qd1-d5+ Kf7-e8 9. Qd5xc5±.)

Using the Initiative

- **7. 0-0 d7-d6** (7. ... Ng8-f6? is another trap!: 8. e4-e5 Nf3-g4 9. Bc4xf7+! Ke8xf7 10. Nf3-g5+ Ke7-e8 11. Qd1-g4±.)

- **8. Qd1-b3 Qd8-e7** (You create a battery against f7. Both 8. ... Qd8-f6 9. Bc1-g5 Qf6-g6 10. e4-e5!, and 8. ... Qd8-d7 9. Rf1-e1, with

e4-e5 to follow, are also uncomfortable for Black.)

- **9. e4-e5 d6xe5** (If 9. ... Nc6xe5, then 10. Nf3xe5 Qe7xe5—or 10. ... d6xe5 11. Qb3-a4+, winning a piece—11. Bxf7+!.)

- **10. Bc1-a3** (You develop with major threats.)

but only for a short period of time.

Black has a number of responses to 1. e2-e4, and we'll show you how to play against them. In this chapter, we'll look at an effective way to continue when Black plays one of the most common—and theoretically correct—moves, 1. ... e7-e5.

We can only get you started. There are hundreds of books specializing in openings. Each one of the openings we mention is the subject of entire books. So, if you get especially interested in an opening, you can specialize. (See our final chapter, "Resources.")

Play over these moves on your own board, imagining yourself commanding the white pieces against a real opponent: **1. e2-e4 e7-e5 2. Ng1-f3 Nb8-c6 3. d2-d4.** (See "Scotch Gambit," far left.) Your last move attacks the center again and opens up a diagonal for your queen bishop. Black shouldn't take this pawn with his knight, since it's normally better to recapture with units of equal value. After 3. ... Nc6xd4 4. Nf3xd4 e5xd4 5. Qd1xd4, White dominates the center.

Trapped in the Center

- Black hasn't castled and his king is still in the center in an *open* game—files and diagonals through the center give you avenues of attack. Now Black has to move his threatened queen while still defending f7.

- **10. ... Qe7-f6 11. Nb1-d2 Ng8-e7 12. Nd2-e4 Qf6-g6** (If Black's queen goes to f4 or f5, play can develop similarly.) **13. Ba3xe7 Qg6xe4** (If 13. ... Nc6xe7, 14. Nf3xe5! Qg6xe4 15. Bc4-b5+!. If 13. ... Ke8xe7, 14. Qb3-a3+ Ke7-e8 15. Ne4-g5!.) **14. Rf1-e1 Qe4-f5 15. Be7-a3.**

Verdict: White Wins

- After fifteen moves, Black is lost. He still can't castle, because f8 is controlled by your dark-square bishop on a3. It's hard for Black to develop his queen bishop because his b7-square would be vulnerable.

- You're threatening to capture on e5—for example, 15. ... Ba4-b6 16. Nf3xe5 Nc6xe5 (16. ... Bb6xf2+ 17. Kg1-h1 is even worse for Black.) 17. Bc4xf7+ Ke8-d8 18. Qb3-d5+. You'll capture the piece on e5 with your rook. Black is in deep trouble.

THE GIUOCO PIANO

Black can move his bishop to a more solid square on his fourth move

You shouldn't get the impression that as White you can force a winning position from the first move. But you should maintain an initiative well into the middle game.

One of the advantages of the line we're recommending for you is that it is more *forcing* than a lot of other openings. It avoids a lot of lines that are solid defenses for Black. But chess is a fair and logical game. There is no pattern of moves you can play as White or Black that prevents your opponent from having options.

As we'll see, chess players have lots of different openings to choose from, and even many *subvariations* within those openings. Sometimes people are confused about how an

Developing and Centralizing

- In this line, your opponent doesn't use his bishop to check on b4. Instead, he develops it on c5, where it bolsters his central pawn on d4.

- **5. c2-c3** (You're again willing to gambit a pawn to acquire a strong initiative.)

5. ... Ng8-f6 6. c3xd4 Bc5-b4+ (You've forced Black's bishop off c5 by constructing a pawn center.) **7. Bc1-d2** (You block the check by developing another piece.) **7. ... Bb4xd2+ 8. Nb1xd2 d7-d5!** (For 8. ... Nf6xe4, see panel 3.)

The Equalizing ... d7-d5

- Black's last move is a good example of the freeing potential of ... d7-d5 for Black in the king pawn openings. As White, you must now play with accuracy to maintain an edge!

- **9. e4xd5 Nf6xd5 10. Qd1-b3 Nc6-e7** (Black has to retreat the queen knight to defend d5 and keep blocking your attack on f7.) **11. 0-0 0-0 12. Rf1-e1 c7-c6 13. Ra1-d1.**

- Both sides have played well. White enjoys a small advantage going into the middle game.

opening is chosen, thinking that one side determines what opening a game will begin with. In truth, both players have a role choosing the opening. Each side's choices narrow the possibilities until the opponents mutually reach a recognized opening formation.

Black had other choices in the line above. To prepare you to play our recommended opening moves, we'll go over some of Black's best options. This new line is called the Giuoco Piano and is characterized in our line by 4. ... Bf8-c5. Should you memorize these lines? Well, a tournament player does have his favorite line committed to memory. But it's always more important to understand the ideas behind the moves. Rote memorization will result in your getting in positions you don't understand and leave you unsure of what to do when your opponent varies from the line you have in mind.

Let's look at what you should do if your opponent picks a more solid play on move four in our line: **1. e2-e4. e7-e5 2. Ng1-f3 2. Nb8-c6 3. d2-d4 e5xd4 4. Bf1-c4 Bf8-c5.** (See "Developing and Centralizing," far left.)

The Fork Trick

- In this variation, instead of playing the freeing 8. ... d7-d5, Black grabs your king pawn with **8. ... Nf6xe4.** Now, if you play 9. Nd2xe4, Black uses the pawn-fork trick we saw in Chapter 8: 9. ... d7-d5!. So . . .

- **9. d4-d5! Ne4xd2 10. Qd1xd2 Nc6-e7 11. d5-d6!** (This prevents Black from ever playing ... d6, and cuts off coordination between Black's queen- and king-sides.) **11. ... c7xd6 12. Qd2xd6 0-0** (If 12. ... Qd8-a5+, 13. b2-b4.) **13. 0-0.**

Initiative for White

- You have an initiative in exchange for Black's isolated d-pawn. Black has problems completing his development. The game is dynamically equal. For example, if 13. ... Ne7-f5 14. Qd6-f4 d7-d5 15. Ra1-d1, then Black's best is to bring his knight back to e7.

- The Giuoco Piano means the "quiet game," but as we've seen, the opening can take on quite a dangerous character if White presses for the initiative.

TWO KNIGHTS DEFENSE

Another of Black's fourth-move options, 4. ... Ng8-f6, is logical, aggressive, and time-tested

Let's back up to Black's fourth move to look at another important option he can choose. So far we've only seen Black develop his king bishop—either to b4 or c5. Another logical choice is to develop his king knight, and the square for choice is, as usual, f6. With 4. ... Ng8-f6, he enters another tried-and-true defensive pattern, the Two Knights Defense.

It's one of the oldest openings and one of the most aggressive for Black.

One of the advantages of the exact move order we recommend is that it eliminates some possibilities for Black in this defense. (The more usual way of entering the line is: 1. e2-e4 e7-e5 2. Ng1-f3 Nb8-c6 3. Bf1-c4 Ng8-f6 4. d2-d4.) So if Black

Two Knights Defense

Simple, Strong Development

- **5. e4-e5 Nf6-g4**

- If instead 5. ... Nf6-e4, you can offer an effective pawn sacrifice: 6. Qd1-e2 Ne4-c5 7. c2-c3 d4xc3 8. Nb1xc3 Bf8-e7 9. Bc1-e3 0-0 10. 0-0. For the gambited pawn, you make it difficult for Black to formulate an effec-

tive plan of development, while your pieces are active and aggressive. You will likely follow up with Rf1-d1, and then perhaps Rd1-d2, threatening to double your rooks, forming a powerful battery on the d-file.

- **6. 0-0** (You play simple, strong developing moves. Black can't capture on e5, even though his attackers outnumber your defender, because you would have an embarrassing pin on his remaining knight with Rf1-e1 after the exchanges.)

- **6. ... d6** (If 6. ... d5, then 7. Bc4-b5 and you threaten 8. h2-h3, and if 8. ... Ng4-h6, 9. Bc1xh6! mangles Black's kingside.) **7. e5xd6 Bf8xd6 8. Rf1-e1+ Bd6-e7** (Black would lose the privilege of castling after 8. ... Ke8-f8.)

wants to go into the Two Knights Defense, he'll enter into your playbook.

Because of your move order, you meet Black's 4. ... Ng8-f6 with an immediate 5. e4-e5. Now Black must make a decision. His two best moves are 5. ... Nf6-g4, which we look at in this spread, and 5. ... d7-d5! (that central thrust to try to equalize the game that we've seen before). We'll prepare you for that option in the next spread.

We begin **1. e2-e4 e7-e5 2. Ng1-f3 Nb8-c6 3. Bf1-c4 Ng8-f6 4. d2-d4 e5xd4.** (See "Two Knights Defense," far left.)

(See "Two Knights Defense," far left.)

That Mean e-file

- Black is a pawn ahead. He's had to move his king bishop twice, and now it's pinned to his king. How can you increase the pressure along the open e-file?

- **9. Bc1-g5!** (You double up the attack on the pinned bishop.) **9. ... Be6** (Black develops at the same time he blocks the pin on the e-file. Attractive logic, but he probably minimizes your advantage by castling immediately, allowing 10. Bg5xe7 Nc6xe7 11. Qd1xd4.) **10. Bc4xe6 f7xe6 11. Re1xe6** (You keep the e-file open!)

Dominating the Board

- **11. ... Ng4-f6 12. Qd1-e2** (You "pile up" on the e-file, creating a battery.) **12. ... 0-0 13. Nb1-d2** (You develop your last minor piece.)

- Through logical play, you have built up a very strong, perhaps even winning, game. You threaten to triple on the e-file by playing Ra1-e1, dominating the middle of the board on the open file.

TWO KNIGHTS DEFENSE II

After 5. e4-e5 in the Two Knights Defense, Black's best is the thematic 5. ... d7-d5

We've seen that in the king-pawn openings, ... d7-d5 can be a freeing maneuver if timed properly. In general, striking back in the center is a good principle of play in the openings. Instead of the fifth-move variation we've just looked at, Black can use this central thrust in the Two Knights as the best way to reach a playable middle game.

As White, you're faced with a decision. Your bishop on c4 is threatened by Black's ... d7-d5. At the same moment, your pawn on e5 attacks Black's knight on f6. What should you move? You should have three or four *candidate moves* in mind (see sidebar). Let's go through the list.

First, 6. e5xf6: Attractive at first glance, since it immediately

Counterattacking the Center

- Our game starts: **1. e2-e4 e7-e5 2. Ng1-f3 Nb8-c6 3. Bf1-c4 Ng8-f6 4. d2-d4 e5xd4 5. e4-e5,** but this time Black finds **5. ... d7-d5!** to reach the position above.

- **6. Bc4-b5 Nf6-d7.** (We'll look at 6. ... Nf6-e4 later.) **7. 0-0 Bf8-e7 8. Rf1-e1** (Both sides develop. Your rook thematically goes to the e-file.) **8. ... 0-0 9. Bb5xc6 b7xc6** (You remove the guard on d4 while doubling pawns.) **10. Nf3xd4.**

Cramping e-5 Pawn

- Black must now "undevelop" with **10. ... Nd7-b8**—10. ... Bc8-b7 would allow you to play 11. Qd1-g4! with a strong attack, threatening Bc1-h6.

- Your e-5 pawn cramps Black's game. After 10. ... Nd7-b8, you can play against the kingside with

11. Qd1-h5 and consider fianchettoing your dark-square bishop to b2 after b2-b3 to add pressure along the *long diagonal.*

- Let's back up to look at the more aggressive choice for Black: **6. ... Nf6-e4 7. 0-0** (or 7. Nf3xd4) **7. ... Bc8-g4 8. Nb1-d2 Bf8-c5.**

opens the e-file, but experience has shown that after 6. ... d5xc4, Black gets much the better game—with a powerful advanced center and an extra pawn. White has no initiative to compensate for it.

Second, the other pawn capture, 6. exd6 e.p.: After 6. ... Bf8xd6, White is a pawn down with little to show for it. Black develops easily.

A third choice—6. Bc4-b5: Moves the bishop to a safe square while pinning the black knight. This move turns out to be best.

Dynamic Equality

- Black has chosen an aggressive placement for his minor pieces. You've developed your queen knight on d2 so that it can hop to b3, where it will attack Black's d4 pawn and gain time by hitting the bishop on c5. If Black had played 8. ... Ne4-g5, your knight reinforces f3 to avoid having your

kingside pawns doubled. You have the option to play Bb5xc6 at some point to double Black's pawns and remove a defender of d4.

- The game is dynamically even. A tough fight is ahead.

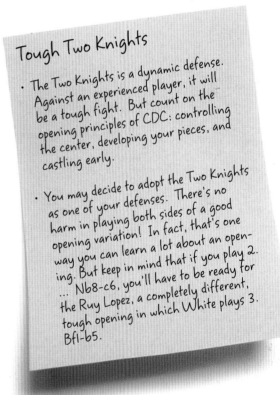

Tough Two Knights

- The Two Knights is a dynamic defense. Against an experienced player, it will be a tough fight. But count on the opening principles of CDC: controlling the center, developing your pieces, and castling early.

- You may decide to adopt the Two Knights as one of your defenses. There's no harm in playing both sides of a good opening variation! In fact, that's one way you can learn a lot about an opening. But keep in mind that if you play 2. ... Nb8-c6, you'll have to be ready for the Ruy Lopez, a completely different, tough opening in which White plays 3. Bf1-b5.

PETROFF DEFENSE

On the second turn, Black can develop his king knight to counterattack rather than defend

We're still considering opening play after 1. e2-e5 e7-e5. We've looked at three important and popular defenses when, after 2. Ng1-f3, Black defended his e5-pawn with the developing 2. ... Nb8-c6. But Black has a different knight move on his second turn. Instead of defending, he can counterattack with 2. ... Ng8-f6, threatening White's pawn on e4. This continuation

is called the Petroff Defense, named after the Russian Alexander Petroff, who analyzed and played the opening moves in the mid-1800s.

Despite the fact that it begins as a counterattack, the Petroff has the reputation of being a tame opening that plays for a draw. But this would be the case only at the top levels of

Petroff Defense

- This is the *tabia* (defining setup) of the Petroff. You play **3. Bf1-c4,** following our normal pattern.

- After **3. ... Nf6xe4,** you continue to develop with **4. Nb1-c3.**

- If Black now plays 4. ... Nb8-c6, just play 5. 0-0, continu-

ing to develop. (5. Nxe4 d7-d5!)

- **4. ... Ne4xc3 5. d2xc3** (Although your c-pawn is doubled, this capture controls d4 and opens the diagonal for your dark-square bishop.)

Quick Development

- Your last move, 5. d2xc3, ignored the opening principle that your pawns should recapture toward the center. This position is an exception. You count on your quick development to give you an initiative.

- **5. ... c7-c6** (Black plans to block the center. Of course

not 5. ... e5-e4 6. Nf3-g5±.) If 5. ... f7-f6?!, given in some opening manuals, continue logically with 6. 0-0, and if 6. ... Bf8-c5 play 7. Nf3-h4, threatening Qd1-h5+, when Black can't play ... g6 because of Nh4xg6!. **6. Nf3xe5 d7-d5.**

tournament chess. Besides, there are a number of sharp lines, and we recommend one of these for you as White.

The line begins: **1. e2-e4 e7-e5 2. Ng1-f3 Ng8-f6.** Now either 3. Nf3xe5 or 3. d2-d4 are the most popular continuations. However, we recommend a surprising but solid move, ignoring the threat and sticking to the themes of our opening repertoire by playing **3. Bf1-c4.** Black could now *transpose*—shift from one opening to another—to the Two Knights Defense by playing **3. ... Nb8-c6,** when you would respond with **4. d2-d4,** reaching familiar territory. (See

"Petroff Defense," far left.) But a Petroff player is unlikely to be comfortable in the Two Knights—if he wanted to see it, he would, after all, play ... Nb8-c6 on the second move!

Bishop with Immunity

- **7. 0-0!** *(D)* Now Black would lose with 7. ... d5xc4 8. Qd1xd8+ Ke8xd8 9. Ne5xf7+.) **7. ... Bf8-d6 8. Rf1-e1 0-0** (Good idea! Your daring bishop is still immune. If 8. ... d5xc4, the discovered check 9. Ne5xc6!+ wins the Black queen.)

- **9. Bc4-b3** (Now it's time to retreat your bishop. 9. Bc4-d3 is another reasonable choice.) **9. ... Nb8-d7 10. Bc1-f4 Qd8-c7** (Black has other choices, but this one develops his queen to a logical square, pressuring e5.) **10. Qc1-d4** (White centralizes his queen.)

Equal but Tricky

- Notice that there's a way for Black to go terribly wrong here: 10. ... Bd6-c5, attacking your queen, loses to another discovery, 11. Ne5xd7!.

- You can see that your pieces are aggressively posted. Black has a few

  moves to go to develop the rest of his queenside pieces.

- Black has threaded his way to a dynamically equal game. The Petroff is a sound defense, so we can't expect to win in the opening against a careful, well-schooled opponent.

OTHER DEFENSES AFTER 1. e4 e5

We've learned a lot, and we're almost finished reviewing the reasonable king-pawn openings

On this page spread, we first look at a very old defense, named after Frenchman André Philidor, the greatest player of the eighteenth century. Later, when we study the end-game, you'll see his name attached to a very important position he discovered. The Philidor is characterized by the opening moves 1. e2-e4 e7-e5 2. Ng1-f3 d7-d6. Theoretically,

we might object because we know that ... d7-d5 can be a thematically important freeing move in a double king-pawn opening. However, 2. ... d7-d6 is logical because it shores up Black's threatened pawn on e5 and opens the diagonal to develop his queen bishop.

Not many modern masters today play the Philidor Defense

Philidor Defense

- Follow your normal pattern: **3. d2-d4 Nb8-d7** (Characteristic of the defense: Black avoids a pin on b5. Other modern Philidor continuations and your suggested replies are: 3. ... Ng8-f6 4. d4xe5 and 3. ... e5xd4 4. Qd1xd4.)

- **4. Bf1-c4 c7-c6** (Black's only good move. If 4. ... Bf8-e7?, 5. d4xe5!—and now whether 5. ... d6xe5 6. Qd1-d5! , or 5. ... Nd7xe5 6. Nf3xe5 d6xe5 7. Qd1-h5!, you're much better.)

- **5. 0-0 Bf8-e7** (If 5. ... Ng8-f6 6. d4xe5 d6xe5 7. Nf3-g5!.)

Bishop Pair Advantage

- You have a forcing series of moves that leads to your advantage: **6. d4xe5 d6xe5** (If 6. ... Nd7xe5, 7. Nf3xe5 d6xe5 8. Qd1-h5!, winning.) **7. Nf3-g5! Be7xg5 8. Qd1-h5** (The mate threat also double attacks Black's bishop on g5.) **8. ... Qd8-e7** (If 8. ... g7-g6 9. Qh5xg5.) **9. Qh5xg5 Qxg5 10. Bxg5.**

- This is the kind of open position, with pawns on both sides of the board, that empowers the bishop pair. You will bolster your center with f2-f3, put a rook on the d-file, and enjoy an advantage.

regularly, but no one really doubts that it is theoretically sound. Probably, the top players find it too passive.

The third and fourth panels on this spread cover two less-respected tries. The Latvian Gambit, 1. e2-e4 e7-e5 2. Ng1-f3 f7-f5 is not sound. It weakens Black's uncastled king and ignores development. It's akin to a pitcher lobbing a slow pitch over the center of the plate, hoping the batter won't connect. Some players will try it, gambling that you're unprepared and that the surprise value of the move will rattle you.

The Elephant Gambit, 1. e2-e4 e7-e5 2. Ng1-f3 d7-d5, is probably the least-often seen of Black's choices in this chapter. It leaves Black with a worse position and doesn't even have the risk-reward potential of the Latvian Gambit. Once again, some players with a penchant for the bizarre will specialize in such an opening for its shock value, desiring to get their white opponents "out of the books." But a few moments of preparation will make you happy to see this move.

After **1. e2-e4 e7-e5 2. Ng1-f3 d7-d6**, we have the Philidor's Defense. (See "Philidor Defense," far left.)

Elephant Gambit

- The Elephant Gambit, also called the Queen's Pawn Counter Gambit: **1. e2-e4 e7-e5 2. Ng1-f3 d7-d5** *(D)*. Although ... d7-d5 is a liberating theme in the double king-pawn openings, it requires preparation.

- **3. e4xd5 Bf8-d6** (If 3. ... e5-e4 4. Qd1-e2, fol-lowed by d2-d3. And if 3. ... Qd8xd5, 4. Nb1-c3 develops another piece while harassing the queen.) **4. d2-d4 e5-e4 5. Nf3-e5 Ng8-f6 6. Bf1-b5+ Bc8-d7 7. Ne5xd7 Nb8xd7 8. c2-c4.**

- You have an extra pawn and easy development.

Latvian Gambit

- The Latvian Gambit: **1. e2-e4 e7-e5 2. Ng1-f3 f7-f5** *(D)* (risky!) **3. Nf3xe5 Qd8-f6** (Others lose—for example, 3. ... f5xe4 and 3. ... Qd8-e7 are both answered strongly by 4. Qd1-h5+!.)

- **3. d2-d4 d7-d6 4. Ne5-c4 f5xe4 5. Nb1-c3.**

- You already enjoy a significant advantage. Black's queen is on an awkward square, while your knights are developed, and you will capture Black's e4-pawn. If Black tries to defend it with 5. ... Qf6-g6, you'll play 6. f2-f3 e4xf3 7. Qd1xf3, with a dominating position.

PLAYING WHITE: OTHER DEFENSES

Black has good defenses against 1. e2-e4 other than 1. … e7-e5; he has the semi-open defenses

Your opponent does not have to respond to your 1. e2-e4 with 1. … e7-e5, resulting in a double king-pawn opening—also called the *open game*. He can instead begin with a *semi-open game*. In this chapter, we'll show you how to play against these semi-open defenses. All of these have this in common: an attempt to create an immediate, dynamic imbalance.

The most popular of these defenses—in fact, the most popular defense to 1. e4 in tournament chess—is 1. … c7-c5, the Sicilian Defense. Its trademark first move controls d4 in a different way than 1. … e7-e5 does. After 1. e2-e4 c7-c5, if you play 2. d2-d4, Black can trade his c-pawn for your more valuable center pawn (see sidebar at right), while keeping both

Sicilian Defense

- We recommend **3. c2-c3**—it's a little offbeat but has been used by even modern world champions. It upsets Black's normal plans, simplifies your task, and is in no way inferior to the more popular lines. Now when you play d2-d4 and Black

captures, you can recapture on d4 with your c-pawn, maintaining your two-pawn center.

- **3. … Ng8-f6** (Black develops while attacking your e-pawn.)

Can Black Capture?

- **4. Bf1-e2!** *(D)* (Can you see why you can ignore Black's "threat" against your important e-pawn? Notice that c2-c3 opened the diagonal for you to check on a4. If 4. … Nf6xe4, 5. Qd1-a4+! wins Black's reckless knight.)

- **4. … Nb8-c6** (Now the diagonal is blocked and there is no check.) **5. d2-d4 c5xd5 6. c3xd4 Nf6xe4 7. d4-d5.**

- Black is ahead one pawn, but your d-pawn push disorganizes his pieces.

his own center pawns. The Sicilian is a riskier defense than 1. ... e2-e5. But the Sicilian offers more chances of winning because of the imbalance it immediately creates. In general, if Black makes it to an endgame in the Sicilian Defense without a serious setback, he will have the better game.

The opening often begins: **1. e2-e4 c7-c5 2. Ng1-f3 d7-d6.** (See "Sicilian Defense," far left.) Normal now is 3. d2-d4 c5xd4 4. Nf3xd4 Ng8-f6 5. Nb1-c3. Then Black can select from a confusing variety of Sicilian formations, each with its own themes and traps.

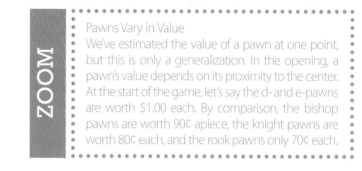
Cramping Bind

- **7. ... Qd8xa5+ 8. Nb1-c3 Ne4xc3 9. b2xc3 Nc6-e5** (If 9. ... Qa5xc3+, 10. Bc1-d2, when Black must move his queen and lose his knight.) **10. 0-0 Ne5xf3 11. Be2xf3.**

- You're still down a pawn, and have another one *en prise*, but you have a cramping bind on d5 that makes it difficult for Black to develop his kingside.

- Taking the c-pawn is now dangerous for Black. You'd play Bc1-d2 and harass the queen, the only developed Black piece, on open diagonals and files.

Trouble Developing

- Black has trouble planning how to castle. If he plays 11. ... g7-g6 to fianchetto his bishop, you centralize your queen with a tempo: 12. Qd1-d4.

- Play could continue 11. ... Bc8-f5; then you play 12. Bc1-b2 g7-g6 13. c2-c4 Rh8-g8 14. Qd1-e2, when the game is dynamically even. Black has a slight material advantage, one pawn, but your pieces and pawns control key squares, and you are safely castled.

THE FRENCH DEFENSE
Black can also choose to play 1. … e7-e6 and after 2. d2-d4, 2. … d7-d5

The French Defense is another popular semi-open defense. After **1. e2-e4 e7-e6 2. d2-d4,** Black plays **2. … d7-d5,** counterattacking your broad pawn center and staking out his own claim to the board's prime territory in the opening. The opening is a solid choice, but like every semi-open defense, it has special advantages and counterbalancing disadvantages.

On the plus side, the French gives Black a bolstered center and the thematic center-counterattacking pawn moves, … c7-c5 and … f7-f6. (Chess players call these *levers*.) On the downside, notice that Black's pawn on e6 blocks in his light-square bishop, tending to make it a "bad" bishop with little mobility and the problem piece of the opening. Black can

French Defense

- Above we show the *tabia* of the French Defense. You play **3. e4-e5,** reducing Black's options while cramping his game.

- After your third move, notice how your pawns "point" toward Black's kingside. In general, you want to

attack in the direction that your center pawns point. So in this variation, your attack is generally on the kingside, while Black's is on the queenside.

- **3. … c7-c5 4. c2-c3 Nb8-c6** (Black keeps counterattacking d4.) **5. Ng1-f3 Qd8-b6**

Piling on d4

- (Black's last move was another good one—piling on d4 while attacking b2.) You play **6. Bf1-d3** (D), developing your key light-square bishop against your opponent's kingside, and we have the position above.

- **6. … c5xd4 7. c3xd4 Bc8-d7** (Not falling into a killing

trap: 7. … Nc6xd4? 8. Nf3xd4 Qb6xd4?? 9. Bd3-b5+!, winning the black queen.) **8. 0-0 Nc6xd4 9. Nf3xd4 Qb6xd4 10. Nb1-c3.**

- You've played a famous line called the Milner-Barry Gambit.

plan to trade off the bishop—for example, with ... b7-b6 and ... Bc8-a6, but he loses time with this maneuver.

Often White continues with 3. Nb1-c3, allowing Black to choose his favorite French variation—perhaps the Winawer with 3. ... Bf8-b4, the Rubinstein with 3. ... d5xe4, or the Classical with 3. ... Ng8-f6.

Again, we recommend a continuation that shortcuts many of Black's choices but is still respected as a theoretically sound move, the Advance French, **3. e4-e5.**

Material vs. Initiative

- This position shows the relationship between material and initiative in the opening. You're safely castled and have your knight and bishop on effective squares. Black's kingside is undeveloped and cramped by your e5-pawn. You are a pawn down—so far.

- **10. ... Qd4xe5** (It's hard for Black to turn down the second pawn before you play 11. Qd1-e2, securing it.)

- **11. Rf1-e1 Qd4-d6** (If 11. ... Qd4-b8 or -c7 or -f6, you have 12. Nc3xd5!.) **12. Nc3-b5 Qd6-b8 13. Qd1-f3 Ng8-e7?**

Find the Finisher!

- Black covers up the pin on the e-file, but he should instead play 13. ... Bf1-d6, when after 14. Nb5xd6+ Qb8xd6 15. Bc1-f4 Qd6-b6 16. Qf3xd5!, you would be better but not "won."

- **14. Bc1-f4!** (Ouch! Black is dead. If 14. ... Qb8-c8, you fork with 15. Nb5-d6+!. If

14. ... Qb8-d8, you checkmate with 15. Nb5-d6#!.)

- And if instead of 12. ... Qd6-b8, Black had tried 12. ... Bd7xb5, you'd play 13. Bd3xb5+ and Black would have to move his king.

111

THE CARO-KANN DEFENSE

The Caro-Kann establishes a supported pawn in the center without blocking in his queen bishop

The Caro-Kann, named after two German-Austrian masters who analyzed it in the 1890s, is another trusted semi-open defense. Compare the first photo below to the first two moves of the French opening. You'll see that the Caro seeks to bolster a pawn on d5 without hemming in Black's light-square bishop.

The disadvantage—there is one, since chess is a logical game—of this approach is that Black will have to move his c-pawn a second time to challenge a white pawn on d4, whereas, in the French, Black could play the lever ... c7-c5 in one move. Partially because of this difference, the Caro-Kann is known as a more passive defense than the French or

Caro-Kann

- This is the Caro-Kann *tabia*, the position after **1. e2-e4 c7-c6 2. d2-d4 d7-d5**. *(D)*

- As against the French, you play the restricting **3. e4-e5**.

- To get an idea of the tactical possibilities, we'll take a look at a game between

two Argentine grandmasters: Pablo Ricardi–Daniel Campora, 1997: **3. ... Bc8-f5 4. Ng1-f3 e7-e6 5. Bf1-e2 Nb8-d7 6. 0–0 Ng8-e7** (Black puts his knights on e7 and d7 because c6 is blocked by his own pawn, and f6 is guarded by White's pawn on e5.) **7. h2-h3.**

Struggling for Space

- Black must battle for space: **7. ... c6-c5 8. c2-c4 d5xc4 9. Nb1-a3** (The knight attacks c4 and quickly jumps toward the center.) **9. ... Ne7-c6 10. Na3xc4 Nd7-b6 11. Bc1-g5 f7-f6 12. e5xf6 g7xf6 13. Bg5-h4 c5xd4 14. Nf3-e5!** (White uses the pin on the

f6-pawn.) **14. ... Nb6xc4 15. Ne5xc6 b7xc6 16. Be2xc4 Bf8-e7 17. Rf1–e1** (Black should now castle, even though White would play 18. g2-g4 Bf5-g6 19. Re1xe6, with an advantage.) **17. ... e6-e5?** (to block the center) **18. Re1xe5!.**

Sicilian. And the defense offers no immediate way for Black to develop his dark-square bishop. Nevertheless, the Caro is a rock-ribbed defense, relied on by three of the greatest world champions: José Capablanca, Mikhail Botvinnik, and Anatoly Karpov.

The Caro-Kann allows Black to develop without creating any serious weaknesses. But it allows you, as White, freedom for your pieces and a space advantage. The struggle revolves around your using these advantages to create a permanent advantage before Black can equalize.

Blindfold, Please!

- Before looking at the specifics of White's last bombshell, let's evaluate this position. White's king is safely tucked away behind an intact kingside string of pawns. Black's king is in the center and suffers from an exposed h5-e8 diagonal. In fact, Black resigned in this position, the equivalent of wearing a blindfold in front of his firing squad. Let's look at what he "saw" coming.

- **18. ... f6xe5 19. Qd1-h5+** (A key check to relocate the queen.) **19. ... Bf5-g6 20. Qh5xe5 Rh8-f8.**

Pinned, Piled On

- **21. Ra1-e1!**

- Although White is a rook down, he pins Black's bishop on e7 and attacks it three times. It's defended only twice. White threatens to play 22. Bh4xe7, setting up a discovered check. Black would have no answer.

- So Black has to try **21. ... Rf8-f7**, but then **22. Bc4xf7+ Ke8xf7 23. Bh4xe7.** Black is lost, for example: 23. ... Qd8-c8 24. Be7-c5 Qc8-f5 25. Qe5-e7+ Kf7-g8 26. Bc5xd4 Bg6-f7 27. Re1-e3, when Black's king has no place to hide.

PIRC/MODERN DEFENSE

The hypermodern defenses encourage White to build up a big center, so Black can attack it

The Pirc and Modern are related "hypermodern" defenses that refrain from moving a center pawn to the fourth rank in the early going. They intentionally permit White to build up a big center, making the struggle about whether White can maintain such a center to his advantage, or whether his proud center will disintegrate under pressure. The hypermoderns

preferred to control the center rather than occupy it.

Hypermodern defenses are difficult to play. You need to know what to do when confronted with them, but we recommend that you avoid playing them yourself until you have the hang of classical principles.

The solid Pirc Defense begins 1. e2-e4 d7-d6 2. d2-d4 Ng8-f6

Pirc Defense

Making Space

- We get the Classical Pirc *tabia* above: **1. e2-e4 g7-g6 2. d2-d4 Bf8-g7 3. Nb1-c3 4. Ng1–f3 Bf8-g7.** *(D)*

- As White, you have a broad pawn center. Black has fianchettoed and is ready to castle.

- **5. h2-h3** (You restrict Black's queen bishop.)

- **5. ... 0-0 6. Bf1–e2 c7-c6** (6. ... c5 is also possible: 7. d4xc5 Qd8-a5 8. 0-0, with a tough game.) **7. 0-0 Nb8-d7** (We look at 7. ... b7-b5 in the last panel.) **8. a2-a4.**

- White's last move restrains Black from expanding on the queenside with ... b7-b5.

- **8. ... e7-e5** (Black has to counterpunch to give his pieces space.) **9. d4xe5 d6xe5 10. Bc1-e3 Qd8-e7 11. Qd1-d3** (White devel-

ops his queen, connecting his rooks and preparing to assemble a queen-rook battery on the d-file.) **11. ... Rf8-d8** (Black tries to oppose your buildup on the d-file, but he may be a bit better off playing 11. ... Rf8-e8.) **12. Ra1-d1.**

while the provocative Modern Defense begins 1. e2-e4 g7-g6 2. d2-d4 Bf8-g7. In both defenses, Black fianchettoes his bishop to g7, making control of the long-dark diagonal a very important theme.

We recommend that you play 3. Nc3 against both defenses. The Modern player must then merge into the Pirc with 3. ... Ng8-f6—or get stuck in an odd mixture of the Caro-Kann and Modern most players would not care to try, the Gurgenidze. In the sidebar at right, we take a quick look at that line in case you run into it.

Into the Middle Game

- You have a slight advantage in space and are entering the middle game with more space. Black must find a way to develop his queen bishop and connect his rooks.

- The purpose of your opening is to give you a playable middle game. Don't get the impression that you can force a winning position in any of the openings we've studied so far. As White against a savvy opponent, you should get a small advantage.

What If 7. ... b7-b5?

- "What if?" is the chess player's question. Let's look at a different seventh move for Black in the above game: **7. ... b7-b5** (D) (a thematic move in the defense—Black expands on the queenside) **8. e4-e5 d6xe5 9. d4xe5** (9. Nf3xe5 is also good.) **9. ... Nf6-d7 10. Bc1-f4.**

- Now if 10. ... Qd8-c7, White plays 11. Qd1-d4 with an advantage. If 10. ... b5-b4, you play 11. Nc3-e4. Black's best may be 10. ... Nd7-c5, planning ... b5-b4, when you can play 11. a2-a3.

ALEKHINE & SCANDINAVIAN

These two defenses aren't used much at the top echelons, but they are still dangerous

The Alekhine Defense was named after one of the greatest world champions, Alexander Alekhine, who used the defense in only two tournament games that we know of!

The Alekhine, 1. e2-e4 Ng8-f6, is the final hypermodern opening we'll look at and the least popular. But don't underestimate it. Against any solid defense, it's a mistake to try to

force a winning position. Your goal as White should be to obtain an advantage—in space or mobility—going into the middle game. It's only if Black makes a serious mistake, like the failure to castle in our Caro-Kann example, that you can expect to get a winning game out of the opening.

The Scandinavian Defense, often called the Center Counter

Alekhine

- The standard follow-up is **2. e4-e5 Nf6-d5** (Now 3. d2-d4 or 3. c2-c4—the "Chase Variation"—is normally played, with a complicated game. But we offer another shortcut to reduce your prep time and take your opponent "out of his book"—away from his favorite lines.

- **3. Nb1-c3 Nd5xc3 4. d2xc3** (Instead of capturing toward the center, you accentuate development. There are a number of ways the game can continue from here. Let's look at one reasonable example to give you an idea.)

Piece Play vs. Pawn Structure

- We reach the position above after: **4. ... d7-d6 5. Ng1-f3 d6xe5 6. Qd1xd8+ Ke8xd8** (With queens off the board, Black isn't concerned about losing his right to castle.) **7. Nf3xe5 Kd8-e8 8. Bf1-c4 e7-e6 9. 0-0.** (D)

- You have an advantage in

space and development. You should pressure Black with piece play. His pawn structure would be a plus in a pawn endgame, since he has four effective pawns against three on the kingside, while his three pawns can stop your queenside because of your doubled c-pawn.

Defense, is a very old answer to the king-pawn opening: 1. e2-e4 d7-d5. We've seen that, in the king-pawn openings, ... d7-d5 can be an equalizing counter if prepared properly. The question with the Scandinavian is whether or not Black can play the center thrust without any preparation! Played extensively by top German master Jacques Mieses in the 1900s, the Scandinavian lived under a cloud for a very long time. After 2. e4xd5 Qd8xd5, modern players felt that the defense exposed the queen to early harassment, permitting White to develop his queen's knight while gaining time. The defense

gained some credence at the end of the last century, even appearing in a world championship match.

The modern Center Counter Defense actually offers another second move choice: 2. ... Ng8-f6, keeping open the possibility of recapturing on d5 with ... Nf6xd5. But White has a number of options that make the knight-developing alternative less popular these days.

Scandinavian Defense

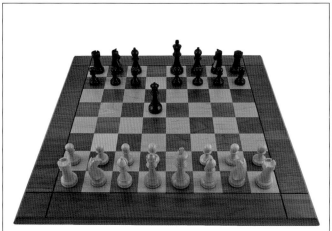

- We reach the Scandinavian (above) after **1. e2-e4 d7-d5 2. e4xd5 Qd8xd5.** *(D)* (If instead 2. ... Ng8-f6, one good line is 3. Bf1-b5+ Bc8-d7 4. Bb5-e2!, when Black's bishop will have to move again, since it blocks the d-file.)

- Now you have **3. Nb1-c3,** developing while gaining time by attacking Black's queen. The game can continue **3. ... Qd5-a5 4. d2-d4 Ng8-f6 5. Ng1-f3 c7-c6** (Defends d5 and at the same time creates an escape square, if necessary, for Black's queen.) **6. Nf3-e5 Bc8-e6 7. Ne5-c4.**

Bishop Pair Advantage

- After **7. ... Be6xc4 8. Bf1xc4 e7-e6,** you have the advantage of the two bishops. But there is a lot of chess left in this position, and the best player will win.

- You should castle short (kingside) and develop your dark-square bishop, probably to e3.

- If earlier, on move five, Black had played 5. ... Bc8-g4, you had 6. h2-h3, when Black must choose between surrendering the bishop pair immediately with 6. ... Bg4xf3 or 6. ... Bg4-h5 7. g2-g4! with the threatening idea of Nf3-e5-c4.

ODDS & ENDS

Faced with an opening "surprise," stay calm and don't try to refute it—play solid moves

On this page spread, we finish our review of Black's responses to the opening move we recommend for you, 1. e2-e4. The three openings we review here are not often used at top levels—although they do serve on occasion as surprise weapons. In fact, the British grandmaster Tony Miles used the second opening on this page, the St. George Defense, to

defeat one of the greatest modern world champions, Anatoly Karpov, in 1980.

As usual, you should look at these openings to understand the ideas behind the moves, rather than trying to memorize all of the possibilities. We give you only some sampling of lines. If you become really interested in opening play, there

Nimzovich Defense

- After **1. e2-e4 Nb8-c6,** we recommend **2. Ng1-f3.** Black may now transpose into normal lines with 2. e7-e5, or play a Scandinavian-like line: 2. ... d7-d5 3. e4xd5 Qd8xd5 4. Nc3 Qa5 5. Bf1-b5 Bc8-d7 6. 0-0, when you lead in development.

- A thematic try is 2. ... d7-d6 3. d2-d4 Ng8-f6 (the position in the photo above) 4. Nb1-c3 Bc8-g4 5. Bc1-e3 e7-e6 6. h2-h3 Bg4-h5 7. d4-d5 Nc6-e5 8. g2-g4 Bh5-g6 9. Nf3xe5 d6xe5 10. Bf1-b5+ Nf6-d7 11. d5xe6 f7xe6. You have the better game.

St. George Defense

- Tony Miles named 1. ... a7-a6 after the famous dragon-slaying saint, appropriate after Miles beat the world champion with the move. We get to the photo above with **1. e2-e4 a7-a6 2. d2-d4 b7-b5 3. Bf1–d3 Bc8-b7 4. Ng1-f3.** *(D)* Now play could continue **4. ...** **Ng8-f6 5. Nb1-d2 e7-e6 6. 0-0 c7-c5 7. d4xc5 Bf8xc5 8. e4-e5 Nf6-d5 9. Nd2-e4 Bc5-e7 10. a2-a4.**

- You have a significant advantage. You're strong in the center, safely castled, and have weakened Black's queenside pawns.

are many good books that specialize in them.

The Nimzovich Defense (not to be confused with the Nimzo-Indian Defense in the closed defenses, also named after hypermodernist Aaron Nimzovich) begins 1. e2-e4 Nb8-c6 and can land Black into cramped positions if White doesn't try to overrun the position too early.

The St. George Defense begins with 1. e2-e4 a7-a6, ignoring the center, with the flank-developing plan of ... b7-b5 and ... Bc8-b7. React solidly in the center and develop methodically, and you should get an opening edge.

Owen's Defense is the least-often seen after 1. e2-e4. White gets a broad center and quick development—recipe for an advantage.

Our last photo discusses a very frequent and very bad way of opening the game seen all too often in the games of beginners. You are bound to see it as you play friends who haven't read a book on the game! Ironically, as appealing as it seems to be to novices, the "opening" is one of the worst that can be chosen.

Owen's Defense

- We reach the position in the diagram above after: **1. e2-e4 b7-b6 2. d2-d4 Bc8-b7 3. Bf1-d3 e7-e6.** *(D)* You have a broad center and an easy path to development.

- After **4. Ng1-f3 c7-c5 5. d4-d5!?** (a gambit!) **e6xd5**

  6. e4xd5 Bb7xd5 7. 0-0 Ng8-f6 (7. ... Nb8-c6 8. Nb1-c3 Bd5-e6 9. Bc1-f4 Ng8-f6 10. Nc3-b5) **8. Nb1-c3 Bd5-b7 9. Bc1-g5 Bf8-e7 10. Bg5xf6 Be7xf6 11. Rf1-e1+ Bf6-e7 12. Qd1-e2 Nb8-c6 13. Nc3-d5,** life is hard for Black.

Novice Mistake

- This "opening" actually has no name. But many beginners will adopt it as Black, probably because they know that the rook is a powerful piece and want to get it into the game early through a6.

- But, in the opening, your rooks should stay on their back rank on an open file and not run around the center of the board, harassed by lowly pawns.

- If White seizes the center, as above, he guards ... a6 anyway! And Black's plan doesn't work on the h-file either.

PETROFF DEFENSE

Here's a reliable set of openings to use as Black against any opening move

In this chapter we'll look at a system for you to play as Black. You need to be prepared for any move White can throw at you. Fortunately, there are a limited number of truly good openings. On the other hand, each of the good openings has a number of popular variations for both sides. At times the possible moves branch out like the many limbs of a tall tree.

We'll do our best to prune them down to size for you.

Whenever you grow tired of studying openings, feel free to move ahead to Chapter 13, "The Middle Game." You can always come back to our review of the openings later. In fact, here's a word of warning: Some chess amateurs spend too much time trying to find the "perfect" opening (which doesn't

Petroff after 3. Nf3xe5

Giving Back the Exchange

- **3. Nf3xe5 d7-d6** (A hasty 3. ... Nf6xe4 allows an uncomfortable 4. Qd1-e2!.) **4. Ne5-f3 Nf6xe4 5. d2-d4 d6-d5 6. Bf1-d3 Bf8-d6 7. 0-0 0-0 8. c2-c4 c7-c6 9. Qd1-c2 Nb8-a6** (If White captures twice on e4, ... Rf8-e8 gives you an initiative.) **10. a2-a3** (to prevent ... Na6-b4)

- **10. ... Bc8-g4** (No pin here, but you threaten ... Bg4xf3, ruining White's kingside pawns.) **11. Nf3-e5 Bd6xe5 12. d4xe5 Na6-c5 13. f2-f3 Nc5xd3 14. Qc2xd3 Ne4-c5 15. Qd3-d4 Nc5-b3.**

- Your last move forked White's queen and rook. But White can continue with a line in which your best play is to return the favor!

- **16. Qd4xg4 Nb3xa1** (White has netted a bishop; you've bagged a rook.) **17. Bc10-h6** (Threatens checkmate on g7!) **17. ... g7-g6**

(The only defense.) **18. Bh6xf8 Qd8xf8** (Material is even again.) **19. c4xd5 Qf8-c5+** (A good move, centralizing your queen. Next you'll play 20. ... c6xd5, getting a passed pawn and opening the c-file for your rook.) It's an equal, fighting game.

exist), to the detriment of their skills in the other two stages of the game—the middle game and endgame. If you become serious about continuing to improve your chess after completing this book and study openings as part of your curriculum, don't make opening study more than 25 percent of your total study time. And combine your book-study with finding a chess club and play many offhand games against other players. Ask them questions after the game about moves and positions you didn't understand.

Since this chapter is for you from Black's point of view, we've made an exception to the tradition of putting the White pieces at the "bottom" of the board. We've put the Black pieces there—to simulate your point of view. The first opening as Black we recommend to you is the Petroff.

The Petroff begins: **1. e2-e4 e7-e5 2. Ng1–f3 Ng8-f6**. Your second move develops and counterattacks. Now White has two popular moves: 3. Nf3xe5 and 3. d2-d4. We'll look at both.

Petroff after 3. d2-d4

- We reach the position above after: **3. d2-d4 Nf6xe4 4. Bf1-d3 d7-d5 5. Nf3xe5 Nb8-d7** (You can't allow White to keep this dominating e5 *outpost*.)

- **6. Ne5xd7 Bc8xd7 7. 0-0 Bf8-d6** (D) (You develop your dark-square bishop to its best square.) **8. c2-c4**

(White attacks your center pawn.) **8. ... c7-c6** (You back it up.) **9. c4xd5 c6xd5 10. Qd1-h5 0-0 11. Qh5xd5 Bd7-c6**. (A good move that keeps your own knight on its outpost.)

Lead in Development

- You're a pawn down but have the lead in development. Your bishops bear down on the white kingside through the center. The game is dynamically equal.

- White must move his threatened queen.

- **12. Qd5-h5 g7-g6** (Forcing the White queen to a worse square.) **13. Qh4-h3 Ne4-g5 14. Qh3-g4 Ng5-e6 15. Nb1-c3 h7-h5 16. Qg4-h3 Ne6xd4.**

- Now material is even, and you have an active game. You must be careful, however, to guard the dark squares around your king.

121

OLD STANDBYS
These four old openings are sometimes still played on a club level

Most of the time that you answer 1. e2-e4 with 1. … e7-e5, you will wind up in the Petroff Defense that we just examined. But there are some other openings that you will occasionally see in response. Below we give you some basic ideas of how to handle these.

The first one we look at is the Four Knights Game—so named because both players bring out both their knights before developing a bishop. It was the most popular opening

of the 1920s, but is now seldom used in tournament chess, seen as too tame.

The next opening we study below is the King's Gambit, the darling of the Romantics, who favored attack at all costs. Modern masters have shied away from it in favor of positional lines that keep White's first-move advantage more clearly in hand. A few great modern players, notably former world champion Boris Spassky, have shown that the opening

Four Knights

- **After 1. e2-e4 e7-e5 2. Ng1-f3 Ng8-f6 3. Nb1-c3 Nb8-c6.** *(D)* (There's nothing illogical about this debut. It's simply played out.)

- We recommend a temporary gambit, the Rubinstein Defense. Here's a sample of play: **4. Bf1-b5 Nc6-d4**

5. Bb5-a4 c7-c6 6. Nf3xe5 d7-d6 7. Ne5-f3 Bc8-g4 (The pin is uncomfortable because White's light-square bishop is unable to break it.) **8. d2-d3 d6-d5 9. Bc1-e3 Nd4xf3+ 10. g2xf3 Bg4-h5 11. Be3-d4 d5xe4 12. d3xe4 Bh5xf3 13. Qd1xf3.** (The game is even.)

King's Gambit

- **1. e2-e4 e7-e5 2. f2-f4.** *(D)* (A declaration of war. Players who make this old and aggressive move tend to be specialists who want complications.)

- **2. … e5xf4** (This makes it a King's Gambit Accepted.) **3. Ng1-f3** (Less popular is

3. Bf1-c4 Ng8-f6 4. Nb1-c3 c7-c6 5. Bc4-b3 d7-d5 6. e4xd5 c6xd5 7. d2-d4 Bf8-d6 8. Ng1-f3 0-0 9. 0-0 Bc8-e6=.) **3. … d7-d5 4. e4xd5 Ng8-f6 5. Bf1-b5+ c7-c6 6. d5xc6 Nb8xc6 7. d2-d4 Bf8-d6.** (The game is even.)

can still score points.

The Vienna Game is a related attempt to reach a favorable version of the King's Gambit but peters out to equality with best play.

The Bishop Opening points an early attack against Black's pre-castling weak point, f7. But because it declares White's intentions too early, it too lacks any long-lasting sting.

YELLOW LIGHT

As Black, Equalize First!
White starts out with the advantage of the first move. After centuries of experimentation in master play, most modern experts subscribe to the opinion that Black should play to nullify this starting advantage before making plans to seek his own advantage. So, whether you're faced with an opening you know or a surprise weapon as Black, don't try to frantically attack. Play solidly, with an eye to the future!

Vienna

- **1. e2-e4 e7-e5 2. Nb1-c3 Ng8-f6 3. f2-f4.** *(D)*

- A King's Gambit–like line; White can also try 3. Bf1-c4, when you should continue: 3. ... Nf6xe4 4. Qd1-h5 (if 4. Nc3xe4 d7-d5!, equalizing with the pawn fork trick) 4. ... Ne4-d6 5. Bc4-b3 Bf8-e7 6. Qh5xe5 0-0=.

- **3. ... d7-d5 4. f4xe5 Nf6xe4 5. Ng1-f3 Bf8-c5.**

- Black is doing well.

Bishop's Opening

- **1. e2-e4 e7-e5 2. Bf1-c4** (the Bishop's Opening) *(D)* **2. ... Ng8-f6 3. d2-d3 c7-c6 4. Ng1-f3 d7-d5 5. Bc4-b3**

- No better for White is 5. e4xd5 c6xd5 6. Bc4-b3 (if 6. Bc4-b5+ Bc8-d7 7. Bb5xd7+ Nb8xd7=) 6. ... Bf8-b4+ 7. c2-c3 Bb4-d6=.

- **5. ... Bf8-d6 6. Nb1-c3 d5xe4 7. Nf3-g5 0-0 8. Ng5xe4 Nf6xe4 9. Nc3xe4 Bc8-f5.**

- **10. 0-0 Nb8-a6=.**

- You'll play ... Na6-c5, hitting White's centralized knight and important light-square bishop.

123

UNUSUAL CHOICES

Let's take a look at what to do when your opponent tries something really unusual

Some players will choose to start a game with very unusual openings, even variations that are not well respected, hoping that the surprise will catch you off guard.

We'll take a look at three such openings as examples. The third is almost never played by experienced players, but you'll see beginners sometimes choosing it.

The Danish opening is an old swashbuckler from the Romantic era that gambits two pawns to develop both bishops quickly in menacing positions against Black's kingside. Learning how to handle it will help you understand the antidote to other such kingside gambits, ... d7-d5.

The Center Game, which brings out White's most powerful

Danish

Center Game

- The attack-at-all-costs Danish gambits two pawns! It can be devastating against a greedy defender.

- **1. e2-e4 e7-e5 2. d2-d4 e5xd4 3. c2-c3 d4xc3 4. Bf1-c4 c3xb2 5. Bc1xb2.** *(D)*

- **5. ... d7-d5!** (The classic antidote, returning a pawn for an even game.) **6. Bc4xd5** (6. e4xd5 Ng8-f6 7. Ng1-f3 Bf8-b4+ 8. Nb1-d2 Qd8-e7+) **6. ... Ng8-f6 7. Bd5xf7+ Ke8xf7 8. Qd1xd8 Bf8-b4+ 9. Qd8-d2 Bb4xd2+ 10. Nb1xd2 Rh8-e8 11. f2-f3 b7-b6 12. Ng1-e2 Bc8-a6=.**

- **1. e2-e4 e7-e5 2. d2-d4 e5xd4 3. Qd1xd4.** *(D)* (This move makes it a Center Game.) **3. ... Nb8-c6** (Naturally, you gain time on White's queen.) **4. Qd4-e3** (If 4. Qd4-a4 Ng8-f6 5. Bc1-g5 Bf8-e7 6. Nb1-c3 0-0 7. Ng1-f3 d7-d6 8. 0-0-0 Bc8-d7=.)

- **4. ... Ng8-f6 5. Nb1-c3 Bf8-b4** (5. ... Bf8-e7 is also a good move.) **6. Bc1-d2 0-0 7. 0-0-0 Rf8-e8 8. Qe3-g3** (8. Bf1-c4 d7-d6=) **8. ... d7-d6.**

piece on the second move, ironically peters out to an equal game quickly, since Black can develop his pieces while threatening the white queen, thereby gaining time.

The variation we take up last in this section, 1. e2-e4 e7-e5 2. Qd1-h5, is sometimes called the Patzer Opening. (A *patzer* is chess-player slang for a poor player.) This opening has long been disparaged as a premature attack by White. But occasionally and very rarely, a good player will experiment with it. Indiana master Bernard Parham has even developed the opening into a "Matrix" system he teaches his students.

And current U.S. champion Hikaru Nakamura has played the opening.

These examples go to show us that we should never jump to the conclusion that our opponent is a *patzer* because he makes unusual moves.

All this aside, however, we don't recommend 2. Qd1-h5 for White and would love all of our opponents to play it against us. We'll show you ideas to combat it.

Unusual Choices

- When you're confronted with the unfamiliar, don't play by rote, rolling out your "normal" moves. Carefully examine the threats of your opponent's moves. Let's look at this example: **1. e2-e4 e7-e5 2. Qd1-h5.** *(D)* (See position above.)

- Reacting automatically with

2. ... Ng8-f6? would allow 3. Qh5xe5+. So, **2. ... Nb8-c6 3. Bf1-c4** (Careful. You're threatened with 4. Qh5xf7 checkmate!) **3. ... g7-g6! 4. Qh5-f3** (Still threatening mate!) **4. ... Ng8-f6.**

- You'll follow up with ... Bf8-g7 and ... 0-0, with a good game.

Dos and Don'ts of Playing Black in the Openings

- Do work to understand ideas and principles.

- Don't try to memorize every possible move.

- Do play to equalize as Black before going on the attack.

- Don't try to checkmate your opponent unless he makes some terrible blunders.

- Do ask yourself, "What did my opponent's last move threaten?"

- Don't spend more than 25 percent of your chess study time on the openings.

QUEEN'S GAMBIT

White has another great first move—1. d2-d4; after 1. ... d7-d5, the popular choice is 2. c2-c4

White, of course, doesn't have to play 1. e2-e4, even though that's a great move. Another first-class master choice is 1. d2-d4, normally leading to a *closed* game, in which a direct clash is generally put off until later in the middle game. Chess players would say that these openings are generally more *positional*—that is, long-term strategy takes a front seat to tactics.

We recommend you respond with 1. ... d7-d5, following sound classical principles of getting your own stake in the center. Then, White's most popular and most challenging continuation is 2. c2-c4, establishing the Queen's Gambit. The first thing to say about the Queen's Gambit is that it's not a true gambit. Black cannot successfully hold on to the pawn

The Queen's Gambit

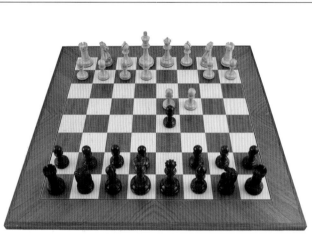

- The starting position of the Queen's Gambit. You play **2. ... d5xc4,** making it a QGA.

- White then has two main choices; the most aggressive is **3. e2-e4,** immediately setting up a classical broad pawn center. But you play **3. ... c5.**

- Naturally, White doesn't want to play 4. d4xc5, allowing 4. ... Qd8xd1+.

- **4. d4-d5 Ng8-f6 5. Nb1-c3 b7-b5 6. Nc3xb5** (6. e4-e5 b5-b4 7. e5xf6 b4xc3 8. b2xc3 Qd8-a5 9. f6xg7 Bf8xg7) **6. ... Qd8-a5+.**

QGA, 3. e2-e4

- To save his knight, White must play **7. Nb5-c3**. Now, because your queen pins White's knight on c3, you can play **7. ... Nf6xe4.**

- After **8. Bc1-d2 Ne4xd2 9. Qd1xd2 g7-g6,** you have an equal game with lots of activity.

- You'll fianchetto your Black bishop on g7, pressuring the long dark diagonal.

- Let's back up to see what to do if White chooses **3. Ng1-f3.**

on c4 if he captures it—later we'll take a look below at what would happen if Black tries.

White's second move puts immediate pressure on your center pawn. You don't want to allow 3. c4xd5 Qd8xd5 4. Nb1-c3, developing while gaining time against your queen. So you should prop up your pawn or simply capture on c4. Defending your center pawn with either 2. ... e7-e6 or 2. ... c7-c6 makes the opening a Queen's Gambit Declined (QGD), either the Orthodox or Slav Variation, respectively. But we recommend that you play 2. ... d5xc4, the Queen's Gambit Accepted (QGA).

The great world champion Emanuel Lasker taught us that if we haven't violated basic principles, we should accept a pawn offered to us in the opening, or it will likely come back to haunt us. He further pointed out that we should take the pawn, not with the intention of keeping it at all costs, but of giving it back after our opponent ties himself in a knot to try to gain it back. Lasker's chess logic is impeccable and can guide us in playing the Queen's Gambit Accepted.

QGA, 3. Ng1-f3

- **3. Ng1-f3 Ng8-f6 4. e2-e3 e7-e6** (You can't hold the pawn with 4. ... b7-b5 5. a2-a4 c7-c6 6. a4xb5 c6xb5 7. b2-b3.)

- But if 4. Nb1-c3, play to hold the c4-pawn: 4. ... a7-a6 5. e2-e4 b7-b5 6. e4-e5 Nf6-d5 7. a2-a4 Nd5xc3 8. b2xc3 Qd8-d5 9. g2-g3 Bc8-b7 10.

Bf1-g2 Qd5-d7 11. Bc1-a3 g7-g6 12. 0-0 Bf8-g7 13. Rf1-e1 0-0=.

- **5. Bf1xc4 c7-c5.** *(D)* **6. 0–0 a7-a6 7. Qd1-e2 b7-b5 8. Bc4-b3 Bc8-b7 9. Rf1-d1 Nb8-d7 10. Rf1-d1 Qd8-b8.**

A Fighting Game

- Black could also have played 10. ... Qd8-c7. Your idea is to get the queen off the d-file to be able to answer d4xc5 with ... Nd7xc5.

- It's a complicated, fighting game.

- For example, 11. d4-d5 e6xd5 12. Nc3xd5 Nf6xd5 13. Bb3xd5 Bb7xd5 14. Rd1xd5 Bf8-e7 15. e3-e4 Nd7-b6 16. Rd5-d1 0-0.

QUEEN PAWN OPENINGS

White can play 1. d2-d4 and follow up with moves other than 2. c2-c4

When the game begins 1. d2-d4 d7-d5, and White doesn't play 2. c2-c4, chess players call it a Queen Pawn Opening. These beginnings are generally not considered as strong a follow-up as the Queen's Gambit because White forgoes his lever against your center. But these opening variations do have their devotees.

The first opening we look at—or actually, learn to avoid—is the Colle System, named after Belgian champion Edgar Colle. His countryman George Koltanowski moved to the United States and promoted the system widely to club-level players. There's a pretty good chance you will run up against it. Colle players generally like to keep their game within a narrow range

(Attempted) Colle

- After **1. d2-d4 d7-d5 2. e3-e3,** White wants to play Bf1-d3, Ng1-f3, c2-c3, and 0-0. Take him out of his road map with **2. ... Bf5.** *(D)*

- Now 3. Bf1-d3 has no sting. You can either capture with 3. ... Bf5xd3, when best for White is 4. c2xd3—or play 3. ... e6 4. Bd3xf5 e6xf5 5.

Qd1-d3 Qd8-d7, and if 6. Qd3-b3 c7-c6.

- White may choose 3. c2-c4 e7-e6. If then 4. Qd1-b3 Nb8-c6 5. Qb3xb7? (5. c4xd5 Qd8xd5 6. Qb3xb7 Nc6xd4! 7. Qb7xd5 Nd4-c2+ is crushing.) 5. ... Nc6-b4!, and you're better.

Veresov

- The Veresov occurs after **1. d2-d4 d7-d5 2. Nb1-c3 Ng8-f6 3. Bc1-g5.** *(D),* when we once again recommend developing your light-square bishop to a good square with **3. ... Bc8-f5.**

- Then White can double your f-pawns but give you

the bishop pair with **4. Bg5xf6** (4. f2-f3 Nb8-d7 5. Nc3xd5 Nf6xd5 6. e2-e4 h7-h6 7. Bg5-h4 c7-c6=) **4. ... e7xf6 5. e2-e3 c7-c6 6. Bf1-d3 Bf5xd3 7. Qd1xd3 Bf8-b4 8. Ng1-e2 0-0 9. 0-0 Nb8-d7 10. e3-e4 Nd7-b6 11. Ne2-g3 g7-g6=.**

of possibilities in the opening and play for a kingside attack. We suggest you dash their hopes quickly with 2. ... Bf5.

Next, the Veresov opening quickly develops White's queenside. With 3. ... Bc8-f5, you put your bishop on a natural square and help to control e4.

The London System was named after the London tournament of 1922, where it was played by the then-older generation as a way of dealing with the hypermodern masters' non-classical approach to the openings from the Black side. Against your 1. ... d7-d5, it offers no special threat.

The Blackmar-Diemer Gambit has become almost a chess cult among a small group of amateurs, who devote books and Web sites to its variations. Theoretically, it is not one of the good openings for White, resulting in a slight disadvantage for him with best play, but it can be dangerous unless you know a good defensive setup.

As usual, when you're confronted with an opening you're not familiar with, don't panic or lash out, trying to prove how bad it is. Rely on the guiding principles we've practiced. Think CDC: Centralize, Develop, and Castle!

London System

Blackmar-Diemer Gambit

- After **1. d2-d4 d7-d5 2. Ng1-f3 Ng8-f6 3. Bc1-f4** *(D),* we get the London System. This is known as a quiet, almost boring opening, but the American world championship candidate Gata Kamsky has used it with success.

- Once again, you can

develop your queen bishop with **3. ... Bc8-f5**. Play can proceed: 4. e2-e3 e7-e6 5. Bf1-d3 Bf5xd3.

- White has other plans as well, but whatever he tries—continue to control the center, develop, and get castled. You'll be in good shape for the coming middle game.

- **1. d2-d4 d7-d5 2. e2-e4** *(D)* **d5xe4 3. Nb1-c3.**

- Now White wants to play 4. f2-f3 to gambit a pawn to get an early kingside attack. (If 3. f2-f3 immediately, 3. ... e7-e5!.) You cross him up.

- **3. ... e7-e5 4. Bc1-e3** (4. Qd1-h5 e5xd4 5. Bf1-c4

Qd8-d7 6. Qh5-e5+ Qd7-e7 7. Qe5xd4 Nb8-c6, when you're better.) **4. ... e5xd4 5. Be3xd4 Nb8-c6 6. Bf1-b5 Bc8-d7 7. Ng1-e2 Ng8-f6 8. 0-0 Bf8-e7 9. Bd4xf6 Be7xf6 10. Nc3xe4 Bf6-e7 11. Qd1-d5 0-0=.**

FLANK OPENINGS

White can eschew the classical pawn moves and begin with pressure from the flanks

Some players as White will play in the hypermodern spirit, not moving one of the center pawns. On a tournament level, this happens less than 20 percent of the time. Our first variation below, the English Opening, accounts for the majority of the games in this non-classical 20 percent.

The English is a respected opening, a kind of Sicilian Defense

with colors reversed and White having an extra move. Its first move, 1. c2-c4, does control d5. Although White can play the opening a number of ways, he will often fianchetto his king bishop on g2, influencing the long light-square diagonal, which also runs through d5.

The Reti Opening has more of the hypermodern spirit,

English Opening

- The principled reply to the English's **1. c2-c4** (D) is **1. ... e7-e5.**

- Play often develops: **2. Nb1-c3 Ng8-f6 3. g2-g3 d7-d5 4. c4xd5 Nf6xd5** (The opening is a Sicilian Dragon reversed. So White has an extra move.) **5. Ng1-f3 Nb8-c6 6. Bf1-g2 Nd5-**

b6 (best) **7. 0-0 Bf8-e7 8. d2-d3 0-0 9. a2-a3 Bc8-e6 10. b2-b4 a7-a5 11. b4-b5 Nc6-d4 12. Nf3-d2** (If 12. Nf3xe5 now, ... Be7-f6!.) **12. ... Be6-d5 13. Nc3xd5 Nb6xd5=.**

Reti Opening

- **1. Ng1-f3 d7-d5** (Other moves allow a transposition to the English with 2. c2-c4, when Black must play a line without an early ... e7-e5.)

- **2. c2-c4** (D) **c7-c6 3. b2-b3 Ng8-f6 4. g2-g3 Bc8-g4 5. Bf1-g2 e7-e6 6. 0-0 Nb8-d7 7. Bc1-b2** (The double fianchetto!) **7. ... Bf8-d6**

8. d2-d3 0-0 9. Nb1-d2 a7-a5.

- Your light-square bishop is outside of your pawn chain, so it's not condemned to being a bad bishop, and you restrain queenside expansion. The game is level.

playing 1. Ng1-f3 and, if Black plays 1. ... d5, levering against Black's d5 with c2-c4.

Larsen's Opening, named after the great modern Danish player Bent Larsen, takes a different tack, announcing with an immediate fianchetto of his queen's bishop with 1. ... b2-b3. The move puts pressure on White's kingside, but commits early, allowing you to equalize quickly.

In the second half of the last century, the Bird's Opening probably endured a worse reputation than it deserved, but it is an odd duck. With 1. f2-f4, White pushes a non-center pawn, weakens his kingside, and does not contribute to his development. So we can see why lovers of classical principles turn their noses up at the Bird's. But it does take charge of e5—and White, having the advantage of the first move, does have latitude. So it doesn't give White a worse game, but it's probably fair to say that it squanders White's advantage quickly. Like the other offbeat openings, the Bird's has its fans, who enjoy its surprise value.

Larsen's Opening

- **1. b2-b3** *(D)* **d7-d5** (White is after the dark squares; you stake out the center's light squares.)

- **2. Bc1-b2** (If 2. Ng1–f3, you still play 2. ... Bc8-g4 3. Bc1-b2 Bg4xf3 4. e2xf3 e7-e6) **2. ... Bc8-g4 3. h2-h3 Bg4-h5 4. Ng1-f3 Bh5xf3 5. e2xf3**

Ng8-f6 6. f3-f4 e7-e6 7. g2-g3 g7-g6.

- Your pawns control the light squares, and you will fianchetto your dark-square bishop to counter White on the long diagonal. The game is even.

Bird's Opening

- **1. f2-f4** *(D)* (The Bird's indicative move.) **1. ... d7-d5 2. Ng1-f3 Ng8-f6 3. e2-e3 g7-g6 4. b2-b3** (4. d2-d4 Bf8-g7 5. Bf1-d3 0-0 6. Nb1-d2 c7-c5 7. c2-c3 b7-b6 8. Qd1-e2 Bc8-b7 9. 0-0 Nf6-e4=, or 4. Bf1-e2

Bf8-g7 5. 0-0 0-0 6. d2-d3 c7-c5 7. Qd1-e1 Nb8-c6=) **4. ... Bf8-g7 5. Bc1-b2 0-0 6. Bf1-e2 c7-c5 7. 0-0 Nb8-c6 8. Nf3-e5 Qd8-c7 9. Nb1-c3 Nc6xe5 10. Nc3-b5 Qc7-c6 11. Bb2xe5 Bc8-f5=.**

RUY LOPEZ

Your suggested opening repertoire avoids these popular openings, but you may want to know their ideas

We've seen that both players have a say in what opening takes shape in a game. Your opening repertoire—the series of openings we've recommended for you in the three previous chapters—does not permit your opponent to play certain popular openings. This chapter shows you the basic ideas in these other openings.

Why should you learn about theses other openings? Well, first of all, we want to repeat our advice that if you're not very interested in studying openings right now, you can skip ahead to the next chapter on the middle game. But as you progress in chess, there are good reasons to know something about openings you don't play. Here are a few:

Ruy Lopez

- Since we're no longer looking at openings you play only as Black, we've returned to the normal convention of White moving "up" the photos and diagrams.

- Ruy Lopez, sometimes called the Spanish Game, opens: **1. e2-e4 e7-e5 2. Ng1-f3 Nb8-c6 3. Bf1-b5.** (D)

- White's third move doesn't really pin the knight. But the bishop threatens, at a key moment, to remove the knight guarding e5.

- The Ruy Lopez now separates into two main branch defenses, those without 3. ... a7-a6, and those with this move.

Berlin

- **1. e2-e4 e7-e5 2. Ng1-f3 Nb8-c6 3. Bf1-b5 Ng8-f6** (the defining Berlin Defense move).

- Less-played third-move choices include the over-aggressive Schliemann Defense, 3. ... f7-f5, and the interesting Bird's Defense, 3. ... Nc6-d4.

- **4. 0-0 (White's best) 4. ... Nf6xe4 5. d2-d4 Ne4-d6 6. Bb5xc6 d7xc6 7. d4xe5 Nd6-f5.** (D)

- White will exchange queens and retain a slight edge. Black will have some trouble developing, but owns the bishop pair.

1. Sometimes a wily opponent will find a way to trick you into an opening you're unfamiliar with.

2. You may find a new opening you like—one that better meets your style.

3. You can better understand the games of others.

4. The ideas and themes of openings you don't play can give you ideas for the openings you do play.

Until the last quarter of the twentieth century, the Ruy Lopez was the king of openings and the training grounds of master chess. Then times changed. It was a bit like the battles we've all read about the U.S. War of Independence, when the British would march into combat in an "agreed upon" deployment, but the American militia had their own ideas, firing from behind any available cover. Top chess players began seeing that they didn't have to enter a predetermined battlefield rehearsed hundreds of times by their famous older opponents. So they chose equally good alternatives.

The "Ruy" has been analyzed many moves deep in many different variations. We give you the highlights below.

Exchange Variation

- The Exchange Variation occurs after: **1. e2-e4 e7-e5 2. Ng1-f3 Nb8-c6 3. Bf1-b5 a7-a6 4. Bb5xc6 d7xc6** (best).

- White has doubled Black's c-pawns but has given Black the bishop pair.

- **5. 0-0** (5. Nf3xe5? Qd8-d4, Black is better; or 5. d2-d4 e5xd4 6. Qd1xd4 Qd8xd4 7. Nf3xd4=) **5. ... f7-f6 6. d2-d4 e5xd4 7. Nf3xd4** *(D)* **7. ... c7-c5!** (Black heads for the endgame.)

- Black will trade queens, play Bc8-d7 and castle long. The game is equal.

Open Defense

- **1. e2-e4 e7-e5 2. Ng1-f3 Nb8-c6 3. Bf1-b5 a7-a6 4. Bb5-a4 Ng8-f6 5. 0-0 Nf6xe4** (Black is following Lasker's advice—he doesn't intend to try to keep this pawn, but give it back for positional considerations. 5. ... Bf8-e7 is often played.) **6.** **d2-d4 b7-b5** (An important move that breaks the attack on Black's queen knight.) **7. Ba4-b3 d7-d5!** *(D)* (A familiar counter-thrust by Black in the king pawn openings!)

- **8. d4xe5 Bc8-e6=.**

QUEEN'S GAMBIT

You've learned about the Queen's Gambit Accepted—here's how the other half plays

The first move 1. d2-d4 is one of the two best choices, as is 1. e2-e4. Like 1. e2-e4, the queen-pawn move occupies the center and opens a path to develop a bishop, but—unlike 1. e2-e4—it does not help prepare for kingside castling. On the other hand, 1. d2-d4 advances a pawn that is supported. The two moves are equally great.

As we've already seen, the Queen's Gambit is the most popular follow-up for White after 1. d2-d4 d7-d5, using the second move 2. c2-c4 to immediately attack Black's center. Possibly second only to the Ruy Lopez, the QGD has been chosen most often by the world's best, until the Hypermodern School popularized options. There are many variations,

Orthodox Defense

- The QGD begins: **1. d2-d4 d7-d5 2. c2-c4 e7-e6.**

- **3. Nb1-c3 Ng8-f6 4. Bc1-g5 Bf8-e7** (Or 4. ... Nbd7 first because White's attempt to win a pawn loses: 5. c4xd5 e6xd5 6. Nc3xd5? Nf6xd5 7. Bg5xd8 Bf8-b4+.) **5. e2-e3 0-0** (D)

- **6. Ng1-f3 6. ... Nb8-d7 7. Ra1-c1.**

- **7. ... c7-c6 8. Bf1-d3 d5xc4** (Black waited to make White move the bishop twice.) **9. Bd3xc4 Nf6-d5 10. Bg5xe7 Qd8xe7 11. 0-0 Nd5xc3 12. Rc1xc3=.**

Tarrasch Defense

- **1. d2-d4 d7-d5 2. c2-c4 e7-e6 3. Nb1-c3 c7-c5** (D) The Tarrasch. 3. ... Ng8-f6 4. Ng1-f3 c7-c5 5. c4xd5 Nf6xd5 is the Semi-Tarrasch.)

- **4. c4xd5 e6xd5 5. Ng1-f3 Nb8-c6 6. g2-g3** (To further pressure Black's isolated d-pawn.) **6. ... Ng8-f6 7.**

Bf1-g2 Bf8-e7 8. 0-0 0-0 9. Bc1-g5 c5xd4 10. Nf3xd4 h7-h6 11. Bg5-e3 Bc8-g4 12. h2-h3 Bg4-e6=.

- Black supports his isolated pawn with his bishop, and if 13. Nd4xe6 f7xe6, the pawn would no longer be isolated. Black will play ... Qd8-d7.

examined many moves deep, in the Queen's Gambit.

The Queen's Gambit Declined Orthodox Defense, characterized by 2. ... e7-e6, separates into many variations. This defense was at one time "the" way to play the opening. Although it is still viable, nowadays the variation is generally seen as too cramped, focusing on holding the fort and offering few chances of winning.

The Tarrasch Defense takes a very different approach, concentrating on piece activity at the cost of an isolated d-pawn in order not to be stuck with such a cramped position. In fact, it was the great Dr. Siegbert Tarrasch who sarcastically named the Orthodox Defense to poke fun at so many players following what he thought to be an inferior opening.

The Slav Defense elects to prop up Black's center with 2. ... c7-c6 and has been very popular during the past twenty years. It keeps the diagonal open for the traditional "problem" light-square bishop of the Queen's Gambit Declined.

The Catalan is really White's challenge to the Queen's Gambit, Orthodox Defense. The Catalan is a kind of hybrid of the Queen's Gambit and Reti openings, combining d2-d4 with g2-g3.

Slav Defense

- The Slav begins **1. d2-d4 d7-d5 2. c2-c4 c7-c6.** *(D)*

- Black's idea is to support d5 without locking in his queen bishop, and then to play that bishop to f5.

- Now 3. c4xd5 is the drawish Slav Exchange Variation.

- **3. Ng1-f3 Ng8-f6 4. Nb1-c3 d5xc4! 5. a2-a4 Bc8-f5 6. Nf3-e5 Nb8-d7 7. Ne5xc4 Qd8-c7 8. g2-g3 e7-e5 9. d4xe5 Nd7xe5 10. Bc1-f4 Nf6-d7 11. Bf1-g2 g7-g5 12. Nc4xe5 g5xf4 13. Ne5xd7 0-0-0! (Cute!) 14. Qd1-d4 Qc7xd7 15. Qd4xf4 Bf8-d6=.**

Catalan

- **1. d2-d4 d7-d5 2. c2-c4 e7-e6 3. Ng1-f3 Ng8-f6 4. g2-g3** *(D)*

- **4. ... d5xc4** (Following Lasker's advice.) **5. Bf1-g2 Bf8-e7 6. 0-0 0-0 7. Qd1-c2 a7-a6 8. a2-a4** (White restrains Black from expanding with ... b7-b5.) **8. ... Bc8-d7 9. Qc2xc4**

Bd7-c6 10. Bc1-g5 a6-a5 11. Nb1-c3 Nb8-a6 (Black's knight won't be "on the rim" for long.) **12. Ra1-c1 Na6-b4.**

- Black's knight has found an unassailable outpost. **13. Rf1-d1 Ra8-c8=.**

135

THE NIMZO-INDIAN DEFENSE

Black can answer 1. d2-d4 with the Indian Defenses, beginning with 1. ... Ng8-f6

The hypermoderns of the 1920s made a particularly long-lasting impact in devising flank defenses against 1. d2-d4. Instead of 1. ... d7-d5, these defenses all begin with 1. ... Ng8-f6—preventing 2. e2-e4—and often follow up by fianchettoing at least one of Black's bishops. We call this group of openings the "Indian" defenses because in the 1800s

Moheshunder Bonnerjee, from Calcutta, played similar openings.

One of these openings is the Nimzo-Indian Defense, named after the great spokesman for hypermodernism Aaron Nimzovich, who worked out many of the effective ideas in the variation. The Nimzo is now a popular mainstream opening

Nimzo-Indian Defense

- **1. d2-d4 Ng8-f6 2. c2-c4** (White doesn't have 3. e2-e4, but he plays another pawn move that controls d5.) **2. ... e7-e6 3. Nb1-c3** (Now White threatens to play 3. e2-e4, since his knight supports that square.)

- **3. ... Bf8-b4** (This is the Nimzo. *(D)* We'll see different defenses against 3. Ng1-f3.)

- Black's last move pins White's knight, preventing 4. e2-e4.

Saemisch Variation

- **1. d2-d4 Ng8-f6 2. c2-c4 e7-e6 3. Nb1-c3 Bf8-b4 4. a2-a3** (the Saemisch).

- Black must capture on c3 (4. .. Bb4-a5 5. b2-b4 Ba5-b6 6. c4-c5 traps the bishop. Other retreats waste time). White plans f2-f3 and e2-e4, building a big center.

- **4. ... Bb4xc3+ 5. b2xc3 c7-c5 6. f2-f3 d7-d5 7. c4xd5 Nf6xd5** *(D)* **8. Qd1–d3.**

- If 8. d4xc5 f7-f5 (preventing e2-e4) 9. Qd1-c2 0-0.

- **8. ... b7-b6 9. e2-e4 Bc8-a6 10. Qd3-d2 Ba6xf1 11. Ke1xf1 Nd5-e7=.**

at all levels. Like other Indian defenses, its asymmetrical quality leads to a dynamic game in which both players fight for a win. Even White can be quickly punished for being passive or inaccurate.

The Nimzo has a lot of theory. We review only some of the major variations below to give you a good start at seeing whether the play suits your tastes.

The Saemisch Variation, 4. a2-a3, is both an intuitive response and a critical test of the Nimzo's underlying idea. Black must immediately trade his dark-square bishop and in return doubles White's c-pawns. White then strives to open the game to give his bishops attacking scope, while Black tries to keep the game closed to maneuver against White's weakened pawns.

The Classical Variation, 4. Qd1-c2, is appealing because it avoids double pawns and reinforces e4.

The Rubinstein Variation, 4. e2-e3, may look like a modest response, but White's logical plan continues with straightforward kingside development.

We've given you these defenses from Black's point of view, moving "up" the board.

Classical Variation

- **1. d2-d4 Ng8-f6 2. c2-c4 e7-e6 3. Nb1-c3 Bf8-b4 4. Qd1-c2** (White protects his pawn structure and reinforces e4.)

- **4. ... 0-0** (Another way to play is an immediate 4. ... b7-b6.)

- **5. a2-a3 Bb4xc3+ 6. Qc2xc3 b7-b6.** (D) Black puts his queen bishop to good use on the long light-square diagonal.

- **7. Bc1-g5 Bc8-b7 8. f2-f3 h7-h6 9. Bg5-h4 d7-d5 10. e2-e3 Nb8-d7 11. c4xd5 Nf6xd5=.**

Rubinstein Variation

- In this variation, White decides to rely on solid development.

- **1. d2-d4 Ng8-f6 2. c2-c4 e7-e6 3. Nb1-c3 Bf8-b4 4. e2-e3 0-0** (As usual, Black can delay castling for a while: 4. ... b7-b6 5. Bf1-d3 Bc8-b7 6. Ng1-f3 0-0 7. 0-0 c7-c5.)

- **5. Ng1-f3 d7-d5 6. Bf1-d3 c7-c5** (Black's last two center-pawn pushes have prevented White from placing a pawn on e4.) **7. 0-0 c5xd4 8. e3xd4 d5xc4 9. Bd3xc4 b7-b6 10. Rf1-e1 Bc8-b7=.** (D)

137

KING'S INDIAN DEFENSE

Another popular Indian defense encourages White to build a big pawn center—and then counterattacks!

The King's Indian Defense has been a favorite of modern grandmasters, including the two highest-rated players of all time, world champions Bobby Fischer and Garry Kasparov. The opening is provocative, taunting White into a big center, and then counterattacks it, hoping to prove that such an occupation has overextended White's early resources.

As he has against other popular Indian systems, White developed many different plans against this defense, some scoring well until their surprise value wore off and Black found antidotes. We give you a sampling of the important ideas and variations below.

The Classical Variation sees White build a three-pawn center.

King's Indian

Classical Variation

- **1. d2-d4 Ng8-f6 2. c2-c4 g7-g6** (Black makes no moves in the center, instead hurrying to get his king bishop on the long diagonal and castle.)

- **3. Nb1-c3 3. ... Bf8-g7** *(D)* (Instead of preventing

e2-e4, as in the Nimzo-Indian, Black encourages White to build up a big center.)

- A classical-versus-hypermodern battle of ideas is shaping up.

- **1. d2-d4 Ng8-f6 2. c2-c4 g7-g6 3. Nb1-c3 Bf8-g7 4. e2-e4 d7-d6 5. Ng1-f3 0-0 6. Bf1-e2 e7-e5!** (Well-timed!)

- **7. 0-0** *(D)* (White can't win a pawn with 7. d4xe5 d6xe5 8. Qd1xd8 Rf8xd8 9. Nf3xe5 Nf6xe4.)

- **7. ... Nb8-c6 8. d4-d5 Nc6-e7 9. Nf3-e1 Nf6-d7** (Black unblocks his f-pawn.)

- **10. Bc1-e3 f7-f5 11. f2-f3 f5-f4 12. Be3-f2 g6-g5,** with a fighting game. White plays on the queenside while Black attacks on the kingside.

Black fianchettoes, castles, and counterpunches.

The Saemisch Variation of the King's Indian (another opening idea developed by the Berlin grandmaster Friedrich Saemisch, who lived from 1896 to 1975) reinforces White's center with f2-f3. The disadvantage is that it delays his development.

Some King's Indian (KI) fans like the defense because they can play their KI setup against a variety of closed openings, including the English Opening. And it doesn't really matter which knight White develops on his third move—as it does

with the Nimzo-Indian and the Queen's Indian. So although no opening is all-purpose, the King's Indian can cover a lot of possibilities in the closed openings, making it a practical defense to spend time learning.

Our last variation in this section, the Gruenfeld Defense, is a separate opening, an offshoot of the King's Indian, which combines a kingside fianchetto with ... d5.

Saemisch Variation

Gruenfeld

- **1. d2-d4 Ng8-f6 2. c2-c4 g7-g6 3. Nb1-c3 Bf8-g7 4. e2-e4 d7-d6 5. f2-f3** (The Saemisch. White protects e4 with a pawn.)

- **5. ... 0-0 6. Bc1-e3 c7-c5.** (D)

- Black has half a dozen other sixth moves but 6. ... c7-c5

is an interesting gambit.

- **7. d4xc5 d6xc5 8. Qd1xd8 Rf8xd8 9. Be3xc5 Nb8-c6 10. Nc3-d5 Nf6-d7 11. Bc5xe7 Nc6xe7 12. Nd5xe7+ Kg8-f8 13. Ne7-d5 Bg7xb2** (Black has initiative and open lines for his pawn deficit.)

- **1. d2-d4 Ng8-f6 2. c2-c4 g7-g6 3. Nb1-c3 d7-d5** (D). (If Black wants to play a Gruenfeld, he must do it now, before White gets in e2-e4.)

- **4. c4xd5 Nf6xd5 5. e2-e4 Nd5xc3 6. b2xc3** (White gets a big center, which Black plans to undermine.)

- **6. ... Bf8-g7 7. Bf1-c4** (White can also play 7. Ng1-f3.) **7. ... c7-c5.**

- Black attacks on the dark squares controlled by his prize bishop. The fight will largely be about the center.

BOGO- & QUEEN'S INDIAN

If White plays 3. Ng1-f3 rather than 3. Nb1-c3, Black has a different set of Indian defenses

When White plays 3. Ng1-f3, he wants to avoid the Nimzo-Indian, but Black has other solid Indian defenses.

The Bogo-Indian Defense is named after Efim Bogoljubov, the German-Ukrainian grandmaster who in the 1930s played twice for the world championship but never took the title. The Bogo is played at all levels these days. It is a straightforward,

logical approach that allows Black to develop quickly.

The Queen's Indian is so-named because Black fianchettoes his queen bishop. (As we've seen, the King's Indian fianchettoes the king bishop.) The Queen's Indian is perhaps the least risky of any of the Indian defenses, since it generally maintains the bishop pair and a sound pawn structure. On the

3. Nf3 Bogo-Indian

- **1. d2-d4 Ng8-f6 2. c2-c4 e7-e6 3. Ng1-f3 Bf8-b4+** *(D)* (Makes it a Bogo-Indian.) **4. Bc1-d2.**

- 4. Nb1-d2 b7-b6 5. a2-a3 Bb4xd2+ 6. Bc1xd2 h7-h6=; 4. Nb1-c3 transposes to the Nimzo-Indian.

- **4. ... Qd8-e7 5. g2-g3** (If 5. e2-e3 Bb4xd2+ 6. Qd1xd2 0-0 7. Nb1-c3 d7-d6 8. Bf1-e2 e6-e5 9. 0-0 e5-e4=.) **5. ... Nb8-c6 6. Bf1-g2 Bb4xd2+ 7. Nb1xd2** (7. Qd1xd2 Nf6-e4 8. Qd2-c2 Qe7-b4+) **7. ... 0-0 8. 0-0 d7-d6 9. e2-e4 e6-e5 10. d4-d5 Nc6-b8=.**

Classical Queen's Indian

- **1. d2-d4 Ng8-f6 2. c2-c4 e7-e6 3. Ng1-f3 b7-b6.** *(D)* (The characteristic move of the Queen's Indian [QI]. Black will pressure the light squares through the center.)

- **4. g2-g3** (The classical way of handling the Queen's Indian.) **4. ... Bc8-a6** (This is

the modern way of playing the QI. Also still good is the original intention: 4. ... Bc8-b7 5. Bf1-g2 Bf8-e7 6. 0-0 0-0.)

- **5. b2-b3 Bf8-b4+ 6. Bc1-d2.**

negative side, it is a bit cramped. But Black aims to exchange pieces, the formulaic solution to playing a position with less space.

White makes an important choice on his fourth move in the Queen's Indian. He can play the classical approach, 4. g2-g3, intending a fianchetto of his light-square bishop to pressure the center. Or he can make use of former world champion Tigran Petrosian's 4. a2-a3, a move with both positional finesse and hidden aggression.

Many players combine the Nimzo-Indian with either the Bogo-Indian or the Queen's Indian for a complete Indian defensive system, whichever knight White develops on his third move. If you play over the lines we give for these openings and like the feel of the positions they produce, then by all means test them out in your own play.

There is a lot more to know about these lines before you venture into tournament play, where most players of White will have made a study of pet lines, but you can see the "Resources" section for information on how to find out more about opening variations.

Continuing the Classical

- **6. ... Bb4-e7** (After causing White to misplace his own dark-square bishop, Black retreats his bishop to look after the dark squares.) **7. Nb1-c3** (or 7. Bf1-g2 c7-c6 8. 0-0 d7-d5=).

- **7. ... 0-0 8. e2-e4 d7-d5!** (This push breaks up White's center and knocks out White's king bishop.) **9. c4xd5 Ba6xf1 10. Ke1xf1 e6xd5 11. e4-e5 Nf6-e4 12. Kf1-g2 Qd8-d7 13. Qd1-e2 Ne4xc3 14. Bd2xc3 c7-c5 15. Ra1-d1 Nb8-c6=.**

Petrosian Variation

- **1. d2-d4 Ng8-f6 2. c2-c4 e7-e6 3. Ng1-f3 b7-b6 4. a2-a3** (This is an aggressive move that prevents Black from playing Bf8-b4.)

- **4. ... Bc8-b7 5. Nb10-c3 d7-d5 6. c4xd5 Nf6xd5** *(D).* (Of course, Black doesn't block the long light-square diagonal with a pawn.

He gives his fianchettoed bishop scope.)

- **7. e2-e3 Bf8-e7 8. Bf1-b5+ c7-c6 9. Bb5-d3 0-0 10. Qd1-c2 h7-h6 11. 0-0 c6-c5 12. Nc3xd5 Qd8xd5 13. e3-e4 Qd5-h5 14. d4xc5 Be7xc5=.**

141

OTHER DEFENSES TO 1. d2-d4

Four more openings complete our review of asymmetrical defenses against 1. d2-d4

Not all of the following four openings are technically Indian defenses, but this is a logical place to cover them nonetheless, at the end of our openings review. Each one of the four defenses below champions a different set of ideas about how to answer White's choice of opening moves.

The Budapest Defense is an aggressive counter after 1.

d2-d4 Ng8-f6 2. c2-c4. It's not often seen on top levels, but it is more popular among amateurs, since it can be particularly effective against an unprepared opponent. After 2. ... e7-e5 3. d4xe5, Black can choose between 3. ... Nf6-g4 and the extra-tricky 3. ... Nf4-e4.

The Benoni Defense is another risky opening that seeks

Budapest Defense

- **1. d2-d4 Ng8-f6 2. c2-c4 e7-e5** *(D)* (the Budapest) **3. d4xe5** (Not grabbing the pawn gives Black an easy game: 3. d4-d5 Bf8-c5 4. Nb1-c3 d7-d6; 3. e2-e3 e5xd4 4. e3xd4 d7-d5.)

- **3. ... Nf6-g4** (3. ...Nf6-e4 4. a2-a3 Nb8-c6 5. Ng1-f3

d7-d6 6. Qd1-c2 Bc8-f5 7. Nb1-c3 Ne4xf2 8. Qc2xf5 Nf2xh1±.)

- **4. Bc1-f4 Nb8-c6 5. Ng1-f3 Bf8-b4+ 6. Nb1-d2 Qd8-e7 7. e2-e3 Ng4xe5 8. Nf3xe5 Nc6xe5 9. Bf1-e2 0–0 10. 0-0 a7-a5=.**

Benoni Defense

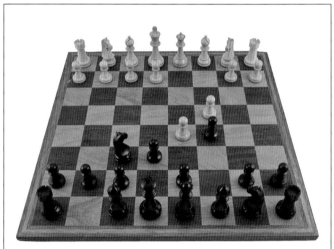

- **1. d2-d4 Ng8-f6 2. c2-c4 c7-c5** *(D)* (the Benoni's key move) **3. d4-d5 e7-e6 4. Nb1-c3 e6xd5 5. c4xd5 d7-d6.**

- Black is cramped but has a mobile queenside majority that can cause trouble for White.

- **6. e2-e4 g7-g6 7. f2-f4** (7. Ng1-f3 Bf8-g7 8. h2-h3 0-0) **7. ... Bf8-g7 8. Ng1-f3** (8. Bf1-b5+ Nf6-d7.)

- The game is very complicated. The best prepared and most tactically alert will likely win.

hand-to-hand combat from the beginning. It has more of a positional justification than the Budapest, and has been used by world champions Mikhail Tal, Bobby Fischer, and Garry Kasparov. Today, there aren't many top players who will regularly risk the cramped positions it produces for Black in the opening. But on an amateur level, like any of the openings we look at, it can be very effective.

The Benko Gambit—named after the American grandmaster Pal Benko and developed into a complete weapon by U.S. grandmasters Walter Browne and Lev Alburt—is another matter entirely. It offers a sound positional sacrifice for queenside piece activity that is based on solid principles. Good moves seem more natural for Black than for White in the Benko, and endgames are pleasant for Black, often even when he remains behind by his gambit pawn.

The Dutch Defense was a favorite of the great world champion Mikhail Botvinnik, of the former Soviet Union. Even though it's never been refuted, it has never been a popular choice at any level, although it has its advocates. Black loosens his kingside with 1. ... f7-f5 and often has a weak square on e6.

Benko Gambit

- **1. d2-d4 Ng8-f6 2. c2-c4 c7-c5 3. d4-d5 b7-b5.** *(D)*(This move makes it a Benko Gambit.)

- **4. c4xb5 a7-a6 5. b5xa6 g7-g6** (Best, delaying recapture of the a-pawn.)

- **6. Nb1-c3 Bc8xa6** (If White plays e2-e4, ... Ba6xf1 will spoil his chance to castle.)

- **7. e2-e4 Ba6xf1 8. Ke1xf1 d7-d6 9. Ng1-f3 Bf8-g7 10. g2-g3 (to "castle by hand") 10. ... 0-0 11. Kf1-g2 Qd8-b6 12. h2-h3 Nb8-a6 13. Rh1-e1 Nf6-d7** (Black will play ... Rf8-b8, pressuring White's queenside, with dynamic equality.)

Dutch Defense

- **1. d2-d4 f7-f5** *(D)* (the Dutch) **2. c2-c4** (Or 2. g2-g3 first without too much difference. After 2. ... Ng8-f6 3. Bf1-g2, Black can also play 3. ... g7-g6 4. Ng1-f3 Bf8-g7 5. 0-0 0-0 6. b2-b3 d7-d6 7. Bc1-b2.)

- **2. ... Ng8-f6 3. g2-g3 e7-e6 4. Bf1-g2 d7-d5** (4. ... Bf8-e7 5. Ng1-f3 0-0 6. 0-0 d7-d6) **5. Ng1-f3 c7-c6 6. 0-0 Bf8-d6 7. b2-b3 Qd8-e7 8. Bc1-b2 b7-b6 9. Nf3-e5 Bc8-b7 10. Nb1-d2 0-0=.**

MIDDLE GAME PRINCIPLES

Material, space, time, and pawn structure are the guiding principles of the middle game

Whatever opening you choose, the game is likely to be decided in the middle game, the second stage of the game, when the heavy fighting and maneuvering take place. We can't overstate the importance of learning middle game principles. A player can get off to a poor start in the opening and make up for it in the middle game. Or a player can execute

his opening moves with precision, but play the middle game poorly only to drift into a losing game.

Each stage of a chess game has its own guiding principles. In the middle game, the four main touchstones are:

Material: Look for ways to win material—a pawn, a piece, an Exchange. Tactics will be your tools for this in the middle

Trading Down to Win

- We're back to White moving "up" the board in our pictures and diagrams.

- Remember this important principle: When you're ahead in pawns or pieces (material), you should trade *pieces*.

- In the position above, White

is one pawn ahead and it's his move. That doesn't seem like much, especially with all this firepower still on the board, but look what happens: **1. Qc2xc8 Re8xc8 2. Rf2xf8+ Rc8xf8 3. Rf1xf8+ Kg8xf8 4. a4-a5,** and the black king cannot catch the little pawn. It will queen. White wins.

Avoid Cramped Positions

- The great José Capablanca played White against the talented woman champion Vera Menchik in 1935 in Moscow. Menchik has let herself be pushed into a cramped position.

- All of Black's pieces are on the back rank and lack coordination.

- Capablanca broke through and won with: **24. g4-g5! f6xg5 25. h4xg5 h6-h5 26. Ng3-f5 Kg8-f7** (if 26. ... g6xf5 27. e4xf5 wins) **27. Nf5-h4 Qd8-e7 28. Qd2-h2 Ne8-c7 29. Rg1-f1 Kf7-e8 30. f3-f4 e5xf4 31. Be3xf4 Ke8-d7 32. Bf4xd6 1-0.**

game. Avoid losing material.

Space: Play to increase the squares you control and the space your pieces have to maneuver in.

Time: Whenever possible, accomplish your plans and goals with a gain of time. Don't waste time!

Pawn Structure: Play to keep your pawns "healthy"—connected and protected.

Practice the principles and themes you learn here in as many games as you have time for!

Gaining Time

- It's Black's move. He wants to develop his king bishop and castle. The obvious move is 1. … Bf8-e7, where it blocks the pin on Black's knight.

- But the former U.S. champ Larry Evans found a better idea in a game in 1946: **1. … Bf8-b4+!.**

- Now White has to *retreat* one of his knights: **2. Ne4-c3.**

- And now, **2. … Bb4-e7,** and Black has gained time by making two moves rather than one!

Pawn Structure

- This endgame from grandmaster tournament play (Bronstein-Tartakover, 1948) illustrates the results of permitting your pawn structure to be mangled in the middle game.

- The *quality* of pawns can be more important than the *quantity* of pawns.

- Every one of Black's seven pawns is *isolated*—having no neighboring pawn to protect it. And six of the pawns are *doubled*—the rear pawns cannot advance until their leaders move.

- After 33. Na6-b8, Black's queenside pawns fall to White's active king.

MORE MIDDLE GAME TIPS

Center control, initiative, and piece activity are also important goals in the middle game

The center remains critical in the middle game.

Initiative also continues to be an important concept in the middle game. Think of other games—basketball, football, soccer. The team that has possession of the ball can be seen as having the initiative. They have the opportunity to score, and the opponents are on the defense.

Piece activity, related to initiative, is the freedom of movement your pieces enjoy and the influence they have—the number of important squares they control.

Control of the Center

- When one side has well-protected central pawns, he has an advantage (other considerations being equal).

- Here White can open up the game on his terms, bringing his pieces through the center.

- Paul Keres wrapped up the game brilliantly: **1. d4-d5! e6xd5 2. e4xd5 Qd8-e7 3. Nf3-e5 f7-f6 4. Qe2-h5! g7-g6 5. Ne5xg6 h7xg6 6. Bd3xg6 Qe7-g7 7. Rd1-d3 Bb4-d6 8. f2-f4 Qg7-h8 9. Qh5-g4 Bd6-c5+ 10. Kg1-h1 Rc8-c7 11. Bg6-h7+ Kg8-f7 12. Qg4-e6+ Kf7-g7 13. Rd3-g3+,** when it's mate in one.

Initiative

- You've seen this Scotch Gambit position before in our recommended White openings.

- White has given up a pawn to develop a very strong initiative.

- White has developed with attacking moves and Black is on the defensive. In the position above, Black must again move his queen, currently attacked by White's bishop.

- An initiative such as this is well worth a pawn. Black would gladly give the pawn back in return for the ability to develop and castle out of danger.

Avoid Weak Squares

Be very wary of creating weak squares in your territory—squares that cannot be defended by one of your pawns. Such squares can be occupied by enemy pieces. The diagram to the right shows a powerful White outpost—and a terribly weak square for Black—on d6. And if Black captures the knight, White remains with a powerful passed pawn on that square.

Piece Activity

- If chess positions played themselves (they don't!), this one would. (It's Capablanca–Herman Steiner, 1928.)

- White's pieces are all active. His knight is posted powerfully on e5. His queen-and-bishop battery points at the Black kingside.

- But the pride of White's game, and the terror of Black's, is the triple-battery dominating the c-file. Capablanca forces his rook to the seventh rank, ultimately winning material: **20. ... Na6-b8 21. Rc3-c7 Bb7-a8 22. Rc7xa7 Nb8-c6 23. Ra7xa8! Nc6xe5 24. Ra8xd8 Rf8xd8 25. Bd3-e2.**

Weak Squares

- Black has a striking complex of weak squares along the light-square long diagonal.

- Bobby Fischer, in one of his matches leading to his successful world championship challenge, played **1. Bg2-f1!,** forcing **1. ... a6-a5** and the creation of another weak square on b5, which White's king later infiltrated.

- Fischer followed up with **2. Bf1-c4!,** tying down Black's rook to passive defense of f7.

- Fischer won this game against Russian Mark Taimanov in 1971.

TYPES OF PAWN CENTERS

The kind of pawn center in your game can determine which plans are good and bad

Knowing the kind of center your game has can help you find the right long-range plan and the best moves. The center has an important effect on the nature of the ongoing struggle, and on what plans are likely to be effective. Let's divide pawn centers into four general types.

A *mobile pawn center* exists when one side has two pawns in the center and his opponent has none or one. In the previous page spread, the game by Paul Keres, under "Control of the Center," shown in the photo on the far left, is an example of the mobile pawn center. This kind of center is very dangerous for the defender (whether Black or White), who must try to block the center with pieces. We show another example

Mobile Pawn Center

- Here you can see that White's pieces have *open* diagonals and files. White's center is *mobile* because Black has no center.

- This is a very dangerous combination for the defender, who should try to block a mobile center with pieces.

- Paul Morphy, in his 1863 Paris match against De Riviere, gave us a lesson in breaking up such positions: **14. e5-e6! f7-f6** (14. ... f7xe6 15. Nf4xe6 Bc8xe6 16. Bc4xe6 Qf5xe6 17. Rf1-e1) **15. Nf3-h4 Qf5-c5 16. Bc1-e3 Qc5-g5**, and White will win with Qd1-h5+!.

Dynamic Pawn Center

- The above photo illustrates a dynamic pawn center.

- In one master game, White pushed his e-pawn too early, dissolving the tension and giving away his initiative: **1. e2-e4 c7-c5 2. c2-c3 e7-e6 3. d2-d4 c5xd4 4. c3xd4 d7-d6 5. Ng1-f3 Ng8-f6 6. Nb1-c3 Bf8-e7 7.** **Bf1-d3 0-0 8. 0-0 Nb8-c6 9. e4-e5?** (A mistake, erasing White's proud center. A developing move like 9. Bc1-e3 keeps White's normal advantage.) **9. ... d6xe5 10. d4xe5 Nf6-d7 11. Qd1-e2 Nd7xe5 12. Nf3xe5 Nc6xe5 13. Bd3xh7+ Kg8xh7 14. Qe2xe5=.**

below, in the far-left photo under the caption "Mobile Pawn Center."

A *dynamic pawn center* is not yet clearly resolved. Our example on this spread shows White mistiming the push e4-e5, pushing it only to allow Black to eliminate White's center pawns while keeping one of his own center pawns. White's ideal center is achieved by a pawn on e4 and a pawn on d4, side-by-side. Unless forced to, White should disturb such a center only if doing so achieves a meaningful advantage.

A *closed pawn center* exists when the center is blocked with interlocking pawns, and no open files or unblocked diagonals run through the center. Our final two photos on this spread show such a center.

An *open center* exists when there are no pawns in the center, or perhaps one of little importance. In this case, both players must strive to control the e- and d-files with their rooks, and augment this control with other pieces.

Closed Pawn Center

- The pawn center above is closed. White's e- and d-pawns interlock with Black's e- and d-pawns in a way that makes it impossible for them to move.

- A locked center helps the attacker on the wing because the defender has no access to the most

effective counter to a wing attack, counterpunching in the center!

- Additionally, here all of White's pieces have easy access to the kingside, while Black can't quickly shift reserves from the other flank through a blocked center.

Closed Center, Friend of the Attack

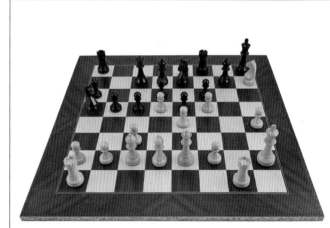

- From the previous position, English international master C.H. O'D Alexander, a famous World War II code breaker, began a kingside *pawn storm*. The photo above shows the position after twenty-five moves.

- Black can't capture the knight because of 26. Qe2-

h5+ Kh7-g8 27. Rg1xg7+ Kg8xg7 28. Ra1-g1+.

- Play continued: **25. ... Bd7-e8 26. Rg1xg7! Kh8xg7 27. Nh7xf8 Kg7xf8 28. Bd2-h6+ Kf8-f7 29. Qe2-h5+.**

- White will bring his queen rook to g1. His mating attack is unstoppable.

149

PAWN STRUCTURE I

The backbone of your position is your pawn structure, so avoid weakening it

As early as the 1700s, André Philidor wrote that "pawns are the soul of chess." His remarks weren't understood fully for another 200 years, but today we recognize the truth of his idea. Unless your pawns remain strong and healthy, your game will suffer. Here we'll look at four kinds of pawn weaknesses. If your opponent is a good player, he will try to saddle you with as many of these pawn weaknesses as he can. You should have an eye to inflicting these pawn weaknesses on your opponent.

A *backward pawn* has lagged behind its fellow peons, so that it can't be protected by another pawn. Such a pawn is usually a weakness that has to be defended in the middle game by pieces, tying them down.

Backward Pawn

- A backward pawn has been left behind by its neighbors, so it must be protected by pieces.

- Backward pawns can become liabilities, tying down your pieces to a defensive task.

- And sometimes your opponent can "pile up" on such a pawn. The position above is a good illustration.

- **1. Ne3-c4!** attacks the pawn for a third time. If Black tries to defend it with **1. ... Nf6-e8**, White has **2. Nc4xe5!,** because the backward pawn is pinned. Try to "see" this in your head.

Isolated and Doubled Pawns

- This is a position from a game for the world championship in 1937. Max Euwe is White against Alexander Alekhine, who has a wrecked queenside pawn structure.

- Alekhine's c-pawn is *isolated*. It has no neighboring pawns to defend it. His a-pawns are *doubled*. They share the same file. They are also isolated.

- White wins material: **20. ... Be6-d5 21. Ra1xa6 Bd5xg2 22. Kg1xg2 Rf8-f7 23. Rf1-a1 Qc7-d6 24. Qc5xd6 Rd8xd6 25. Ra6xa7 Rf7xa7 26. Ra1xa7 Ne5-c4 27. Be3-c5 Rd6-e6 28. Bc5-d4,** and White won.

An *isolated pawn* "casts gloom over the entire chessboard," according to the poetic Nimzovich, and he had a point. Isolated pawns have no pawns next to them, so they are weak and must be babysat by pieces. However, in modern chess, an isolated center pawn, normally the d-pawn, can be a powerful weapon in the middle contest. But as the game tends toward an endgame, the isolated pawn becomes more and more of a liability.

Doubled pawns share the same file. Obviously, the one in back can't move until the one in front does, and, in some respects, two pawns are doing the work of one. In the middle game they can have an upside. They open an adjacent file for a rook. And sometimes the doubled pawn can cover a key group of squares.

A *pawn island* is a connected group of friendly pawns separated from other friendly pawns by one or more files. Both armies start out with one united pawn island. But, through exchanges, more files are created and smaller pawn islands emerge. Separated pockets of pawns are weaker than a united group of pawns.

Strong Isolated Pawns

- Not all isolated pawns are weak.

- The photo above shows a well-known opening position. White's d-pawn is isolated but controls important center squares while allowing White's pieces great activity through the center.

- Black should play to block the pawn with a knight until, hopefully, he can trade off enough pieces that the pawn will be weak in an endgame.

- Notice that 1. ... Nc6xd4 fails to 2. Nf3xd4 Qd8xd4 3. Bd3xh7+!, *discovering* to win the queen.

Pawn Islands

- White has two pawn islands (connected groups of pawns), while Black has three.

- Pawns are generally stronger in larger groups, rather than many small groups scattered around the board.

- In general, the fewer the pawn islands, the better.

PAWN STRUCTURE II

Learn to recognize passed pawns, hanging pawns, pawn majorities, and minority attacks

Understanding the nature of pawns is critical to playing chess well. On this spread, we'll look at four more important thoughts about pawn play. Unlike the previous section, not all of these ideas are about pawn weaknesses.

Our first photo below shows the power of the *passed pawn*, a great plus for its proud owner, and the goal of much

jockeying in the middle game and ending. The great Emanuel Lasker pointed out that a passed pawn must be captured or blocked—or it will be promoted.

Hanging pawns, our second example, can be strong or weak, depending on the piece placement of a specific position. Normally, the side with the hanging pawns needs to

Passed Pawn

- White's pawn on e6 is *passed*. It has no adjacent enemy pawns ahead of it.

- As Nimzovich put it, "A passed pawn has a lust to expand."

- In the position above, Black uses his queen to block

the pawn—not a proper job for her majesty. Notice here that White can play **1. Bc1-a3!.** If **1. ... Qe7xa3 2. e6-e7,** and Black will have to give up his queen to stop the pawn from promoting.

Hanging Pawns

- Two pawns that stand abreast but make up a separate pawn island, separated from other friendly pawns, are called "hanging pawns."

- Black's pawns on d5 and c5 in the photo above, which shows the pawn structure in the sixth game of the

1972 Fischer-Spassky world championship match, are "hanging pawns."

- Hanging pawns can be a weakness, especially if one is forced to advance without getting something in return. Fischer forced ... d5-d4 and won the endgame.

have superior piece activity to make this smallest of pawn islands strong.

Pawn majorities can be a powerful threat, since in an endgame, without the intervention of pieces, they can produce a passed pawn.

Minority attacks developed as a successful idea about 1900. Under certain circumstances, a player can advance his pawn minority against a majority to cause weaknesses he can then attack with pieces.

Pawn Majorities

- A *pawn majority* occurs when a larger pawn island opposes a smaller one.

- In the photo above, White has a queenside majority and Black has a kingside majority.

- Pawn majorities are very important in the endgame,

since a healthy majority can produce a *passed pawn*.

- In a middle game with the pawn structure above, Black should consider a kingside attack with pawns. White should play for the endgame, where he would try to produce a passed pawn.

Minority Attacks

- The *minority attack* takes place when one player pushes a pawn *minority* against a pawn *majority* to create weaknesses.

- In the position above, White should begin the minority

attack 1. b2-b4, intending to follow up with b4-b5. Then Black either captures on b5, taking on isolated pawns, or allows White to capture on c6, creating a backward pawn.

MIDDLE GAME PIECE EVALUATION
The value of pieces can vary with the stage of the game and the exact position

The chart of relative piece values you learned early in this book is very useful and is an excellent general guide. But the relative value of pieces (and even pawns) can vary with the stage of the game—and these values can vary in different types of middle game formations as well.

A bishop pair is, as a general rule, more valuable than a knight and bishop. But it can depend on the pawn structure. If the bishops are blocked by pawns (becoming what we call "bad" bishops), the knights excel because of their leaping ability.

When each side has only one bishop, and one player owns a light-square bishop while his opponent has a dark-square

Bishop Pair

- The middle game power of the bishop pair on open diagonals can be very dangerous and create surprising opportunities. In the position above, on the move, Black's bishops are overwhelming, of much more value than White's bishop and knight.

- Black to move plays **1. ... Qa2xb2+!**. After **2. Kc1xb2 Be5xd4+ 3. Kb2-c1 Ra5-a1+ 4. Kc1-d2 Rc8xc2#**.

- It's interesting to note that if it were White's move in the position above, he could play 1. Re2xe5! d6xe5 2. Nd4-c6, winning.

Good vs. Bad Bishop

- Black's light-square bishop has mobility because Black's pawns are all on dark squares. With this arrangement, both color squares are controlled—and the bishop's activity is not restricted.

- White's light-square bishop is very much a bad bishop,

what chess players call a "tall pawn." All of White's pawns except one are on light squares. Because of this, the bishop has few moves, and White's game is very weak on the dark squares.

- Black's bishop is much more valuable than White's.

bishop, the situation takes careful play. Since opposite-color bishops can never travel or control the same squares, they can't defend attacks from each other. A mating attack on the "wrong" color squares (the squares your bishop can't cover) can be difficult to defend.

Outposts are strongpoints on squares (in enemy territory) that are unassailable by pawns and occupied by a knight, or rook, or a bishop. An outpost piece has very enhanced relative value. For example, a white knight on e6 or d6 (or a black knight on e3 or d3) is normally worth a rook.

Opposite-Color Bishop Attack

- Here the players are castled on opposite sides and are attacking the enemy king position. They have *opposite-color bishops*; that is, their bishops move on different-colored squares.

- Although material is equal, Black has a mating attack on the dark squares, over

which White has no control. No matter who is to move, White loses.

- When the opponents have opposite-color bishops, attacks on the squares that the opponent's bishop doesn't guard can be extremely dangerous.

Superior Knight Outpost

- The position above illustrates two important middle game ideas.

- First, notice White's *outpost* on Black's weak c5-square. The white knight is unassailable by enemy pawns and reaches deep into the Black position.

- Also notice that this middle game position shows a superior knight that should be valued much more highly than the inferior black bishop, a "bad" bishop that is blocked in by his own pawns.

- White's knight is worth much more than Black's bishop.

ATTACKING THE KING IN THE CENTER

One of the most exciting middle game plans is the attack on the enemy king

Most players love the opportunity to attack. Three big ideas go into making a successful attack—knowing *where* and *when* to attack, and *how* to carry on the attack. An attack suggests itself when you have more power in one area of the board than your opponent. Planning an attack often involves transferring pieces to the area you want to attack.

Having more pawns on one wing than your opponent suggests the possibility of an attack.

The enemy king does not have to be the object of every attack. In fact, in many games, one player attacks on the king-side, where the kings are, while the other player attacks on the queenside. Of course, not all attacks succeed. Defense in

Sacrificing Two Pieces

- Morphy finds the one good move! Any other leaves Black with an advantage.

- Morphy played **8. Ng5xf7! Ke8xf7** (Otherwise, Black loses material.) **9. Qd1-f3+ Kf7-e6** (If Black wants to

hold his extra knight, this is the only move. Better is 9. ... Be7-f6, but after 10. Bc4xd5+, Black has nothing for his pains, and a worse position.) **10. Nb1-c3!** (See next photo.)

The King Walk

- Kings should not be walking around the center of the board in the opening! White's tenth move is another brilliant hammer-blow. White threatens to capture Black's horseman on d5. So . . .

- **10. ... d4xc3 11. Rf1-e1+** (Morphy's dashing play

has forced open the queen file—now there is just too much artillery gunning for the black monarch.)

- **11. ... Nc6-e5** (Again, the only move that holds material.) **12. Bc1-f4** (piling up on the pinned knight) **12. ... Be7-f6 13. Bf4xe5 Bf6xe5** (See next photo.)

chess is as important a skill to develop as offense.

Attacking the enemy king is probably the most fun, of course—and is certainly the most promising. Attacks on the king divide themselves into three categories, helpful when we study how to conduct them:

1. Attacking the king in the center;

2. Attacking the king when both kings have castled on the same side;

3. Attacking the king when the kings have castled on opposite sides.

Sacrificing to Activate Reserves

- **14. Re1xe5+** (Morphy sacrifices his rook for the bishop in order to bring his last piece into the game.) **14. ... Ke6xe5 15. Ra1-e1+ Ke5-d4 16. Bc4xd5 Rh8-e8** (If 16. ... Rh8-f8, Morphy forces mate in four: 17. Qf3xc3+! Kd4xd5 18. Re1-e5+ Kd5-d6 19. Qc3-c5+ Kd6-d7 20. Qc5-d5#.)

- But now it's mate in seven! **17. Qf3-d3+ Kd4-c5 18. b2-b4+ Kc5xb4** (If 18. ... Kc5-d6 19. Bd5-f3, checkmate, illustrating the power of White's ownership of the e-file. See next photo.)

On this spread, we look at a famous example of attacking the king in the center. The game, contested more than 150 years ago, was played as White by Paul Morphy, considered by many to be the greatest chess mind of all time. His opponent was an amateur whose name history has forgotten. There's a lot to learn from Morphy-Amateur, New Orleans, 1858. The game began: **1. e2-e4 e7-e5 2. Ng1-f3 Nb8-c6 3. Bf1-c4 Ng8-f6** (the Two Knights Defense) **4. d2-d4 e5xd4 5. Nf3-g5** (Nowadays we would prefer 5. e4-e5.) **5. ... d7-d5** (5. . . Nc6-e5 is a good alternative) **6. e4xd5 Nf6xd5? 7. 0-0 Bf8-e7.**

Final King Hunt

- It's a king hunt. Morphy knows by calculation that he has checkmate in five more moves. But even if he did not visualize each move, he would know that Black's king is defenseless, trapped on the side of the board, without blockers.

- **19. Qd3-d4+ Kb4-a5 20. Qd4xc3+ Ka5-a4 21. Qc3-b3+ Ka4-a5 22. Qb3-a3+ Ka5-b5 23. Re1-b1#.**

- So in the end, it is the open b-file, created by Morphy's eighteenth-move sacrifice, that makes it possible to checkmate.

MODERN ATTACK IN THE CENTER
The principles of attack from Morphy's games 150 years ago are still valid

Were such attacks played only in the old days? Well, at the top levels, defensive technique has certainly improved, but the principles of attack remain valid. Let's take a look at a modern world champion using the same methods against one of his chief rivals. Most modern masters know to get castled early, but sometimes they can still get caught by surprise, waiting just a little bit too long to get their king into safety. The game below, between Vladimir Kramnik (White) and Peter Leko, took place during a televised match in Europe in 2000.

Is this game between the best of modern chess? Yes—two months after this game was played, Kramnik went on to defeat Garry Kasparov, winning one "belt" of the chess world

Preventing Castling

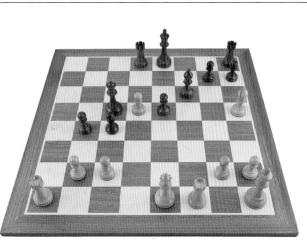

- Kramnik has just played **22. Be2-h5+!,** preventing Black from castling. If 22. ... g7-g6, 23. Rf1xf6 g6xh5 24. Qe1xe5+ Qc5-e7 25. Rf6-e6.

- **22. ... Ke8-e7** (With Black's king stuck in the center, White has an eye on open files and open light diagonals.)

- **23. Qe1-g3 g7-g6** (to discourage 24. Rf1xf6) **24. Rf1xf6!** (Anyway! See next photo.)

The Hunt Begins

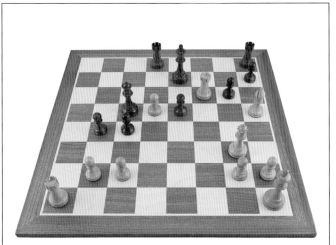

- You should see some similarity now to the other king hunts in the center we've looked at. Black's bishop was holding Black's center and guarding the dark squares around Black's king.

- **24. ... Ke7xf6 25. Ra1-f1+** (Of course—White jumps on the file with a gain of time, pushing Black's king back from the defense of his e5-pawn.) **25. ... Kf6-g7.**

- **26. Bh5xg6!** (Kramnik sees that opening the h-file will be lethal for Black.) **26. ... h7xg6 27. Qg3xe5+** (See next photo.)

championship. In October 2006, Kramnik went on to defeat World Chess Federation world champion Veselin Topalov in a unification match. Kramnik became the first undisputed world champion since Garry Kasparov broke away from FIDE in 1993.

In 2000 the Hungarian Peter Leko became a grandmaster in 1994 at only fourteen, a record at the time. One of the top-ranked players in the world, Leko later drew a match with Kramnik. Both players were in the world's elite.

We'll pick the game up below after twenty-one moves for White. Later, if you want to play over the whole game,

here's how the game started: **1.e2-e4 c7-c5 2.Ng1-f3 e7-e6 3.d2-d4 c5xd4 4.Nf3xd4 Nb8-c6 5.Bf1-e2 Qd8-c7 6.Nb1-c3 a7-a6 7.0-0 b7-b5 8.Nd4xc6 d7xc6 9.Bc1-e3 Bc8-b7 10.f2-f4 c6-c5 11.f4-f5 Ra8-d8 12.Qd1-e1 Ng8-f6 13.f5xe6 f7xe6 14.Be3-f4 e6-e5 15.Bf4-g5 Bf8-e7 16.a2-a4 c5-c4 17.a4xb5 a6xb5 18.Kg1-h1 b5-b4 19.Bg5xf6 Be7xf6 20.Nc3-d5 Bb7xd5 21.e4xd5 Qc7-c5.**

Kramnik has said that chess is the art of carrying out a long-term plan. Here he combines planning with a sharp eye for tactics!

Forcing the King Forward

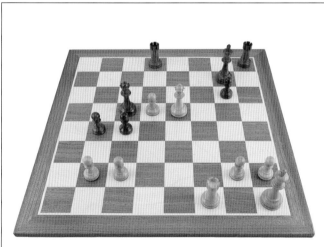

- **27. ... Kg7-g8** (If 27. ... Kg7-h7 or 27. ... Kg7-h6, 28. Rf1-f4, we have the game-ending position. Black struggles to avoid it.) **28. Qe5-e6+ Kg8-h7 29. Rf1-f7+ Kh7-h6 30. Qe6-h3+** (Once again, we see the attacker forcing the defending king to march forward into a crossfire.)

- **30. ... Kh6-g5 31. Qh3-g3+ Kg5-h5** (If 31. ... Kg5-h6, it's mate on the move: 32. Qg3-h4#) **32. Qg3-e5+ Kh5-h6** (32. ... g6-g5 33. Rf7-g7; 32. ... Kh5-g4 33. Rf7-f4#) **33. Rf7-f4.**

No Way Out

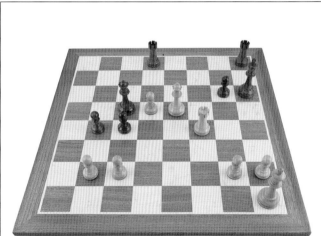

- Black resigns, forced into the hopeless position he sought to avoid.

- White is a full rook down, but as we've seen before, the defender's extra material can't get into play before it's too late.

- White threatens 34. Rf4-h4

mate. If Black tries 33. ... g6-g5, White forces mate in three: 34. Qe5-f6+ Kh6-h5 35. Qf6-f7+ Kh5-h6 36. Rf4-f6#.

- If Leko tries 33. ... Kh6-h7, it's a different mate in three: 34. Rf4-h4+ Kh7-g8 35. Qe5xh8+ Kg8-f7 36. Rh4-h7#.

ATTACKING: SAME-SIDE CASTLING
Here the attacker often pushes pawns in front of his own king

When the opponents are castled on the same side of the board—most often on the kingside—the attacker can use pieces and pawns in his assault on the enemy king's position, but he must be careful not to leave his own king under-defended and subject to counterattack. In the game below, we see White employing four important and frequently used techniques in the same-side attack.

1. He stabilizes the center, cramping Black with a pawn on e5;

2. He moves a superior amount of force to the side of the board where the kings are castled;

3. He "lifts" a rook in front of his own pawns to use as heavy artillery;

4. He pushes a kingside pawn to use, if needed, as a battering

Rook Lift

- **18. Rd1-d3** (a typical rook "lift" to attack—White readies his rook to swing in front of White's kingside pawns to attack) **18. ... Nb6-d5.**

- **19. Bf4-c1** (White preserves his dark-square bishop, keeping it on the c1-h6 diagonal) **19. ... Nd7-f8** (Black adds a kingside defender.) **20. h3-h4** (White threatens to push the pawn to h6 to weaken Black's pawn-guard.) **20. Nd5xc3 21. b2xc3 Qd8-d5 22. Qe4-g4 f7-f5.**

Weakened Kingside

- **23. e5xf6 ep** (Black takes on an isolated pawn on e6, but he has a more immediate goal—avoiding checkmate!)

- **23. ... Be7xf6 24. Nf3-g5 Qd5-f5 25. Qg4-e2** (White avoids exchanging his biggest gun.) **25. ... h7-h6?** (Black is anxious to chase away the invading white knight. But he weakens his kingside pawn formation.) **26. Ng5-e4 Bf6-e7 27. Rd3-f3** (White points up the problem with the black queen's position.) **27. ... Qf5-d5?** (Unappetizing as it looks, 27. ... Qf5-h7 gave stiffer resistance.) **28. Bc1xh6!**

ram against the opposing king's defenses.

Victor Korchnoi has been at the top tier of chess for fifty years—he has had the longest tournament-winning career in the history of chess. Below we see him conducting a kingside attack against fellow Russian Andrey Peterson in 1965. Korchnoi (White) opens the game with a Queen's Gambit. The game began: **1. d2-d4 d7-d5 2. c2-c4 d5xc4 3. Ng1-f3 Ng8-f6 4. e2-e3 Bc8-g4 5. Bf1xc4 e7-e6 6. h2-h3 Bg4-h5 7. Nb1-c3 Nb8-d7 8. 0–0 Bf8-e7 9. e3-e4 Nd7-b6 10. Bc4-e2 0–0 11. Bc1-e3 Bh5-g6 12. Be2-d3 Nf6-d7 13.** **Be3-f4 Be7-d6 14. e4-e5 Bg6xd3 15. Qd1xd3 Bd6-e7 16. Ra1-d1 c7-c6 17. Qd3-e4 Rf8-e8.** (See photo below, far left.)

Korchnoi has a cramping pawn on e5 and a centralized queen. Black's pieces are not in the best position to defend his king and will have to be relocated. White sees that he has accumulated more material force on the kingside and decides to attack the king. Let's see the master at work.

Stripping Away Defenders

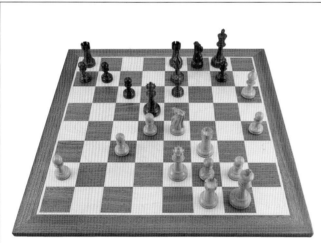

- White "sacs" (chess-speak for "sacrifices") a bishop to strip the black king of defenses.

- **28. ... g7xh6 29. Rf3-g3+ Kg8-f7 30. Qe2-g4** (Good enough to win, but 30. c3-c4! was a killer, with the idea of removing the black queen's guard on h5. For

example, if 30. ... Qd5xd4, 31. Qe2-h5+, with mate in three, or 30. ... Qa5 31. c4-c5, followed by 32. Qe2-h5!.)

- **30. ... Re8-d8** (Falls into a pretty mate in four, but Black was lost anyway.) **31. Qg4-g7+ Kf7-e8 32. Qg7xe7+!!**

Knight-and-Rook Checkmate

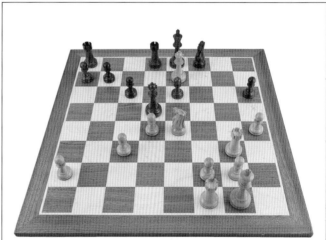

- Ouch! The kind of move that looks obvious after someone makes it for you!

- **32. ... Ke8xe7 33. Rg3-g7+ Ke7-e8 34. Ne4-f6#.**

- The resulting knight-and-rook mate pattern is worth remembering.

161

ATTACKING ALONG THE DIAGONAL

When you have an advantage, you have the obligation to attack

Let's take a look at another great attack against an enemy king in a game featuring kings castled on the same side, a common situation. This time the attack is conducted by the Russian Mikhail Botvinnik, the only player ever to hold the world championship title on three separate occasions, from 1948 to 1963. Here he is in his twenties, polishing off one of the greatest chess masters of the previous generation, Milan Vidmar, who lived in present-day Slovenia.

Although the game begins as an English Opening, it transposes into a Queen's Gambit Declined. White takes on an isolated queen pawn in exchange for lots of piece activity, including a threatening light-square bishop on the a2-g8 diagonal. Additionally, the d-pawn helps White control e5, occupying the square with a knight. Black tries to follow the traditional prescription of blocking the square in front of the *isolani*—an isolated pawn, one with no adjacent

Opening a Key Diagonal

- **17. f2-f4 Ra8-c8 18. f4-f5** (Botvinnik advances his f-pawn to weaken Black's defenses along the a2-g8 diagonal, a classic pathway of attack. He will then lift his rook into the game along the f-file.)

- **18. ... e6xf5?** (Black had a difficult but not outright losing game—until this mistake. He should go straight to 18. ... Qd8-d6. If then 19. f5xe6, f7xe6, and the a2-g8 diagonal remains blocked.) **19. Rf1xf5 Qd8-d6?** (But now, with the diagonal open, the move falls into a combination.) **20. Ne5xf7!** (See the next photo.)

Diagonal Lineup

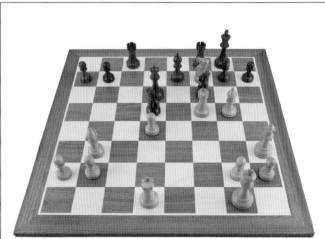

- **20. ... Rf8xf7** (Black's knight, rook, and king are lined up on the a2-g8 diagonal, now wide open for White's bishop on b3.) **21. Bg5xf6 Be7xf6** (This leaves Black's knight on d5 *en prise*, but if 21. ... Nd5xf6, then 22. Rf5xf6!, next capturing the rook with 23. Qh3xc8.)

- **22. Rf5xd5 Qd6-c6** (White has gotten his piece back plus a pawn—and Black's king and f7-rook are still lined up on the killing diagonal.) **23. Rd5-d6!** (See the next photo.)

colleagues—with a knight, hoping to live through the middle game and get into an endgame, in which White's singleton becomes a permanent weakness.

In the position pictured in the first photograph below right, Botvinnik sees that, like White in the previous game, he has an advantage on the kingside—and is therefore *obligated* to attack. There is an important principle of attack that tells us that if we fail to attack when we have the advantage, we will lose our advantage.

The game, Botvinnik-Vidmar, 1936, began: **1. c2-c4 e7-e6**

2. Ng1-f3 d7-d5 3. d2-d4 Ng8-f6 4. Bc1-g5 Bf8-e7 5. Nb1-c3 0-0 6. e2-e3 Nb8-d7 7. Bf1-d3 c7-c5 8. 0-0 c5xd4 9. e3xd4 d5xc4 10. Bd3xc4 Nd7-b6 11. Bc4-b3 Bc8-d7 12. Qd1-d3 Nb6-d5 13. Nf3-e5 Bd7-c6 14. Ra1-d1 Nd5-b4 15. Qd3-h3 Bc6-d5 16. Nc3xd5 Nb4xd5. (See photo below, far left.)

Poison Rook

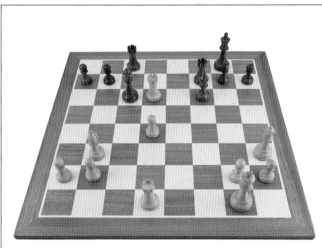

- The rook is poison. If 23. ... Qc6xd6, then White plays 24. Qh3xc8+, and his pin on the diagonal guarantees that he will win more material.

- **23. ... Qc6-e8 24. Rd6-d7**

- Black must now lose a whole rook. Vidmar gives up.

Tips on Same-Side Castling Attacks

- If you have a strong advantage on the kingside you must attack or lose the initiative!

- Don't attack so wildly that you expose your own king to a dangerous counterattack.

- Before starting your attack, be sure that the defender can't counterpunch in the center to get a better game.

- Keep rook lifts in mind and same-side pawn pushes to add pressure against the enemy king.

When kings are castled on opposite sides, the first attack to break through normally wins

We've looked at two brilliant attacks against the king when the defending monarch was stuck in the center. Then we looked at two games that illustrate a skillful assault on the king when both sides had castled on the same side of the board.

Now we'll look at two exciting games in which the opponents have castled on opposite sides. When this happens,

both sides may begin a plan of attacking the other's king. In such games:

1. The quick advance of pawns against the enemy king (a *pawn storm*) is frequently used to open lines to the enemy king; 2. The attacker can push these pawns without exposing his own king, since his king is not behind them; 3. Time

Pawn Majority Attack

Missing the Best Defense

- White's 14. Q d2-e3! prevents Black from castling long, since it attacks a7.

- **16. f2-f4** (White gets his pawn majority rolling right away with a gain of time.)

- **16. ... Qe5-e6 17. e4-e5**

- Alekhine's pawn push

opens the important diagonal to Black's h7 and drives a wedge into the middle of the defender's position.

- **... Rf8-e8 18. Rh1-e1** (White's e5-pawn is pinned to his queen at the moment, so Black's knight is temporarily safe.) **18. ... Ra8-d8** (See next photo.)

- **19. f4-f5** (Alekhine still can't take the knight on f6, but he advances the pawn attack with a gain of time.)

- **19. ... Qe6-e7 20. Qe3-g5 Nf6-d5?** (Marshall retreats his knight too soon! Black should play 20. ... Qe7-f8 immediately. If then 21.

e5xf6 Re8xe1 22. Rd1xe1 Rd8xd3 23. Re1-e7 h7-h6=.)

- **21. f5-f6! Qe7-f8** (Now it's the only move.) **22. Bd3-c4 Nd5xc3** (If 22. ... h6, 23. f6xg7 wins) **23. Rd1xd8** (White doesn't hurry to recapture the knight.) **23. ... Re8xd8** (See next photo.)

(getting there first) and initiative (putting the opponent on the defensive) are crucial; 4. Control of the center is very important; 5. An advantage in attacking force in the area of the enemy king is crucial.

The game below was played in 1925 between two of the greatest attacking players in the world. Alexander Alekhine (White) would become the fourth world champion. Frank Marshall reigned as champion of the U.S. for twenty-eight years. The game began: **1. d2-d4 d7-d5 2. c2-c4 Ng8-f6 3. c4xd5 Nf6xd5 4. e2-e4 Nd5-f6 5. Bf1-d3 e7-e5 6. d4xe5 Nf6-g4**

7. Ng1-f3 Nb8-c6 8. Bc1-g5 Bf8-e7 9. Bg5xe7 Qd8xe7 10. Nb1-c3 Nc6xe5 11. Nf3xe5 Qe7xe5 12. h2-h3 Ng4-f6. (See photo below, far left.)

Alekhine sees that he has a majority of pawns on the kingside and plans to castle long and attack on the kingside. 13. Qd1-d2 Bc8-d7 14. Qd2-e3! Bd7-c6 15. 0-0-0 0-0.

Attempted Swindle

- **24. f6xg7** (24. e5-e6 also wins.) **24. ... Nc3xa2+** (If 24. ... Qf8-Qe8 25. Bc4xf7+!. White picks up Black's rook.)

- **25. Kc1-b1** (If 25. Bc4xa2, 25. ... Qc5+ 26. Kc1-b1 Rd8-d7, and Black is slightly better.) **25. ... Qf8-e8** (If 25. ... Na2-c3+, 26. b2xc3 wins.)

- **26. e5-e6 Bc6-e4+** (Marshall saved so many bad games that he was known as a swindler. Now if 27. Kb1xa2, 27. ... Qe8-a4 is checkmate! It may have worked against a hasty opponent! See next photo.)

Smiling at the Trap

- Alekhine doesn't fall for Marshall's trap. **27. Kb1-a1** (27. Re1xe4 wins as well, but White's move is a smile at Marshall's attempted ploy.)

- **27. ... f7-f5** (If 27. ... f7xe6, 28. Bc4xe6+ Qe8xe6 29. Qg5xd8+) **28. e6-e7+** (discovered attack) **28. ... Rd8-**

d5 29. Qg5-f6! Qe8-f7 30. e7-e8Q+ (An undermining deflection! Now Black's rook on d5 is under-defended and his game is in ruins. In fact, it's mate in two.) **1-0.**

- There are no tricks or traps left for Marshall now. He resigns.

OPPOSITE-SIDE FIANCHETTO

When Black castles behind a kingside fianchetto, White can castle long to start a pawn storm

This is the last game of the section. It's another attack on the king with the opponents castled on opposite sides. But this time we look at a Black formation that includes a kingside fianchetto. Such an attack can come from an opening like the Sicilian Dragon or the Modern Defense. Black's pawn on g6 can become a target for White's advancing h-pawn,

giving White a chance to open the file by exchanging pawns or gambiting his h-pawn.

The kind of pawn storm that follows can be straightforward and easy to play for the attacker. Your author played the game below to test ChessMaster 5000, a 1998 chess-playing software program for Windows, set on its expert level, to see

h-file Attack

Winning, but Not Best!

- **1. ... Qd8-c7** (A human master, knowing that counterattacking in the center is normally the best reaction to an attack on the flank, would likely play 1. ... d6-d5.) **2. h4-h5 Nf6xh5 3. g2-g4** (advancing the pawn storm with a gain of time.) **3. ... Nh5-f6.**

- **4. Be3-h6** (thematic, eliminating Black's important bishop) **4. ... Bg7xh6 5. Qd2xh6 Nb8-d7.**

- **6. g4-g5** (Kicking the knight again, I didn't want to play this move before using the diagonal to exchange off Black's fianchettoed bishop.) **6. ... Nf6-h5** (See next photo.)

- **7. Rh1xh5!** This move is so thematic in this kind of position that I didn't analyze. It was my only candidate move.) **7. ... g6xh5.**

- In a previous game I had played: 8. Qh6xh5 e7-e6 9. Ng1-e2 Rf8-e8 10. Rd1-h1 Nd7-f8 11. e4-e5 d6-d5 12.

Bc4-d3 and won. This time I found better.

- **8. g5-g6!** (The little chip-reader's f-pawn is pinned by my bishop. If he could feel emotions, he'd certainly regret not playing 1. ... d6-d5, blocking this diagonal. See next photo.)

how a computer would defend against this kind of attack and if such an attack "played itself," as so many chess writers would say. I set up a middle game position from a 1960 game between future world champ Boris Spassky and the great American champion and writer Larry Evans. From that point on, the computer program and I were on our own. I resolved to play intuitively and very quickly, relying on general principles, not extensive calculations.

The resulting game was indeed easy to win and fun to play.

Familiar Rook Lift

- **8. ... h7xg6 9. Qh6xg6+** (I have mate in nine moves, but I needed to do no such heavy calculations. The moves suggest themselves.)

- **9. ... Kg8-h8 10. Qg6xh5+** (clearing the file with a gain of time) **10. ... Kh8-g8 11. Qh5-g5+ Kg8-h8 12. Rd1-d2** (The familiar rook lift threatens mate on the move. 12. Ng1-e2 is also good.)

- **12. ... Nd7-f6 13. Rd2-h2+ Nf6-h7 14. Qg5-h6.** (See next photo.)

Thematic Ideas

- There's no way out of checkmate. Black can throw away a bishop with 14. ... Bc8-f5 or 14. ... Bc8-h3, but after White captures it, there's no preventing 16. Qh6xh7 mate.

- The thematic play in this game is quite useful to understand, since the ideas occur frequently when Black is castled kingside and fianchettoes his king bishop.

- Notice how often we see a defeated defender with much of his army sitting idle, distant from his helpless king.

ONE-MOVE KILLERS

Studying realistic tactical problems is probably the single most effective exercise to improve your chess results

Let's look at some chess puzzles. They're fun and will develop your tactical eye.

Chess enthusiasts from club player to grandmaster know that working tactical puzzles is one of the best ways to improve and keep sharp. Since most games are decided by tactics, having a trained instinct for tactical themes will win

you many, many games. You can find books full of tactical puzzles, and find such puzzles in magazines and online.

We should emphasize that the benefits result from working practical puzzles—positions that did or could occur in a real chess game. There is another type that uses very improbable, artistic positions that are not at all likely to happen in a game.

White Mates in Two

- Try to visualize this one without using a set. White could mate Black on the back rank with either rook—except that Black's bishop covers both potential mating squares, a8 and e8.

- If we attack the bishop with, say, 1. Re1-c1, Black could

play 1. ... Bc6-d5 or even 1. ... Bc6-e8, and there's no way to mate in the one move we have left.

- Is there a way to *deflect* the bishop?

- **ANSWER: 1. Ra1-a8+! Bc6xa8 2. Re1-e8 mate.**

What's White's Best Move?

- Can you do this one in your head?

- Whichever rook White checks with on the back rank, Black can block with one of his own.

- Let's look at an example, 1. Ra7-a8+. Any ideas?

- **ANSWER: 1. Ra7-a8+! Rb3-b8 2. Rh7-h8+ Rd3-d8 3. Ra8xb8+** (Deflection again, taking the king away from the defense of the other rook.) **3. ... Kc8xb8 4. Rh8xd8+** (White can actually begin by checking with either rook. It's the method that's important.)

Generally, this sort of chess puzzle is called a chess "problem," and those who compose them or just like to solve them are called "problemists." So if you see a book of chess "problems," make sure it's what you want before buying it.

The goal of any puzzle is to find a win (or draw, if that's the direction) in as few moves as possible. If the directions require "Mate in Two," solving it in three moves doesn't qualify. Sometimes the directions may be "White to Move and Win." In that case, the best move is the only one that counts.

When you approach each puzzle, think back to our discussion of tactics. Solutions to all these problems employ one or more of the tactical tools we learned in Chapter 7. Read the title above each photograph or diagram carefully—it tells you what you are supposed to find and whether White or Black moves first. Try to solve the problem without looking at the bullets below the photo. But if you can't, then cover the bullets with a piece of paper and read them one at a time, from top to bottom. Each bullet is another hint. The last bullet, in bold, is the answer.

White to Move and Win

- This is another to first try solving in your head.

- We don't know whether we should look for mate or just material gain. So we have to assess the entire position. Actually, there's only one check available for White—and it's a winner!

- **ANSWER: 1. Nc4-d6+!** (This move uncovers an attack on Black's queen. White's next will be 2. Be2xb5, winning the queen for two pieces.)

Black to Move and Win

- Black is winning and can win long term with a number of different moves. But instructions like this always mean to find the best, most forcing win.

- Black attacks f2 with his bishop and queen. The square has two defenders, White's rook and king.

- **ANSWER: 1. ... Ba6!** (White must move his rook or lose the Exchange. White's game falls apart.)

UNPLEASANT SURPRISES

Most winning combinations are unpleasant surprises for the victim—here's a collection, from simple to stunning

A combination is a short series of forced moves—the opponent has no good way out—that accomplishes a certain goal. In solving these chess puzzles, you're really finding the winning combinations in realistic game positions. In a way, you're walking in the shoes of the great masters who played the moves originally.

You should try to solve each of the problems in this chapter before looking at the answers. Some are simple enough to try in your head. But if you don't see the answer after a few minutes of analysis, set up a board with the starting position in each photo and move the pieces to help you visualize. You can always reset the pieces to match the photo to start over.

White to Move and Win

- White's rook is attacked. Black's knight is defended. Black's pawn on e4 is *en prise*.

- Look for a way for White to win a piece in one move.

- The Black pawn on e4 and the Black king are on the same diagonal.

- **ANSWER: 1. Qh4xe4+** White's queen forks the black king and bishop. Black's King must move, and White will win the bishop.

White to Move and Win

- Black attacks White's bishop on a6 twice, and it's defended only once. With his rook on c5, White attacks Black's knight on e5. But look for a surprise White move.

- What square needs to be covered to keep Black's king trapped on the back-rank?

- **ANSWER: 1. Ba6-d3!** (Covers the black king's escape square, h7. If **1. ... Ra8xa1 2. Rc5-c8#.** If 1. ... Ra8-b8 2. Rc5xe5 and White collects a piece, and wins easily. This is a position from Capablanca-Rossolimo, 1933.)

When you first examine a puzzle, look over the diagonals, files, and ranks to see what pieces are threatening or controlling what squares. Recall the tactics we've studied. Look for *discoveries* that uncover a second threat when a piece moves. See if there are *undermining* moves that deflect a piece from its important duty. Look for checks, of course, although not all checks are good moves.

Remember that we give you hints in the bullets below the photos, and the last bullet gives you the answer.

Black Mates in Five

- This seems like a difficult assignment. But, this section is about surprises!

- Black controls the e-file, limiting the white king's movement. Black's bishops have open diagonals.

- If White's knight were taken, g2xf3 would open the f1-h3 diagonal to White's king.

- **ANSWER: 1. ... Qh5xf3+! 2. g2xf3 Bc8-h3+ 3. Kf1-f2 Bf6-h4+ 4. Kf2-g1 Re8-e1+ 5. Qc4-f1 Re1xf1#**. Each of White's moves is forced after 1. ... Qh5xf3+!. The great German champion Adolf Anderssen played this move in 1876.

White to Play and Win

- Black has just tried to "break" the pin on his f6-knight by playing g7-g5. But White has a surprise.

- What if White could eliminate Black's g- and h-pawns and remain with a pin on Black's threatened knight?

- **ANSWER: 1. Nf3xg5!**. After **1. ... h6xg5 2. Bh4xg5**, White will get his piece back because the knight on f6 is pinned and attacked. What's more, Black's kingside has just about disappeared. White can easily work up an attack. Black is lost.

WINNING "SACRIFICES"

Many combinations begin by sacrificing a valuable piece for a lesser man, or sometimes for nothing at all

Recall that a sacrifice (or a "sac," as chess players sometimes call it for short) gives material away as a kind of investment, expecting a high rate of return. The four examples on this spread begin with a sacrificial idea. When a player gets his investment back immediately, it's not a true sacrifice, but the idea, and the method of thinking, are the same.

Of course, when you know you should be looking for a sacrifice, it's easier to find. In your own games, no one will tell you that the position you're in requires a sacrifice. But practicing with many different types of tactical problems will prepare you for your games. You'll develop a sense for what kind of positions may contain that chance for a brilliant combination

Discovered Attack

- The solution involves a *very* temporary sacrifice.

- Look for a discovery.

- **ANSWER: 1. ... Bd6xh2+! 2. Kg1xh2 Rd8xd1 3. Rfxd1.**

- Black has won the white queen and pawn for rook and bishop. Now he has 3. ... Qe7-c5, winning more material. But you didn't have to see this far to know that 1. ... Bd6xh2+! was good.

White to Move and Mate in Three

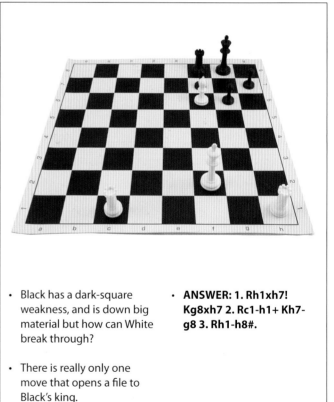

- Black has a dark-square weakness, and is down big material but how can White break through?

- There is really only one move that opens a file to Black's king.

- You need only a bishop and one rook for the final mate.

- **ANSWER: 1. Rh1xh7! Kg8xh7 2. Rc1-h1+ Kh7-g8 3. Rh1-h8#.**

that checkmates your opponent, or leads him to tip over his king, the traditional gesture of resigning.

······· GREEN ● LIGHT ·······

Reversing the Move Order
Sometimes you can "feel" there is combination in a position, but you can't find it. If you're stuck in this way, try reversing the move order in your candidate-move lines. For example, if you're looking at capturing a piece with your knight and then moving your queen—look at moving the queen first. The fourth puzzle below is an example of a position in which this technique may help you.

White to Move and Win

White to Move and Win

- 1. Qb1xh7+ Kf7-e6 2. Qh7-h3+ Ke6-e7 3. Qh3-h7+ forces a draw by repetition, which we'll study on page 184, (... Ke6-d6? runs into Rc1-d1+)—a save, but no win.

- But if the queen were only one more square farther away from her king. . .

- **ANSWER: 1. Rc1-c7!** (An undermining deflection, putting the Black queen where we want her.) **1. ... Qd7xc7** (The queen is pinned to her king, so she must take or be taken.) **2. Qb1xh7+ Kf7-e6 3. Qh7xc7.** From here, White wins easily.

- White's rook is attacked by Black's queen. White's knight attacks Black's bishop, which is guarded by the black queen.

- 1. Nf5xe7+ Qb7xe7 2. Qd1-d5 Nb8-d7 doesn't win anything. Black keeps an advantage.

- When you're stuck, try changing the order of the moves you're considering. Try this on the line above.

- **ANSWER: 1. Qd1-d5!!** **Qb7xd5** (If 1. ... Qb7-d7 2. Nf5xe7+ Qd7xe7 3. Qd5xa8) **2. Nf5xe7+ Kg8-h8 3. Ne7xd5.** White has won a piece and the game.

COMMANDING QUEENS
Whenever the powerful queen moves, she changes the balance of forces in some area of the board

The four puzzles on this page spread all involve initial queen moves. This is a big hint that you normally don't get when looking at such puzzles. But the goal here is to give you practice in seeing and making combinations.

When confronted with a puzzle, first evaluate the position. What are the pluses and minuses of the side to move? There have to be threats, even if they are concealed. What are the special weaknesses of the defending side? Make sure to study the diagonals and files to make sure you see all the squares that are threatened and controlled. Look for surprise tactics like discovered attacks. Look for checks, but realize that not all checks are useful—they can even be a mistake.

White Mates in Three

- White is down material. He needs a big move.

- Uncovering on the black queen gets nowhere: 1. Nb1-d2 Qa1-c3, and Black is winning.

- 1. Qe7xc7 Qa1xa2, and Black is still winning.

- Try a sacrificial deflection.

- **ANSWER: 1. Qe7xf8+! Kg8xf8 2. Be3-c5+ Kf8-g8 3. Re1-e8#.**

White to Win Black's Queen

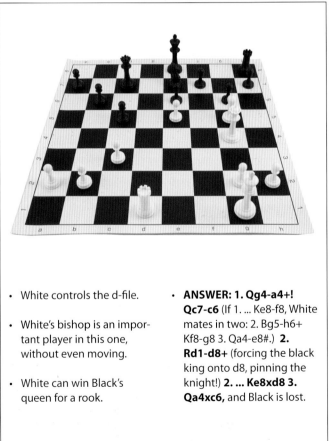

- White controls the d-file.

- White's bishop is an important player in this one, without even moving.

- White can win Black's queen for a rook.

- **ANSWER: 1. Qg4-a4+! Qc7-c6** (If 1. ... Ke8-f8, White mates in two: 2. Bg5-h6+ Kf8-g8 3. Qa4-e8#.) **2. Rd1-d8+** (forcing the black king onto d8, pinning the knight!) **2. ... Ke8xd8 3. Qa4xc6,** and Black is lost.

Look at the first puzzle. Since it's a mate in three, you know you need to find forcing moves. There's no time for a long maneuver. And you know that, since it's in this section, the first step will be a queen move.

As always, try to solve the problem without looking at the bullets below the puzzle. Look at the photo to see if you can solve it "in your head." But have a set and board handy if you need it. Move the pieces around if you need to. Then, if you still need help, look at the bullets below, one at a time. The last bullet gives the answer.

Don't be concerned if you can't solve these problems. But be sure to play over the moves until you get the idea. Even if you solved a problem, play over the lines carefully to make sure you've seen all the ideas in the position.

White to Mate in Six

- Don't be overly impressed with the six-move requirement. Threaten mate in one.

- Black will then throw checks at you until you walk out of them, leaving him helpless.

- **ANSWER: 1. Qe4-g6** (This is the key move. The hanging [*en prise*] rook and checks are meaningless in a few more moves.) **1. ... Rd8xd1+ 2. Kh1-g2 Rd1-d2+ 3. Kg2-h3 Rd2xh2+** (The last desperate check.) **4. Kh3xh2 b7-b5** (or any other legal move) **5. Qg6xh6#** (Another brilliancy from master play: Nimzovitch-Rubinstein, 1928.)

White to Mate in Five

- Daydream a little. Wouldn't it be great to be able to push White's e-pawn with check?

- To do that, we need to deflect Black's blockading queen.

- **ANSWER: 1. Qc3-g7+! Qe7xg7 2. e6-e7+ Rd8-d5** (It's hopeless. If 2. ... Kg8-h8 3. e7xd8Q+ Qg7-g8 4. Qd8xg8#) **3. Bb3xd5+ Kg8-h8 4. e7-e8Q+ Qg7-g8 5. Qe8xg8#.**

GRANDMASTER MOVES

Here's another collection of puzzles that can start with any kind of move—see what you can do

You've had some practice, so let's try some puzzles that can begin with any sort of move. But go about solving them in much the same way. First evaluate the position to identify the weaknesses the defender has and the threats the attacker has. Go over the diagonals, ranks, and files to make sure you see the interplay of all the pieces.

Try some candidate moves. Analyze them first in your head. Then, if you need to, try them on a board, moving the pieces to help you analyze, and read the hints from top to bottom.

Don't be discouraged if you don't solve any of the problems! The important thing at this stage is to understand and

Black to Move and Win

- White's tripled pawns and restricted king are clues.

- Black's bishop on c5 restricts White's king to the h-file corridor his pawns create.

- Black's queen is attacked. But if only that h-file could be forced open...

- **ANSWER: 1. ... h7-h5! 2. Rf5xg5 h5xg4+** (Now it's mate in two, but if 2. g4xh5, Black captures the rook with 2. ... Qg5xf5.) **3. Rg5-h5 Rh8xh5#.**

Black to Discover

- Black has active pieces, some aimed at White's king. Note Black's bishop on a7 and rook on g8.

- Sometimes "daydreaming" or "fantasizing" about the changes you'd like to see in the position can help you find combinations.

- If White's pawn on f2 weren't there, Black would have a pawn-push discovery.

- **ANSWER: 1. ... Be6xf5** (removes a g3-protector) **2. Be4xf5 Rg8xg3+! 3. f2xg3** (If 3. Kg1-h2 Qd8xh4+ 4. Bf5-h3 Qh4xh3#.) **3. ... d4-d3+,** winning material, as White has to play **4. Qe2-f2.**

start to recognize the patterns that make these combinations possible in your own games.

If, even after looking at the answer, you can't understand how the solution worked, make sure that you're starting from the exact position pictured. Check each square and compare it to your own board. Then look at the final position of the solution. Three of the positions end in checkmate. In the second puzzle, Black wins a big material advantage. Confirm that the final positions correspond to these results.

White Mates in Three

- Remember, your moves must force mate in three, with no escape for Black.

- White's rook on the seventh rank and pawn on f6 are two of the four key players in this combination.

- But the first move is a queen sacrifice.

- **ANSWER: 1. Qd3-g6! f7xg6** (Black must capture. Everything else allows 2. Qg6xg7#.) **2. Rb7xg7+ Kg8-f8 3. Nf4xg6#** (This one's also from an actual high-level game, Bronstein-Geller, 1961. The rook-and-knight mate crops up every once and a while and is worth remembering.)

Find Black's Best Move

- It's Black's move and White has a back-rank weakness. How can Black take immediate advantage of it?

- Deflection may work. And this is a section on commanding queen moves. . .

- **ANSWER: 1. ... Qd6-c6! 2. Rc1xc6** (If 2. f2-f3, then of course, 2. ... Qc6xc1; and if 2. Rc1-d1, then ... Re4xe1+ discovers an unstoppable mating attack on g2.) **2. ... Re4xe1#.**

KNIGHT MARES

The leaping knight is a tricky piece—the problems below show it at its surprising best

Three of the puzzles below begin with a knight move. Knowing that will help you solve them. On the other hand, the puzzles here can be complicated. Keep in mind that the longer you think trying to solve the problem, the more you will learn. Don't be concerned with trying to be fast. Instead, be thorough and analytical. Assess the strengths and weaknesses of both sides and unearth the threats hiding in the position—especially for the side on move.

Then, just as if you were playing one of your own games, decide on candidate moves and begin to analyze—visualize the move and the responses it could get.

The second puzzle below is the most complicated

White to Move and Win

- The open g-file in front of Black's castled king is an invitation to White's rook. But is there a better move first?

- Notice the White queen-and-bishop battery along the long dark diagonal.

- **ANSWER: 1. Nc3xd5!**

e6xd5 (If 1. ... Nf6xd5, then 2. Qd4xg7#. And if Black doesn't capture the knight, White has won a pawn and will go on to shatter Black's kingside. Perhaps Black's best is 1. ... e6-e5, closing the diagonal.) **2. Qd4xf6!** (A nice touch!) **2. ... g7xf6 3. Rh1-g1+ Kg8-h8 4. Bb2xf6#.**

White to Move and Win

- This one is complicated. White has a number of pieces aiming at Black's kingside.

- Start with a forcing move. A check would be handy.

- **ANSWER: 1. Nf7-h6+ Kg8-h8** (If 1. ... g7xh6 2. Rf1-f8+ Re8xf8 3. Qb3xe6+ Kg8-h8

4. Qe6-e5+, and White will soon mate Black.) **2. Rf1-f8+ Re8xf8 3. Ba3xf8** (Black was threatened with mate on f1.) **3. ... Qe6xh6** (3. ... Qe6xb3 4. Bf8xg7#; 3. ... Ra8xf8 4. Rb7-b8! Rf8xb8 5. Qb3xb8+) **4. Bf8xg7+ Qh6xg7 5. Rb7xg7 Kh8xg7 6. Qb3-b7+.**

178

combination that starts with a knight move. But it is especially pleasing, since White has all Black's responses worked out. See if you can discover the first few moves and analyze some of the lines on your board before confirming the solution.

The last puzzle of this section does not begin with a knight move. We saved it for last because it is a bit difficult, but very interesting. Boris Spassky, as White, is threatened with mate in three by Victor Korchnoi, beginning with 1. ... Rf3xh3+.

But, fortunately for Boris, it is his move. Find the best defense and you'll find a win for Spassky.

White to Move and Win

- Material is even. But is White's knight trapped on a6?

- White has already "lifted" a rook to the third rank and his own king is safe.

- If White can break up Black's queenside pawns, he may mate Black.

- **ANSWER: 1. Na6-c5!** (White simultaneously threatens checkmate on b7 and the rook on d7.) **1. ... b6xc5** (If 1. ... d6xc5 2. Rd1xd7.) **2. Rf3-a3! Ka7-b8 3. Ra3xa5,** and Black can't escape checkmate on a8. He can only delay it with the spite check 3. ... Qf7xa2+.

White to Move and Win

- Remember, this one does not start with a knight move.

- Not 1. g2xf3, because of 1. ... Qh4xh3+ 2. Qg1-h2 Qh3xh2 mate.

- **ANSWER: 1. Qg1–h2** (To stop mate, White gives up this queen—but he'll get a new one.) **1. ... Bf4xh2** (If 1. ... Rf3-f2 2. e7-e8=Q, with similar play.) **2. e7-e8=Q Rf3-f2 3. Re1-e7+ Kg7-f6** (If 3. ... Kg7-h6, 4. Re7-h7+ wins the queen.) **4. Re7-f7+ Kf6-g5 5. Bb4-e7+,** winning Black's queen. (If you worked out a line beginning 1. e7-e8=N+, take full credit!)

MIDDLE GAME MASTERPIECE

Black's attempt to force a win in the opening boomerangs against accurate play by White

Susan Polgar is the oldest of the three famous Polgar sisters, who were born in Hungary and homeschooled by their parents. Their father Laszlo wanted to prove his theory that genius was made, not born. Laszlo felt that children, if educated in a specialty field from a very early age, would become geniuses in that field. He chose to teach all three girls chess. All three

became chess prodigies—children who can perform at an extremely high level at a skill normally dominated by adults.

Susan became women's world champion. She now lives in the United States and dedicates much of her time to inspiring children to play chess.

Hungarian international master Peter Hardicsay tries to mix

Fighting Benoni

- Black has one less pawn in the center in exchange for a queenside pawn majority and a position with a wild character, full of traps. Perhaps Hardicsay thought that he would have a chance to play a winning combination against the teenage girl across the board from him.

- **9. Qa4+ Bd7**

- Black blocks the check while developing his bishop. Of course not 9. ... b5 10. Nxb5! (or 10. Bxb5+!). Black's a-pawn is pinned.

- **10. Qb3.** (See next photo.)

Playing for Complications

- From b3, White's queen attacks Black's b7-pawn. More importantly, if she captures that pawn, she then attacks the much more valuable black rook. Black needs to hold b7. He could move his bishop back to c8. Or Black can try the riskier but thematic 10. ... b5.

- **10. ... Bg4**

- Black has a different idea, playing for wild complications in order to confuse his teenage adversary.

- **11. Qxb7.** (See next photo.)

it up early in the game, perhaps in an attempt to confuse his young opponent. But Susan's accurate play puts her in a better position. On move seventeen, she launches a bold combination that routs her opponent.

Use this game to practice the short version of notation that most experienced chess players use to record games.

The game began:

1. d4 Nf6 2. c4 c5 3. d5 e6 4. Nc3 exd5 5. cxd5 d6 6. Nf3 g6 7. Bf4 a6 8. e4 Bg7. (See photo below, far left.)

Calm Logic

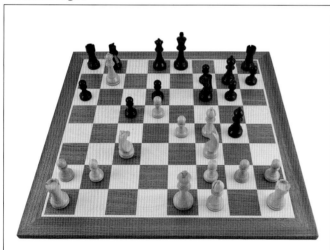

- Such positions, in which neither side has yet castled and tactics have begun on both sides of the board, can be intimidating. But Susan calmly makes logical moves. She knows she hasn't violated any opening principles and that chess is a fair game. If Susan doesn't step into a trap, in the end Black must pay the price for his recklessness.

- **11. ... Bxf3 12. Qxa8 Nxe4.** (See next photo.)

Wild Tries

- Black finds a continuation that gives Susan a chance to go wrong. After the tempting 13. Nxe4 Bxe4 14. f3, Black has 14. ... Bxb2!. Then after 15. Rd1 Bc2, the position is even wilder. But Polgar makes the one move that keeps her clearly in control.

- **13. Rc1! Bd4** (Black throws everything at the uncastled white king.)

- **14. Rc2** (Susan defends f2.) **14. ... Nxf2.**

- 14. ... Nxc3 is better, but Black goes for broke. (See first photo in next spread.)

ACQUIRING ADVANTAGES
Remember, winning combinations come from building a better position, not a worse one

After fourteen moves in a wild game, Susan Polgar has wended her way through the complications, foiling her opponent's attempts to bamboozle her into a mistake. Black's go-for-broke play hasn't yielded him the opportunity for a winning combination. Instead, he's down in material and running out of ideas.

It will be Susan who finishes the game with a stunning series of forceful moves. A player normally gets the opportunity to play winning combinations because she is in a *better* position, not a worse one. It's true that a player with the better game has to be on the lookout for "swindles" by his opponent, combinations that transform a win into a loss or a draw.

Setting the Stage

- Polgar gladly trades her rook and pawn for two of the three developed black pieces. **15. Rxf2 Bxf2+ 16. Kxf2** (White gains a tempo because Black must retreat his remaining bishop.) **16. ... Bg4.**

- Now Susan winds up the game with a beautiful

middle game combination.

- **17. Bb5+!**

- An unpleasant shock for Black. White brings her undeveloped bishop into the game with a *tempo*, at the same time clearing a path for his rook to take over the empty king file.

Unpleasant Surprise!

- **17. ... axb5 18. Re1+ Kf8** (If Black instead tries 18. ... Kd7, White plays 19. Qb7+. After the forced 19. ... Qc7, Susan has seen the beautiful undermining sacrifice 20. Re7+!.)

- **19. Bh6+ Kg8**

- Now Polgar plays two beau-

tiful tactical blows in a row: **20. Re7!**

- The rook can't be taken because of 21. Qxb8+, with mate to follow after Black gives up both his bishop and queen to temporarily block the check.

Susan has acquired one advantage after another. That's generally the process that leads to the opportunity to play a game-winning combination. But only a player of great imagination would see White's opportunity in this game. True, most masters in her position after 16. ... Bg4 would win and chalk up the point, but then the game would join the archives of the unremarkable.

On her seventeenth move, Susan plays the kind of beautiful combination all chess players hope to find at least once in their lives, and that made this game famous.

What's the Follow-Up?

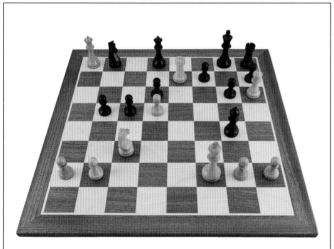

- **20. ... Bd7**

- With this move, Black does much more than defend his pawn on b5. He threatens 21. ... Qxe7, since then he has supported e8 to block check. But Susan has another shocker.

- **21. Qxb8!!**

- Magnificent! Black has no choice but to capture the white queen. But why would Susan trade in her valuable queen for a lowly knight? The black queen still guards the back rank. Did Susan intend to follow up with 22. Rxd7? But a knight and a bishop still don't equal a queen.

Calling Up the Cavalry

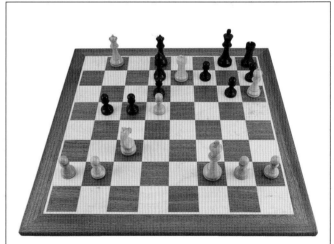

- **21. ... Qxb8** (*forced*) **22. Ne4!,** Black resigns.

- A wonderful finale, reminiscent of Paul Morphy's masterpieces. White can't be prevented from playing 23. Nf6#.

- Now it's easier to understand why Susan played 20.

Re7!. In the final position, we see that it prevents two escapes. Black's queen can't defend by moving 22. ... Qd8 to guard f6, because White's rook blocks the diagonal. And Black can't find relief in 22. ... f5, because f7 is covered by the rook.

FIVE WAYS TO DRAW

Know the five ways that a chess game can be drawn and what material is needed to mate

There are five ways that chess games are drawn: (1) by stalemate, (2) by insufficient material, (3) by mutual agreement, (4) by repetition of position, (5) by a claim of the fifty-move rule.

We've studied the *stalemate draw* in Chapter 4. Take a look at the stalemate positions in Chapter 4 if you need to.

A *draw by insufficient material* occurs when neither side has enough material to mate. (Any position with even one pawn left has enough material, potentially, for one player to mate.)

At any time in the game, the opponents can agree to a draw by mutual consent, although in tournament play, the players must first put up a fight. And there's no use playing chess unless you try to win! In general, we recommend that

Mutual Agreement

- Sometimes a player can see that there is no way to *force* a win and knows his opponent is a good enough player to know how to draw.

- The position above is a good example. Black has an extra rook pawn, but he can't force White out of his perfect defensive position in the corner.

- So—if you were Black in this position, and you knew your opponent had also read this book, you might agree to a draw.

Three-Time Repetition

- It's Black's move in the position above. Black is down a rook. So he would love to force a draw. He begins with **1. ... Qf4-c1+.**

- Now **2. Kg1-h2** is forced. Then Black plays **2. ... Qc1-f4+.** Play could continue **3.** **Kh2-g1** and now we're back in the exact position that we started. **3. ... Qf4-c1+.** Now after **4. Kg1-h2**, **Qc1-f4+ 5. Kh2-g1**, Black can claim a draw by announcing that the same exact position has been repeated three times.

while you're learning, you should play your games out until the end result.

Let's clear up the draw by three-time repetition: Just playing the same move three times in a row does *not* make a draw! Only when the *exact position and conditions (such as the right to castle)* of the entire board are repeated for the third time at any time during the game—not necessarily in a row—with the same player on move, does that player have the *option* to claim a draw. In a tournament, he must claim the draw immediately *before* making the move that repeats a position

three times.

Finally, if no pawn has been moved or any capture made in fifty moves, either side can claim the draw.

Perpetual Check

- After **2. ... Qc1-f4+**, White could try **3. g2-g3**—after all, White is a rook up, and he doesn't want to be trapped into a draw.

- But Black then has **3. ... Qf4xf2+ 4. Kh2-h1 Qf2-**

f1+, and could check in this way forever—that's why they call it a perpetual, or sometimes just a "perp." But it's really a variation of the draw by three-time repetition rule.

Tricky Three-Time Repetition

- Draw by repetition does not require the positions to repeat in a row. Even masters sometimes forget to watch out for this rule.

- In Korchnoi-Portisch, 1970, the players reached the position above with Black to make his sixty-fourth move. Black has two extra

pawns, but. . .

- **64. ... Rd6-h6+ 65. Kh5-g4 Rh6-d6 66. Kg4-h5** (second repetition) **66. ... Kg7-f6 67. Rb8-b2 Kf6-g7** (And White claimed the third repetition and a draw, before moving.) **68. Rb2-b8.**

MATING WITH TWO HELPERS

When there aren't any pawns to promote, know how to mate with what you have

When you get to the end of the game with a big material advantage, you don't want to spoil your result by not knowing how to checkmate your opponent. On these two pages you'll learn how to checkmate when the defender has only his king and the superior side has two men to help his king.

The key idea in all of these mates is forcing the defender to the edge of the board, where he has few escape squares. The educated defender will try to stay in the center of the board, and so must be forced to the edge. Of course, the attacker needs to be careful not to carelessly give away material. And he must keep a keen eye out to avoid stalemating the enemy king.

Queen and Rook

- When one side has a queen and rook against the lone king, the technique is easy—but the attacker must take care to avoid stalemate.

- In the photo above, White mates in four: **1. Rh5-c5** (White fences in the enemy king. With an extra move, White can also set up the "ladder mate": 1. Rh5-e5+ Ke4-d4 2. Qg3-f4+ Kd4-d3 3. Re5-e3+ Kd3-c2 4. Qf4-f2+ Kc2-d1 5. Re3-e1#) **1. ... Ke4-d4 2. Qg3-c3+ Kd4-e4 3. Rc5-e5+ Ke4-f4 4. Qc3-e3#.**

Queen and Rook #2

- The photo above lets us show you the "ladder mate" in its pure form. It's a very useful technique to know.

- **1. ... Rb8-b6+ 2. Ke6-d5 Qa7-a5+ 3. Kd5-d4 Rb6-b4+** (It's like climbing a ladder, one rung at a time, straight "up.") **4. Kd4-c3 Qa5-a3+ 5. Kc3-c2 Rb4-b2+ 6. Kc2-c1 Qa3-a1#.**

- For the record, the quickest is a mate in four, boxing in the enemy king and using the attacker's own king: 1. ... Qa7-d4 2. Ke6-e7 Kh8-g7 3. Ke7-e6 Rb8-e8+ 4. Ke6-f5 Re8-e5#.

The mate with queen and rook is the easiest. Learning and practicing a few techniques will make it a snap. We show you two different starting positions so that you can learn two different approaches to the mate.

The mate with two rooks is likewise easier once you've practiced a bit. The smart defender will play to attack one of the rooks, making the strong side shift his rooks out of reach. But this delaying tactic doesn't amount to a defense. The rooks are quite effective at long range.

Last in this section, we show you that two pawns supported by a king can produce a mate, although it can't be forced. Of course, if the defending king avoids the mate, one of the pawns will promote to a queen—and checkmate is then inevitable.

Don't try to memorize the moves in any of these checkmates. Concentrate instead on learning the ideas.

Two Rooks

- Mating with two rooks is easy as well. Let's look at the "ladder" method using two rooks.

- **1. ... Rb8-b6+ 2. Ke6-d5 Ra7-a5+ 3. Kd5-c4** (Now the difference between the queen and rook and the two rooks shows up. The rooks are unguarded. So: **3.** **... Ra5-h5 4. Kc4-d4** (Trying to stay in the center.) **4. ... Rb6-b4+ 5. Kd4-c3 Rb4-g4** (Black puts his rook as far away as possible.) **6. Kc3-d2 Rh5-h3 7. Kd2-e2 Rg4-g2+ 8. Ke2-f1 Rh3-h2 9. Kf1-e1 Rh2-h1#.**

Two Pawns

- In the photo above, it's Black to move. We wanted you to make sure you know the power of the two marching pawns, supported by their king.

- **1. ... g3-g2** is checkmate. No promotion required!

187

KING PLUS MAJOR PIECE

A king and one major piece can force mate against the lone king

When there is nothing else on the board and the weaker side has only his king, he can be checkmated by his opponent's king and queen or king and rook. Both checkmates are important to know. You certainly don't want to fight through a long, hard game and not be able to finish off your opponent to chalk up a well-deserved win with the checkmate, the goal of every game of chess.

The checkmate with king and queen can arise after the

strong side has promoted a pawn to a queen. From any position, the queen and king can force checkmate against a lone king in ten moves or less. But in the example below we give you an easy method to remember that will always work, rather than concerning ourselves with the shortest mate. The side with the queen should be constantly vigilant to avoid a careless stalemate, throwing away an easy win. (Such a stalemate is possible only with the weaker side's king on the

Queen and King

- In the photo above, White has plenty of power to mate.

- The easiest method is to use only the queen until the enemy king is boxed in. It doesn't much matter whose move it is. Let's give it to Black: **1. ... Ke5-d4 2.**

Qa2-e2 Kd4-c5 3. Qe2-e4 Kc5-d6 4. Qe4-f5 Kd6-c6 5. Qf5-e5 Kc6-d7 6. Qe5-f6 Kd7-c7 7. Qf6-e6 (White's queen corrals the enemy king like a well-trained sheepdog.) **7. ... Kc7-b7 8. Qe6-d6 Kb7-c8 9. Qd6-e7.** Look at the next photo.

Queen and King, Final Stage

- It's Black's move: **9. ... Kc8-b8 10. Qe7-d7** (Or even the simple 10. Kb2.) **Kb8-a8.** Okay, this far and no farther. We have to give the enemy's king two squares to move back and forth on or it would be stalemate!

- The next stage is to move

up the white king while Black marks time. **11. Ka1-b2 Ka8-b8 12. Kb2-c3 Kb8-a8 13. Kc3-d4** (It doesn't matter what squares the White king takes, as long as he winds up on c6, b6, or a6.) **13. ... Ka8-b8 14. Kd4-d5 Kb8-a8 15. Kd5-c6 Ka8-b8 16. Qd7-b7#.**

edge.) The defender will be looking for the opportunity to set a stalemating "trap," since it's his only hope.

A king and rook can checkmate a lone king from any position in no more than sixteen moves. Of course, you can take more, as long as you don't exceed fifty moves and let your opponent claim a draw. The attacker must use his king and rook to keep narrowing the board available to the defending king, forcing him to the edge, where mate can be delivered.

Once again, don't memorize moves. Learn the methods.

Mate with King and Rook

- White will use both his rook and king to herd the Black king to the edge of the board. **1. Rh1-h4** (Fencing in the king.) **1. ... Kd5-e5 2. Ka1-b2 Ke5-d5 3. Kb2-c3 Kd5-e5 4. Rh4-d4** (Boxers call it "cutting off the ring.")

- **4. ... Ke5-f5 5. Kc3-d3 Kf5-e5 6. Kd3-e3 Ke5-f5 7. Rd4-e4 Kf5-f6 8. Ke3-f4 Kf6-g6 9. Re4-e6+** (See the next photo.)

Mate with King and Rook

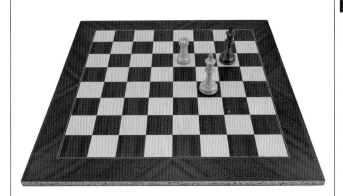

- Black can make different choices along the way, but the technique is the same—White drives him to whatever board edge Black breaks toward.

- **9. ... Kg6-f7 10. Kf4-f5 Kf7-g7 11. Re6-e7+** (Forcing Black to choose his poison—mate on the h-file

or the eighth rank.)

- **11. ... Kg7-f8 12. Kf5-f6 Kf8-g8 13. Re7-d7.** (Remember this finesse.)

- **13. ... Kg8-h8** (If 11. ... Kg7-f8, 12. Rd7-d8 is mate.) **14. Kf6-g6 Kh8-g8 15. Rd7-d8#.**

KING PLUS TWO MINOR PIECES

Since these endings rarely occur, don't waste too much of your study time on them

King plus two minor pieces is the most difficult and complex of the basic mates. From a defending king in the center of the board, the mate with two bishops takes nineteen moves against best defense. Although we show you the whole procedure for mating with the two bishops, it's enough to remember the basic idea. Often the defender is checkmated in the very corner square, but there is actually another final position possible in this mate—the defending king in the square next to the corner square. That's the one we show below.

The mate with bishop and knight—the granddaddy of difficult mates—can take thirty-three moves against a

Two-Bishop Mate

- A two-bishop-vs.-king ending is quite rare. So don't spend too much time on this now. Just learn the ideas.

- The superior side must force the enemy king to the nearest corner. To do this, he arranges his bishops on adjacent squares to create a "wall."

- From the position in the photo above: **1. ... Bc8-b7 2. Kd4-e3 Bf8-c5+ 3. Ke3-d3 Bb7-d5** (the first "wall") **4. Kd3-c3 Kg8-f7 5. Kc3-d3 Kf7-e6 6. Kd3-c3 Ke6-e5 7. Kc3-d3 Ke5-f4 8. Kd3-c3 Kf4-e4.** (See the next photo.)

Two-Bishop Mate II

- Keep in mind that you shouldn't memorize the moves but the method. If you understand the technique, chances are that you'll be able to figure out how to mate if you ever get this ending.

- **9. Kc3-d2 Bc5-d4 10. Kd2-e2 Bd5-c4+** (a second "wall") **11. Ke2-d2 Bd4-f6 12. Kd2-c2 Ke4-e3 13. Kc2-c1 Ke3-d3 14. Kc1-d1 Bf6-c3 15. Kd1-c1 Bc3-b4 16. Kc1-d1 Bc4-b3+ 17. Kd1-c1 Bb4-a3+** (a third "wall") **18. Kc1-b1 Bb3-d5 19. Kb1-a1 Kd3-c3.** (We've reached the next photo.)

defending king starting out in the center making the best defensive moves! So you can see that the fifty-move draw rule becomes a real factor in these endings. Missing the correct procedure even once in the knight-and-bishop mate, for example, can cost you the win against an alert opponent. Below we describe the basic method of how to go about this mating procedure, and show you a sample mating position.

The good news is that the knight-and-bishop ending happens only once in about 5,000 games.

Two-Bishop Mate, III

- We've reached the final stage. The white king has been forced into the corner.

- **20. Ka1-b1 Kc3-b3** (The white king isn't going anywhere.) **21. Kb1-a1**

Ba3-b2+ 22. Ka1–b1 (Now the *coup de grace*. White's king has no moves and all it takes is a check.) **22. … Bd5-e4#.**

Mate with Bishop and Knight

- Because this ending is so complex, and because it happens so rarely, we'll just give you the idea.

- Checkmate can be given only on a corner square the same color as the superior side's bishop. The photo above gives you a final mating position.

- Three stages: Use all three pieces to drive the weaker king to the edge of the board. The knowledgeable defender will then run toward the "wrong" corner. Then drive him to the "right" corner to checkmate.

PAWN ENDINGS, BASICS

Many games boil down to kings and an extra pawn, so learn how to play this ending

We can cover only some of the important endgame basics here. There are great books devoted to the endgame. If you get very interested in chess, you should get one. (See Chapter 23, "Resources.")

Let's start off with king-and-pawn endings—when the game has boiled down to just the opposing kings and one

pawn. We'll need to use the small diagram on the next page, far right, as a building block to our knowledge:

This diagrammed position is a draw, regardless of who moves first and what rank the pawn stands on. It's crucial to understand why. Let's look at a logical line when White moves first: **1. Ke4-f4 Ke6-e7** (Black could go to any of three

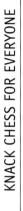
Rule of the Square

- How quickly can you calculate whether the white pawn can reach the eighth rank before the black king can catch it?

- The Rule of the Square can show you at a glance!

- Mentally draw a straight line from the square the

- pawn is on to the queening square—then make it into a square, like the one above.

- If the king, on move, can get inside the square, it can catch the pawn. This one can!

- If it is White's move, however, the pawn strolls into Queen!

Not Blocking the Pawn Loses

- When you're using your lone king to defend against a king and pawn, your whole task is to keep the pawn from being promoted. You don't necessarily have to capture it—but, of course, you should if you can.

- The first defensive rule is

- to *block*—to get your king in front of the pawn. See the building block position diagrammed above.

- On both halves of the board in the photo above, Black has failed to block. The enemy pawn will queen easily, and Black will lose.

squares—d7, e7, or f7—to hold the draw.) **2. Kf4-f5 Ke7-f7 3. e5-e6+** (White's king can't make progress, so he pushes his pawn.) **3. ... Kf7-e7 4. Kf5-e5 Ke7-e8 5. Ke5-f6 Ke8-f8 6. e6-e7+** (The defender *wants* the pawn to check when it reaches the seventh rank.) **6. ... Kf8-e8 7. Kf6-e6 stalemate.**

Now let's go back to the position in the diagram to look

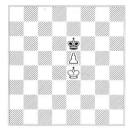

at what would happen if Black moves first: **1. ... Ke6-e7 2. Ke4-f5** (if 2. Ke4-d5 Ke7-d7) **2. ... Ke7-f7** (preventing the opponent's king from making progress) **3. e5-e6+ Kf7-e8** (3. . . .Kf7-e7 is equally good) **4. Kf5-f6 Ke8-f8 5. e6-e7+** (If 5. Kf6-e5, then ... Kf8-e7 or -e8) **5. . . .Kf8-e8 6. Kf6-e6.** (Now White must either abandon his pawn or force stalemate.)

Blocking the Pawn May Draw

- In this example, Black has gotten immediately in front of the pawn. As a defender, you welcome this position.

- As we saw above, no matter whose move it is, the game is a draw with best play by Black.

- Let's look at *bad* play by Black: **1. ... Ke6-e7** (Okay so far.) **2. Ke4-f5 Ke7-e8??** (This move is a clunker. Black should play 2. ... Ke7-f7.) **3. Kf5-f6 Ke8-f8 4. e5-e6 Kf8-e8 5. e6-e7** (Without check!) **5. ... Ke8-d7 6. Kf6-f7 Kd7-d6 7. e7-e8=Q.**

The Opposition

- If two kings stand with one square between them (this is called the *opposition*), as in the photo above, the king who has the opposition is the one who does *not* have to move and give way.

- Here the stronger side is in front of his pawn, his best position. He will win unless the defender has the *opposition*, blocking White's king from making progress. For example: **1. Ke5-f5 Ke7-f7,** and White can't make meaningful progress.

ADVANCED PAWN TRICKS

You should learn a few more key ideas of king-and-pawn endings before going on to more complex endgames

Promoting pawns, or preventing your opponent from promoting them, is frequently the main battle of the endgame. Rook pawns can be the hardest to promote because of stalemating possibilities, since their queening squares are the very corners of the board. Take a look at the first small diagram on the next page.

Sometimes the defender doesn't even need to get to the queening square. He can trap his opponent's king on the rook file. If White is to move, play could continue: **1. Ka6-a7 Kc6-c7 2. a5-a6 Kc7-c8 3. Ka7-a8** (If Black's king gets to the corner, it can never be forced out.) **3. ... Kc8-c7 4. a6-a7 Kc7-c8, stalemate.**

Ready to Oppose

King on the Sixth Wins

- To win, the side with the pawn will have to put his king *in front* of the pawn, and Black must be ready for it.

- On the board above, Black on move must be ready to take the opposition. Thus, he plays **1. ... Kc7-d7**. Now, if White plays 2. Kc3-d4,

Black takes the opposition with ... Kd7-d6. Or if White plays 2. Kc3-b4, 2. ... Kc7-b6 (or d6—opposition on the diagonal counts as well).

- If it's White's move, it's still a draw. Black can eventually grab the opposition however White's king advances.

- When the stronger side's king is on the sixth rank in front of a non-rook pawn, he wins no matter who is to move and no matter where the weaker side's king is. In the photo above, we put Black's king in the best possible position.

- If it's Black's move, he must

step aside: If **1. ... Ke8-f8 2. Ke6-d7**, or if **1. ... Ke8-d8, 2. Ke6-f7.**

- If it's White's move: **1. Ke6-f6 (or d6) Ke8-f8 (or d8) 2. e5-e6 Kf8-e8 3. e6-e7** (without check!), and Black is forced out of the queening square.

If Black moves first, it's still a draw: **1. ... Kc6-c7 2. Ka6-a7** (2. Ka6-b5 Kc7-b7) **2. ... Kc7-c8 3. a5-a6 Kc8-c7 4. Ka7-a8 Kc7-c8 5. a6-a7 Kc8-c7, stalemate.**

On the other hand, here's a trick that favors the offense. We've seen that when the superior side's king is in front of his pawn but stands face-to-face with the enemy king, the attacker needs to have the opposition to win. But

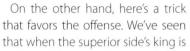

take a look at this position:

Here White wins no matter whose move it is. If White has the opposition, that means it's Black's move and his king must give way. If it's White's move, he leaves his king standing firm and plays **1. d2-d3!** and takes the opposition. Such a

reserve move can be very important. That's one reason the superior side wants to advance his king ahead of his pawn.

Last Attacker Wins

- This is another important trick to remember—call it "Last Attacker Wins."

- Black attacks White's pawn. If it's Black's move, he wins the pawn and the game.

- But with White to move, he plays **1. Ke5-e4!,** defending his pawn and attacking Black's. Black must move away, allowing White to capture on f4. Since Black is out of position to block, White queens his pawn and wins.

Rook Pawn Draw

- This is another way that the defender can draw with the rook pawn.

- All the defender has to do is get to the queening square, and there's no way to force him out, no matter whose move it is.

- If White moves first, pushing

the pawn stalemates: **1. h4-h5 Kh8-g8 2. h5-h6 Kg8-h8 3. h6-h7,** stalemate.

- If Black moves first: **1. ... Kh8-g8 2. h4-h5 Kg8-h8 3. h5-h6 Kh8-g8 4. h6-h7+ Kg8-h8,** when White can either abandon his pawn or force stalemate with 5. Kg6-h6.

MULTIPLE PAWNS & MAJOR PIECES

Before the game simplifies to kings and a pawn, powerful pieces can control the endgame

Let's look at some more complex examples with more pawns and pieces. Our first example involves more than one pawn and illustrates the very important idea of the *distant passed pawn*, which can be a tremendous advantage in the endgame because of its power to divert enemy forces to stop it from queening.

Then we'll take a look at queen vs. pawn on the seventh rank, one step away from queening. Winning with queen against a pawn on the seventh is a simple technique against certain pawns. Once you know it, you will win this ending consistently. You'll see that with the queen on move, her side will always win, wherever her king is on the board, as long

Distant Passed Pawn

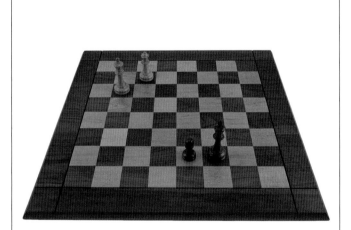

- When a passed pawn is away from the rest of the chessmen, it can be pushed to use as a winning diversion.

- White must capture the pawn. When White's king has been diverted to the b-file, Black captures both white pawns.

- Here's a sample line: **1. ... b7-b5 2. Ke4-d4 Kg7-h6 3. Kd4-c5 Kh6-g5 4. Kc5xb5 Kg5xg4 5. Kb5-c4 Kg4xf5 6. Kc4-d3 Kf5-g4 7. Kd3-e2 Kg4-g3 8. Ke2-f1 f6-f5 9. Kf1-g1 f5-f4 10. Kg1-f1 Kg3-f3,** and Black has the winning position we've studied.

Queen vs. Pawn

- The queen wins against a center or knight pawn even when it is about to queen.

- In the position above, using checks, White repeatedly forces the enemy king to block his own pawn. White uses that moment to advance his own king, and repeats the process until he

can double attack and win the pawn: **1. Qc7-f4+ Kf2-e1** (if 1. ... Kf2-g2 2.Qf4-e3 Kg2-f1 3.Qe3-f3+ Kf1-e1, and White brings up his king) **2. Kb6-c5 Ke1-d1 3. Qf4-d4+ Kd1-e1 4. Kc5-c4 Ke1-f1 5. Qd4-f4+ Kf1-e1 6. Kc4-d3 Ke1-d1 7. Qf4-f3.** The pawn falls.

as a check is available to her on the first move—unless the pawn is a rook pawn or bishop pawn. Take a look at the small diagram at right.

1. Qd5-d2 Kb2-b1 2. Qd2-b4+ Kb1-a2 3. Qb4-c3 Ka2-b1 4. Qc3-b3+ Kb1-a1 (The key point.) **5. Qb3xc2, stalemate!**

But if we put the white king on a square closer to the enemy pawn, it's a different story:

1. Qd5-d4+ Kb2-a2 2. Qd4-a4+ Ka2-b1 3. Qa4-b4+ Kb1-c1 (If 3. … Kb1-a1, then the simple 4. Ke3-d2.) **4. Ke3-d3 Kc1-d1 5. Qb4-d2#.**

Last in this section, we'll take a look at a basic rook-vs.-pawn position.

Queen vs. RP

- The rook pawn about to queen makes this one a draw because of the now-familiar stalemate in the corner.

- After **1. Qg8-f7+ Kf1-g1 2. Qf7-g6+ Kg1-h1,** White's technique of advancing his king doesn't work, because it would leave Black in stale-mate. Since the lone queen can never win the pawn without sacrificing itself, the game is drawn.

Rook vs. Pawn

- If White's king blocked the pawn instead of being distant, White would win easily.

- Black to move draws with **1. … Kd6-d5.** The rook will then have to sacrifice itself to prevent Black's queening.

- If White moves, he wins with **1. Rg8-g5!,** cutting off the enemy king on *its fourth rank*—an important technique to know. Now White's king can advance to win the pawn. If Black tries **1. … c4-c3 2. Rg5-g3 c3-c2 3. Rg3-c3,** the pawn is lost, along with the game.

PAWNS & MINOR PIECES

Let's see how the minor pieces, knight and bishop, handle the challenge of passed pawns

The minor pieces don't inject as much power into the endgame as the major pieces, but the knight and the bishop each bring their own special characteristics to bear.

Our first two examples below illustrate some of the unique characteristics of the bishop. The first example shows the limitation of the bishop when trying to help advance a passed rook pawn whose queening square is a different color than the bishop. If the defending king is blocking the pawn, it's a draw. When the extra pawn is not a rook pawn, however, the stronger side wins easily, regardless of the color of the queening square.

Our second example shows a bishop, without his king's

Bishop and Rook Pawn

- Even though White is a bishop and pawn ahead, he can't force a win against best defense!

- Black's king controls the queening square, h8.

- White's bishop is the wrong color to challenge control of the queening square.

- If White's bishop were on the dark squares, or if we push the position to the queenside corner of the board, where the queening square is a8, White would win easily.

Bishop vs. Two Pawns

- White wins if it's his move: **1. c4-c5! Bb8-e5 2. c5-c6 Kd1-d2 3. f5-f6 Kd2-e3 4.f6-f7 Be5-d6 5. c6-c7,** when the bishop must capture on c7, allowing f7-f8=Q.

- But if it's Black's move, it's a draw because **1. ... Bd6!** permits the bishop to guard the advance of both pawns on one diagonal.

- The farther apart the pawns are, the harder it is for the bishop to defend. If the white pawn is on b5 instead of c5, White would win no matter who moves first.

help, fighting to restrain two enemy pawns. The general rule here is that, the more files that separate the pawns, the harder it is for the bishop to stop them.

Our last two examples show a unique potential of the knight in the endgame. The third position reveals how the knight can single-handedly hold off a rook pawn on the sixth rank, even when the pawn has the help of his king!

And our final position shows the knight, without the aid of his king, holding at bay a knight pawn on the seventh rank, once again, even when the advanced pawn is being aided by his king. Of course, in these two illustrations of the knight's special powers, the key idea is that the advancing pawn has to try to avoid being taken by the knight, even when the knight can be recaptured. The defending side is trying only to secure a draw, since he lacks mating material.

Knight vs. Rook Pawn

- Here Black can draw if he can "sacrifice" his knight for the pawn.

- No matter whose move it is, White's king can't drive away the knight: **1. Kc7-b6 Na7-c8+ 2. Kb6-b7 Nc8-d6+ 3. Kb7-c7 Nd6-b5+ 4. Kc7-b6 Nb5-d6!,** setting up the fork on c8 if the pawn advances.

- White can't make progress.

- If it's Black's move, he shuffles his king anywhere. His knight does all the work in this ending. We should note that rook pawns are the hardest for the knight to handle.

Knight against Knight Pawn

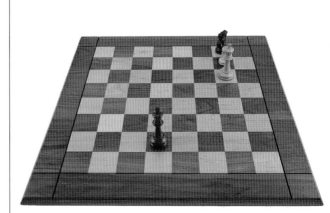

- The lone knight can't stop a rook pawn on the seventh, but it can often stop other pawns on the seventh.

- White on move runs in circles to no effect: **1. Kg6-f7 Ng8-h6+ 2. Kf7-f6 Kd2-d3 3. Kf6-g6 Nh6-g8 4. Kg6-h7 Ng8-e7, draw.**

KEY ROOK & PAWN POSITIONS

This section is one of the most important lessons on the endgame in this book

Half of all chess endgames are rook endings. Learning and practicing the basics of pawn endings and rook endings are two of the most practical investments of time you can make in your chess training.

The endgame in which one player has a rook and an advanced pawn while his opponent has a rook has fascinated chess players for hundreds of years. Our first example shows a position in which the defender uses his rook to passively defend the back rank against a bishop pawn. It doesn't work because the attacker can threaten to skewer the defending rook.

The next three examples concern Philidor's Position and

Bishop Pawn

- In the position above, Black must keep rook on its back rank to prevent mate.

- Such passive defense against a bishop pawn doesn't work here: **1. Rc1-c7 Ra8-b8 2. Rc7-g7+ Kg8-f8** (2. ... Kg8-h8 3. Rg7-h7+ Kh8-g8 4. f6-f7+ Kg8-f8 5. Rh7-h8+, winning the rook.)

3. Rg7-h7 (White threatens 4. Rg7-h8+, skewering White's rook.) **3. ... Kf8-g8 4. f6-f7+,** winning.

- If you move the original position over to the right one square, the position is a draw because White can never threaten the skewers above.

Philidor's Position

- If the pawn has not yet reached the sixth (or third) rank, the defender draws easily if he knows Philidor's Position.

- The three-part method: (1) defender prevents the enemy king from advancing to the sixth rank, forcing him to push his pawn; (2)

then the defender drops his rook back to the rear; (3) defender checks from behind: **1. ... Rb1-b6 2. e5-e6** (2. Rh7-g7 Rb6-a6 3. Rg7-g6 Ra6xg6 4. Kf5xg6 Ke8-e7=) **2. ... Rb6-b1 3. Kf5-f6 Rb1-f1+ 4. Kf6-e5 Rf1-e1+ 5. Ke5-d6 Re10-d1+,** draw.

Lucena's Position, which help us play accurately when one player has a rook and a pawn and his opponent has only a rook. Both positions are very important to chess theory and play. In fact, many rook-and-pawn vs. rook endings reach one of these two positions.

François-André Philidor was the best player of the 1700s. For nearly fifty years he was considered the best player in the world. Interestingly, during much of this time, he was the leading composer of operas in France. Philidor's Position—sometimes called the Third-Rank Defense because of the importance of the rook going to that rank (or to the sixth rank, if the superior side is White)—is a drawing method for the defending side. Lucena's position, named after the fifteenth-century chess player and writer Luis Ramirez de Lucena, on the other hand, is a method to help the superior side win. It applies to any pawn except the rook pawn.

To play rook-and-pawn endgames well, you'll have to know both Philidor's and Lucena's Positions. The good news is that they are both logical and easy to learn, with a little repetition and practice.

Getting to Lucena's Position

- Lucena's Position is a method for the superior side to win when the defender does not block the pawn with his king. From the position in the photo above, let's look at the method.

- **1. Kg7-h7 Rg2-h2+ 2. Kh7-g8 Rh2-g2 3. g6-g7** (reach- ing Lucena's Position.) **3. ... Rg2-h2 4. Rf1-e1+ Ke7-d7 5. Re1-e4 Rh2-h1 6. Kg8-f7 Rh1-f1+ 7. Kf7-g6 Rf1-g1+ 8. Kg6-h6 Rg1-h1+ 9. Kh6-g5 Rh1-g1+ 10. Re4-g4.**

- The whole point is to use the attacker's rook to block the checks on his king.

Lucena's Position: Result

- Using Lucena's method, the superior side proceeds in five stages: (1) advance the pawn to the seventh (reach- ing Lucena's Position); (2) use his rook to push the defender's king away; (3) move his rook to the fourth rank; (4) move his king back to the fifth rank; (5) block the checks with his rook.

- The position above shows the result of Lucena's method. White has blocked the pesky checks, and Black's king is out of play. Black can't stop the pawn from promoting.

PAWNS & LIKE PIECES

This section shows you positions in which the players battle with multiple pawns and the same type of piece

In this section, we take a look at more complex endgames with multiple pawns and the same type of piece for each side. We examine rook vs. rook, same-color bishop vs. bishop (when one is a very "bad" bishop), opposite-color bishop vs. bishop, and knight vs. knight. (To remind you, when we talk about bishops of the same or opposite "color," chess players are referring to the color of the squares the bishops travel on.)

Our first example shows the value of having an active king in a rook ending. Over and over, beginners need to be reminded that the endgame is the stage of the game that the king must march into action, taking part in some of the combat firsthand.

KNACK CHESS FOR EVERYONE

Rook and Pawns

Bad Bishop

- When there are rooks and pawns on the board, having active pieces, including the king, is very important.

- In the above position, White is a pawn down, but his active king makes up for the material deficit.

- **1. Kc4-b5 Rh3xh4** (Black

should think draw: 1. ... Rh3-c3!=) **2. Kb5-c6 Rh4xe4 3. Kc6xd6 Ke8-f8 4. Ra7-a8+ Kf8-g7 5. Kd6-e7** (Ironically, Black's pawns protect White's king from checks.) **5. ... Re4-d4 6. d5-d6 e5-e4 7. d6-d7 e4-e3 8. f2xe3 Rd4-e4+ 9. Ke7-d6 Re4xe3 10. d7-d8=Q,** White wins.

- Black's bad bishop is blocked in by its own pawns.

- If Black moves his king, he loses because White will penetrate Black's position through e5 or c5.

- **1. h2-h4 Bc6-e8** (If 1. ... g4xh3 ep. 2. Bf1xh3 Bc6-d7

3. Bh3-g2 Bd7-e6 4. Bg2-f1 Be6-d7 5. Bf1-d3, Black must move his king or lose a pawn.) **2. Bf1-e2 Be8-c6 3. Be2-d1 Bc6-d7** (3. ... Bc6-e8 4. Bd1-c2 Be8-d7 5. Bc2-d3!) **4. Bd1-b3 Bd7-e6 5. Bb3-c2 Be6-c8 6. a3-a4 b5xa4 7. Bc2xa4 Bc8-e6 8. Ba4-e8 Be6-g8 9. Be8xh5,** winning.

The second position illustrates the drawbacks of a very "bad" bishop, restricted by his own pawns, which are placed on squares the same color the bishop travels on. Such a bishop is relegated to purely defensive tasks, and can't do even these duties effectively because of his constrained mobility. Once again, the kings are a determining factor in this ending. The white king threatens to infiltrate Black's position, and his opposing monarch is overmatched to the task of defending all of Black's weak points.

The third position vividly makes the point that opposite-color bishops can have Black's powerful drawing effect on endgames with pawns. Even though White is ahead by two healthy passed pawns, he can make no progress against Black's fortress-building.

Our final position on this page spread shows the value of the active king when each side has pawns and a knight.

Opposite-Color Bishop Fortress

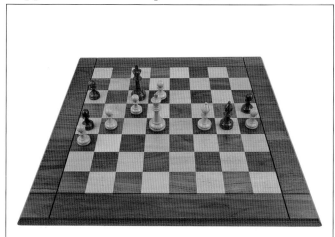

- Opposite-color bishops can make an endgame very drawish. The weaker side looks to build a *fortress*.

- White is two pawns up— normally enough to win easily. But he can't advance

his passed pawns, he can't make new ones, and he can't successfully attack any of Black's pawns.

- Black simply moves his bishop back and forth to draw.

Knight and Pawns

- Black has an advantage: His active king has penetrated White's camp; his two-pawns-against-one queenside is ideal for creating a passed pawn; it's hard for White to make a passed pawn on the king-side because his isolated e-pawn is blocked.

- **1. Ke2-d1** (If 1. g4-g5, then 1. ... b5-b4 2. Ke2-d1 Kc4-d3 3. Nd4-f5 b4-b3, winning.) **1. ... Ne4-f2+ 2. Kd1-c2 Nf2xg4 3. Nd4-f5 f7-f6 4. Nf5-d6+ Kc4-b4 5. e3-e4 Kb4-c5 6. Nd6-b7+ Kc5-d4 7. Nb7-d6 b5-b4 8. h4-h5 Ng4-f2 9. Nd6-f5+ Kd4xe4,** White is lost.

UNLIKE PIECES
Often endgames pit different types of pieces against each other in the struggle to promote a pawn

This section gives you some ideas about the dynamics of endgames that match different types of pieces against each other. Our first position shows a "good" bishop, one not overly restricted by his own pawns, holding the enemy knight at bay. The technique of fencing in the knight on the edge of the board is very handy to know. The position also shows up

the advantage of the bishop as a long-range piece against the short-range knight. But don't overgeneralize, thinking that the bishop is always the better piece. Keep in mind that the exact position of the other men on the board determines whether a bishop or knight is the preferred piece in an ending.

Knight vs. Good Bishop

- The knight is a short-range piece. The bishop is a long-range piece. And a knight on the edge can be completely corralled by a well-placed bishop.

- **1. Bc5-d4!** (Remember this technique: The knight has

no moves! What's more, the pawn on f6 is attacked.) **1. ... Kh7-g7 2. d5-d6! Kg7-f8** (What else? The pawn must be stopped, and the knight can't help.) **3. Bd4xf6.**

- White wins a pawn. He went on to win the game.

Rook vs. Bishop

- When one side has a rook against a bishop with pawns on the board, frequently the winning technique is a well-timed sacrifice of the Exchange.

- **1. Rb8-b7+ Kg7-g8 2. Kg5-f6 Bf5-d3** (It doesn't matter

which square Black chooses for his bishop.) **3. Rb7-g7+ Kg8-h8 4. Rg7xg6 Bd3xg6 5. Kf6xg6.**

- White picks up both pawns and wins easily.

The second position illustrates a very frequently used method of winning when one player is ahead the Exchange; that is, he enjoys a rook over a bishop. When the time is right, the superior side sacrifices the rook for the bishop, transposing into a won king-and-pawn ending (showing again the necessity of knowing the basics of pawn endings).

Example three shows a rook and pawn winning against a bishop, as they should in most positions.

The fourth position shows a knight, aided by his aggressive king, romping to a win over a moderately bad bishop.

Rook and Pawn vs. Bishop

- Most of the time, rook and pawn beat the bishop.

- Here White wins with the pawn sacrifice: **1. g6-g7! Kg8-h7** (1. ... Bc3xg7 2. Kf5-g6 Bg7-e5 3. Rb7-e7, when Black loses the bishop or gets mated.) **2. Rb7-f7! Bc3-d4** (2. ... Bc3xg7 3. Kf5-g5 Kh7-g8 4. Kg5-g6 Bg7-h6

5. Rf7-d7 Bh6-f8 6. Rd7-d8, and Black is lost.)

- **3. g7-g8=Q+ Kh7xg8 4. Kf5-g6 Bd4-g1 5. Rf7-f1 Bg1-h2 6. Rf1-h1 Bh2-g3 7. Rh1-h3 Bg3-d6 8. Rh3-d3 Bd6-c7 9. Rd3-d7 Bc7-a5 10. Rd7-a7 Ba5-d8 11. Ra7-a8,** White wins.

Knight vs. Bad Bishop

- Once again, we see a bishop partially restricted by his own pawns. White will use his active king to infiltrate the dark squares while his knight has more influence than the enemy bishop because the horseman is not blocked in by the pawns.

- **1. Ke5-f6 Ba6-d3 2. Kf6-e7 Bd3-b1 3. a2-a3 Bb1-e4 4. Nd4-e6+** (Black's king is forced to give way. The end is near.) **4. ... Kc7-b8 5. Ke7-d6 Be4-c2 6. Ne6-d4 Bc2-d1 7. Nd4xc6+,** and Black is lost.

205

BIG GUNS IN THE ENDGAME

These four positions illustrate the sudden shocks that can occur when major artillery remains in the ending

We're close to the end of this section on the endgame, but we're hardly at the end of everything important to know about the chess endgame. If you go on to become very interested in chess, you should get a book that specializes in explaining endgame ideas. In the meantime, we can get you started with some more examples of important techniques.

The first position shows the technique of putting a battery of rooks on your opponent's second rank. You'll hear this called "rooks on the seventh," regardless of whether the rooks are on the second or the seventh rank—what counts is that they are on the *enemy's* second rank. The great chess writer and grandmaster Aaron Nimzovich dubbed such rooks "blind

Blind Pigs

- A battery of rooks on the enemy's second rank—generally called "rooks doubled on the seventh"—is a powerful deployment. Watch how quickly Black wins in the above position.

- **1. ... Rd8-d2! 2. Ra1-b1 Rf7-f2** (Nimzovich called such rooks doubled "blind pigs.") **3. Rb1xb6 Rf2xg2+ 4. Kg1-f1 Rg2xh2 5. Rb6-b8+ Kg8-f7 6. Rb8-b7+ Kf7-f6 7. Rb7-b6+** (7. Re4-f4+ Kf6-e5) **7. ... Kf6-g5 8. Kf1-g1 Rd2-g2+ 9. Kg1-f1 Rg2-c2 10. Kf1-g1 Rh2-d2 11. Rb6-b1 Rc2xc3,** Black wins.

Queen and Pawn

- On an open board, the defending queen can make it difficult for his enemy to advance a passed pawn, especially when the defender's king blocks it.

- But remember this technique of simplifying to a won ending.

- With White to move, **1. Qd4-c4+!,** converts the game to an easily won king-and-pawn endgame because he's seen he will have the opposition.

- If it's Black's move, he keeps the draw by playing 1. ... Qf7-d5.

pigs," because they eat everything in their path!

The second example examines a position with two queens that allows White, on move, to check and force the exchange of queens, leaving a basic pawn ending that we already know, which White wins easily. The example shows that we need to be constantly alert for such possibilities that suddenly and drastically change the character of the game.

Example three again shows the sudden explosions that can rock a player when queens dominate a nearly bare board. White simultaneously sets up the threat of exchanging queens and a discovered check. Although he gives up his pawn to accomplish this double-threat, White wins in all variations. We give you some sample lines. Working out other variations for yourself will be good practice.

The final example on this spread is a great photo of how a distant passed pawn—a pawn near the edge of the board, away from other pawns—can be a winning advantage, even when queens remain in the game.

Queen Land Mines

- Endings with the powerful queens still on the board contain a lot of land mines. Black's king is badly placed in the corner.

- **1. Qa2-d5! Qd6xb4+**

- Black's also lost if he doesn't capture. Naturally, he can't exchange queens. But now

White mates in a maximum of six moves, beginning with **2. Ke4-f3!.**

- Sample tries: 2. ... Qb4-c3+ 3. Kf3-f2+ Kh1-h2 4. Qd5-g2#; 2. ... Kh1-h2 3. Qd5-h5+ Kh2-g1 4. Qh5-g5+ Kg1-f1 5. Qg5-g2+ Kf1-e1 6. Qg2-e2#.

Distant Passed Pawn

- Here White has the advantages of a distant passed pawn, an advanced king, and a centralized queen.

- If Black, to move, captures with 1. ... Qf6xa6, White simplifies into a winning king-and-pawn endgame: 2.

Qd5-d7+ Ke7-f8 3. Qd7-d6+ Qa6xd6+ 4. Kc7xd6 Kf8-f7 5. Kd6-d7 Kf7-f6 6. Kd7-e8.

- If Black plays 1. ... Qf6-c3+, then 2. Qd5-c6 Qc3-e3 (2. ... Qc3xg3 3. a6-a7) 3. Kc7-b8, and the pawn queens.

QUEEN VS. TWO PIECES

Let's look at a queen battling against a rook and minor piece in the endgame

When a queen takes on a rook and bishop or a rook and knight in the endgame, the results depend on the specific locations of the kings and the pawns—and of course, the number of pawns. We take you through two examples here, showing two positions in each ending. The first example shows off the mobility of the queen and her ability to make threats all over the board, especially with a fighting king at her side. Our second example shows a very interesting fortress-building technique by Black to draw against the queen and her pawns.

Since this is our last section on the endgame, let's summarize some tips on successful play.

Queen vs. Rook and Bishop

- Black protects his bishop by keeping his rook on the c-file. But the queen is in her element when she can make threats and check. And White's king will march into the center of Black's position.

- **1. ... Rc4-c3**

- If 1. ... f5-f4+, then 2. Kg3-h2 Kh7-h8 3. Qe7-e8+ Kh8-h7 4. Qe8-g6+ Kh7-h8 5. Qg6-f7, and the rook must move, giving up material.

- **2. Qe7-d6 Rc3-c2 3. Qd6-g6+ Kh7-h8 4. Qg6-e8+ Kh8-h7 5. Kg3-f4 Rc2-c1 6. Qe8-g6+ Kh7-h8 7. Kf4-e5 Bc8-d7 8. Qg6-b6 Bd7-c8.**

King Penetration

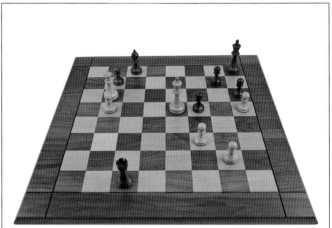

- White's king is threatening to head to f8 to double attack g7.

- White, on move, advances his king: **9. Ke5-d6 Kh8-g8 10. Qb6-e3.**

- This is the end. Now Black can't keep his rook on the c-file because if 10. ... Rc1-c2, then 11. Qe3-b3+; or if 10. ... Rc1-c4, then 11. Qe3-b3, pinning and winning. And if Black's rook leaves the c-file, then 11. Qe3-e8+ wins the bishop.

A Dozen Endgame Dos and Don'ts

1. Use your king!

2. Put your king in front of passed pawns, whether they're yours or your opponent's.

3. If you are a pawn ahead, exchange pieces, not pawns.

4. If you are a pawn down, exchange pawns, not pieces.

5. In choosing which pawn to advance, favor a pawn that doesn't face another pawn.

6. Try to make a passed pawn—if you have one, try to promote it; if your opponent has one, block it.

7. Distant passed pawns and passed pawns protected by pawns are big advantages.

8. Rooks belong behind a passed pawn, whether the pawn is yours or your opponent's.

9. Passive rooks generally lose—activate your rook, even if you have to sacrifice a pawn.

10. Bishops of opposite color increase the odds of a draw.

11. With pawns on both sides of the board, a bishop is generally better than a knight.

12. Don't block your bishop with your own pawns.

Holding the Draw

- When the action is all on one side of the board and there are few pawns remaining, the knight can be quite effective. In fact, Black can draw the position above by setting up a special kind of defensive fortress with ... g6-g5.

- **1. ... Kh7-h8 2. Kh2-g3 g6-g5 3. Kg3-f2 Nh6-f7 4. Kf2-e3 Rg7-g8 5. Qe4-c6 Kh8-g7.**

- Black has finished his fortress. (See the next photo, above.)

The Fortress

- **6. f3-f4** (If 6. Ke3-e4, then 6. ... Rg8-e8+, and White can't make progress.) **6. ... g5xf4+ 7. Ke3xf4 Rg8-f8 8. Qc6-c3+ Kg7-g6 9. Qc3-d3+ Kg6-f6 10. Qd3-a6+** (If 10. g4-g5+, Black has 10. ... Nf7xg5) **10. ... Kf6-g7.**

- Now the rook and knight hold the queen and pawn to a draw.

- **11. g4-g5 Nf7-h6+** (discovered check) **12. Kf4-g3 Nh6-f5+ 13. Kg3-h3 Rf8-h8+ 14. Kh3-g4 Rh8-f8,** draw.

MASTER OF THE ENDGAME

Let's look at a complicated ending by one of the greatest endgame players of all time

Endgame skills separate the master from the non-master—and the great master from the journeyman. Many would say that José Raúl Capablanca y Graupera of Cuba, known affectionately as "Capa" by chess fans, was the greatest player of all time. Everyone knowledgeable would hold that he was one of the best endgame players in the history of the game.

Capablanca was a chess prodigy, learning the game when he was only four by watching his father and uncle play. Nine years later, Capa beat the champion of his native Cuba in a match. Young Capa loved baseball and journeyed to Columbia University in New York City to become shortstop of its freshman team.

Queen Ending

- Both kings are safe, which is important when queens remain on the board. White has a mobile center but his rook and queen are on awkward squares.

- Black has three notable advantages. His rook controls the open c-file. He has a two-to-one queenside pawn majority. His queen, despite appearances, exercises a lot of control—particularly along the f1-a6 diagonal.

- **20. ... Nc3!** (The master's touch. Capa sees that White will soon miss his bishop.)

- **21. Bxc3 Rxc3 22. Nf3 Rfc8.** (See next photo.)

Owning the c-file

- Now Black dominates the c-file. But White couldn't have prevented this with 22. Rc1, because after 22. ... Rxc1 23. Qxc1 Qd3, one of Black's center pawns will fall.

- **23. h3** (White makes an escape square to prevent a future back-rank weakness and marks time.)

- **23. ... Nc4** (Black *discovers a double attack* on White's a-pawn.) **24. a4 Na3!** (Black blocks the a-pawn defender and attacks the white queen with the same move. See next photo.)

But he was soon swept up in the swirl of chess in New York. In 1909 Capa beat longtime U.S. champion Frank Marshall in a lopsided match. In 1921 Capa defeated Emanuel Lasker for the world championship and retained the title until 1927. Capablanca was handsome, charming, always impeccably dressed, and enjoyed the high life of his celebrity. He became an idol of the roaring twenties. He remained one of the world's best players until he died—while analyzing a chess game at the Manhattan Chess Club in New York City in 1942.

We'll once again practice the abbreviated notation, called "standard algebraic," used by most experienced players and in most books and magazines. (Most computers use the longer form, and it's never wrong to use it in your own games—it's your choice.) We're going to focus on the endgame of one of Capa's gems. Havasi vs. Capablanca, Budapest, 1929, began:

1. d4 Nf6 2. c4 e6 3. Nc3 Bb4 4. Qc2 d5 5. Nf3 c5 6. cxd5 Qxd5 7. a3 Bxc3+ 8. bxc3 Nc6 9. e3 0-0 10. Be2 cxd4 11. cxd4 b6 12. Nd2 Bb7 13. Bf3 Qd7 14. 0-0 Rac8 15. Qb1 Na5 16. Bxb7 Qxb7 17. Bb2 Qa6 18. Re1 Nd5 19. Ra2 Rc6 20. e4. (See photo below, far left.)

Missed Combination

Creating a Passed Pawn

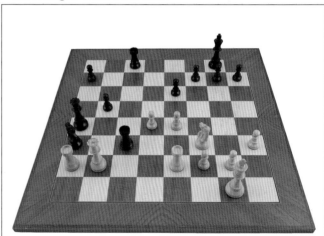

- **25. Qb2** White could also try 25. Qd1, and if 25. ... R(8)c4?!, play 26. d5!. Capa had 25. .... Qc4 or 25. ... Nc2, maintaining a secure advantage.

- **25. ... Qxa4 26. Re2** (if 26. Ra1, Black has 26. ... Qb5, escaping from the pin) **26. ... b5.** (See next photo.)

- Capa pushes his passed pawn and has a winning position. But he could end things with 26. ... Rxf3!. If 27. gxf3, then 27. ... Qd1+ 28. Kg2 Rc1. White must then trade his queen for the black rook to prevent mate.

- **27. d5** (White can't simply sit and wait for Black to advance his queenside pawns. He creates a passed pawn of his own.)

- **27. ... exd5** (Capa could also ignore White's pawn push for now and continue with 27. ... b4.)

- **28. exd5** (White sees a glimmer of hope after this recapture. Now he has a threat: 29. Qxc3 Rxc3 30. Re8, checkmate!)

- The game continued on the next two pages.

CAPABLANCA THE NATURAL

Thousands of players have gotten good at endgame play by studying the endings of "Capa"

Capablanca was one of the greatest natural players ever. He studied little (and once admitted he didn't keep a chess set handy at home). And yet Capablanca's endgame prowess is universally admired. Capablanca himself wrote: "In order to improve your game, you must study the endgame before everything else." He explained that the opening and middle game had always to be studied in relation to the endgame, while the ending can be mastered independently.

Thousands of players have improved their endgame play by studying the natural and clear logic of Capa's play in the ending. The game we're playing over together is an example.

After the twenty-eighth move by White, we've reached

Discovered Protection

Clearing the Path

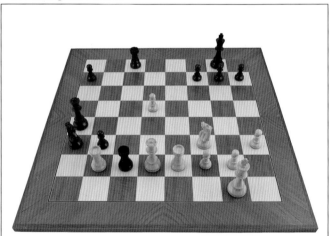

- **28. … b4** (Not only does this move bring Capa's pawn one square closer to promotion, but it clears the a4-e8 diagonal so the queen can protect against White's new threat.)

- **29. Qd2** (White immediately supports his passed pawn with his queen, trying to make her more active. Perhaps stronger resistance was offered by 29. Ra1.)

- **29. … b3** (another step closer, with tempo) **30. Rb2 Rc2.**

- To push his b-pawn farther, Capa must clear away the blockading rook.

- **31. Qe3** (White tries to mix things up. Instead, 31. Rxc2 bxc2 allows 32. … Rb8 and 33. … Rb1, and it's over.)

- **31. … Rxb2 32. Rxb2 Nc4**

- Black forks White's knight and queen. But White uses a pin to get away.

a position in which both players are hoping to advance a passed pawn. Black is a pawn up and has two *united* passed pawns. If necessary, the pawns can protect each other as they advance. With no pawns opposing them, they are potential juggernauts. White's passed pawn, while advanced, is *isolated*. It could require constant protection from White's pieces.

White's main hope in this position is the possibility of his opponent falling into a trap like the one White has just set. But the likelihood of Capablanca missing such a direct threat is extremely remote.

Komel Havasi, Capablanca's opponent in this game, was a Hungarian chess master and champion who had stood up to some of the greatest players of his day. It is only the deceptive simplicity of Capablanca's style that makes this game appear easy for Black to win. Havasi died tragically in 1945 in a Nazi forced labor camp in Austria.

Unstoppable Pawn

Capablanca's Finale

- Black's pawn reaches the eighth rank and is promoted to a queen. In one move, Black has achieved an enormous material advantage. White is lost.

- **33. Qc1 Qa3** (Naturally, not 33. ... Nxb2 34. Qxc8+, with mate to follow next move.) After 33. ... Qa3, White must retreat his rook.

- **34. Rb1 Qxc1+,** White resigns.

- After the straightforward and unavoidable 35. Rxc1 b2 36. Rb1 Rb8 37. Kf1 Na3 38. Rd1 b1=Q (see Capablanca's Finale, right), White would have to trade his rook for the new queen and be too far down in material to have any hope. Such is the effect of a promoted pawn.

THE OPERA BOX GAME

Thanks to chess notation, we can all learn from one of the most famous games in history

You are about to play over the most famous chess game in all of history. Chess notation made it possible to preserve this and thousands of other memorable games for us to learn from. Although played more than one hundred years ago, this short masterpiece continues to capture the admiration of chess players—and undoubtedly will for generations to come. Many expert players know this game by heart.

Paul Morphy was perhaps the most talented player of all time. An American born in New Orleans, he graduated from the University of Louisiana law school and passed the Louisiana bar when he was still too young to practice law. So in 1858 he took a trip to Europe, where he defeated the world's

An Opening Slip-Up

- The game opened **1. e4 e5 2. Nf3 d6 3. d4.** (D)

- The Black team so far plays soundly against the young world-beater. You may recognize that they're employing a still-used opening called the Philidor Defense. It stakes out a share of the center with two

center pawns, the queen pawn supporting the king pawn, while opening up squares for both bishops. Black is ready to develop his pieces. The Duke and the Count, consulting on the moves, may be amateurs, but they're clearly not tyros. (See next photo.)

Knights before Bishops!

- **3. ... Bg4**

- Perhaps Isouard added up (he's a Count, after all) attackers and defenders on e5 to see that it's two-to-one in White's favor. So the Black team pins the attacking knight. Logical, but it flaunts the general principle of "knights before bishops" and

gives White the opportunity to enact a clear, forcing plan to keep Black's king in the center. There are a number of better moves. Many modern players would favor developing while counterattacking with 3. ... Nf6.

- **4. dxe5 Bxf3.** (See next photo.)

best chess players, becoming recognized as the strongest player alive. (It wasn't until 1886 that there was an officially recognized world chess championship.)

While Morphy was in Paris, the Duke of Brunswick and Count Isouard, amateur chess players and admirers of the American phenomenon, invited Morphy to the Paris opera to see *The Barber of Seville*. But once settled in their private box seats, the two challenged Morphy to a game. Although we can be certain young Morphy would have rather relaxed and enjoyed the show than play two unranked amateurs,

the always soft-spoken Morphy politely consented—and we have to be grateful.

We'll use "standard algebraic" notation again. Set up your own board and pieces to play over the game below, using the photos to confirm that you have the correct position set up at each stage of the game. Below each panel, we explain the main ideas of the play.

Play over this game as many times as you want to before going on—and come back to it often. There's lots to learn from Morphy's elegant annihilation of the Duke and Count.

Attacking f7

- If first 4. ... dxe5, White would play 5. Qxd8+ Kxd8 6. Nxe5, winning the important e-pawn.

- **5. Qxf3 dxe5 6. Bc4 Nf6**

- Black develops his knight while blocking the threat of mate on f7. Black could save his b-pawn with 6. ...

Qe7 (if then 7. Qb3 Qb4+). But White could then play 7. Bg5! (7. ... Qxg5 allows 8. Qxf7+) and remain with the better game.

- **7. Qb3 Qe7** (Black's last defensive move blocks his bishop from developing.)

Pinning and Developing

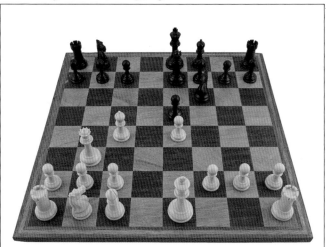

- Morphy has formed a battery with bishop and queen, renewing his attack on the traditionally weak f7 square, gaining time while Black defended. (By the way, Black couldn't have played 7. ... Qd7 because of 8. Qxb7, when White would win the rook.)

- In the game position above, White could also win the b7-pawn (but not the rook after 8. Qxb7 Qb4+). Morphy, however, has more in mind.

- **8. Nc3 c6** (to protect against 9. Qxb7) **9. Bg5.** (See next spread, first photo.)

SACRIFICE TO OPEN LINES

Morphy finds the one move—a striking sacrifice— that refutes his opponents' desperate counterthrust

In the first half of this famous game, Morphy has taken advantage of Black's ill-chosen 3. ... Bg4 in a flawless manner, gaining a strong initiative in the opening stage of the game. Black has been forced into a cramped position. Remember what the great player and chess teacher Siegbert Tarrasch, by profession a physician, wrote: "Cramped positions contain

within them the germs of defeat!"

In the next stage of the game, Morphy's opponents push a pawn in a desperate attempt to develop some play of their own. Their move 9. ... b5 has probably been overly criticized. From a practical point of view, it has an appeal. If White does not continue by sacrificing his knight, Black will get an even

Desperate Counterattack

- White is beautifully developed and ready to castle on either side.

- Black is in a snarl, hard-pressed to find a useful move. If he tries to break the pin with 9. ... h6, White plays 10. Bg5xf6, when Black must recapture with the g-pawn, since 10. ...

Qxf6 allows 11. Qxb7, trapping Black's rook. Black could then resign. After 10. gxf6, White castles long and Black remains in a tangle. So he tries a desperate queenside counterattack.

- **9. ... b5.** (See next photo.)

No Retreat!

- Black wants White to retreat his threatening bishop, taking the pressure off.

- But Morphy has an unpleasant surprise in store. Instead, Black should try 9. ... Na6 to get a piece off the back rank, even though after 10. Bxa6, his queenside pawns would

be *isolated* and *doubled*—a serious long-term weakness. If Black resorts to 9. ... h6 10. Bxf6 gxf6 *(not 10. ... Qxf6 11. Qxb7)*, Morphy would play 11. 0-0-0, with a winning position.

- **10. Nxb5! cxb5 11. Bxb5+ Nbd7.** (See next photo.)

game. And many players would be unwilling to sacrifice without seeing a clear and quick repayment on their investment. But they are up against the best player in the world. Black's ninth move is all it takes for the brilliant Louisianian to demolish his royal opposition and get back to watching the opera.

It's true that it can be difficult to "sit on" a bad position when your opponent seems to have all the options. But the Duke and Count should refrain from lashing out, which only serves to create more weaknesses in their position. Instead, they should try to find moves that keep their position together, making it as hard as possible for White to tear it apart. At some time or another, every player gets into such a game. A tenacious defender can sometimes actually win from an inferior position because his attacker runs out of patience and becomes the one who cracks, making an impulsive and unsound move.

Castling Long

- **12. 0-0-0**

- White castles queenside, also called *castling long*, bringing his king to safety and his rook to the open file. Morphy has sacrificed material to keep Black's king stuck in the center in a jumble of his own men. Both black minor pieces are immobilized by pins. In contrast, White's king is safely tucked away, and all of his other pieces, except his rook on h1, join in the attack. Now watch how Morphy throws this last log on the fire!

- **12. ... Rd8.** (See next photo.)

The Final Reserve

- Black has added a defender to the pinned knight on d7. But ...

- **13. Rxd7! Rxd7 14. Rd1**

- Yes, Morphy trades a rook for a knight, a loss of the Exchange, but he can recapture the Exchange at any time, since his bishop applies an absolute pin to Black's rook. But much more importantly, Morphy has eliminated a key defender, the Black knight on d7, while bringing his own last piece of artillery front and center into the attack.

- **14. ... Qe6.** (See next spread, first photo.)

217

SURPRISING BEAUTY

Morphy unleashes the game-winning combination, employing a striking queen sacrifice to deflect the key defender

After fourteen moves, Black's king is still stuck in the center, unable to move. White, on the other hand, is safely castled. White's queen and queen rook dominate the center of the board. Black offers an exchange of queens, hoping to return a piece and, although two pawns down, stay in the game.

But the American champ is about to force the logical outcome of his previous play. In the position shown in the next game-photo, try to find the forced win Morphy sees. Move the pieces around on your board as you try different moves. If you can find the solution, give yourself a gold star! But don't be ashamed if you can't solve the puzzle. Morhpy's final combination is a thing of surprising beauty.

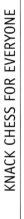
False Hopes

- With their last move, the Duke and Count dream of finally developing their king's bishop and then castling out of the center into safety. If they manage this, they could resist for a while. But Morphy's next blow shakes them from their fantasy.

- We can sense that Black's king is in mortal danger, but how does the great Morphy finish him off?

- **15. Bxd7+! Nxd7 16. Qb8+!!** (See next spread, first photo.)

Deflection Sacrifice

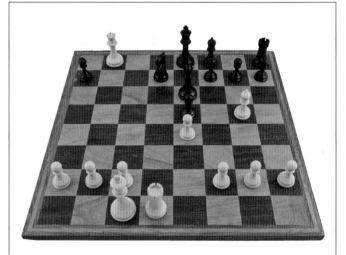

- Inspired! This show-stopping *undermining* deflection sacrifice forces Black's knight to leave his post—blocking the d-file, to capture the white queen. The fat lady of the off-the-stage opera is about to sing, bringing the curtain down on Black.

- **16. ... Nxb8 17. Rd8#.** (See next photo.)

218

Checkmate

- The black king is check-mated on his home square, never having moved. Materially, Morphy is down by the lopsided tally of 25–15 (when comparing material we ignore kings). Indeed, he's left with only two pieces besides his king—the ones necessary to checkmate!

- His army performed like a runner completing the perfect marathon—nothing was left in reserve. This game has been universally admired for more than 150 years as an elegant work of genius. Since 1858, all chess players have dreamed of playing such a game.

Paul Morphy taught us all some very important principles:

1. Get our pieces into play rapidly onto good squares—chess players call this developing quickly.

2. Castle early.

3. When an opponent violates these principles, look for a way to punish him.

4. Chess rewards a combination of creativity and sound logic.

219

ENDLESSLY FASCINATING

Some great games—played decades ago—still inspire controversy and new ideas

One of the endless attractions of chess is that some games seem to present never-ending puzzles. This very famous game by Bobby Fischer falls into that category.

At the age of fifteen, Fischer won the international grandmaster title, the highest awarded in chess, by finishing among the top half-dozen players in the world at the 1958 Interzonal

tournament in the city of Portoroz in what is now Slovenia. Published in 1969, Fischer's book, *My 60 Memorable Games,* became an instant chess classic, known for its objectivity and careful analysis. The second game annotated in the book was Fischer's win in Portoroz against Danish grandmaster Bent Larsen, eight years Bobby's senior and one of the world's great players.

Profile of a Dragon

- Black chooses the Dragon Variation of the Sicilian, a defense that takes its name from the similarity of Black's pawn structure to the outline of the mythical beast. The fire the Dragon breathes may be the power of the bishop that will be fianchettoed on g7, applying force down the long a1-h8 diagonal, which cuts through the center. In addition, Black enjoys an extra pawn in the center and the half-open c-file for a rook.

- **6. Be3 Bg7 7. f3 0-0 8. Qd2 Nc6 9. Bc4.** (See next photo.)

Tabia

- An important *tabia*, or starting formation of the opening battle. White has lined up a queen-bishop battery, threatening Bh6 to trade off Black's Dragon bishop, which would leave Black weak on the dark squares. White has bolstered his center with f3, developed his other bishop to menace f7, and stands ready to castle queenside and launch a kingside pawn storm. (See next photo.)

- **9. ... Nxd4 10. Bxd4 Be6 11. Bb3 Qa5 12. 0-0-0 b5.**

The publishing of that game, more than any other single contest, sullied the reputation of a then very popular defense, the Sicilian Dragon—a variation of the Sicilian Defense in which Black fianchettoes his king's bishop. Fischer's opposite-side castling and kingside pawn storm seemed like an automatic refutation. Fischer himself wrote that he "had it down to a science: pry open the KR-file, sac, sac, mate!" (Fischer was using chess-player slang for *sacrifice*; "KR" refers to king rook.)

Now, fifty years after the game, another of the greatest world champions, Garry Kasparov, has written that Fischer's analysis of an unplayed variation—moves Larsen could have played but didn't—was faulty. This was big news. But there remain mysteries in this game.

Bobby Fischer vs. Bent Larsen, 1958, can teach you a lot about attacking, defending, and formulating a middle game plan. Like the other classic contests we show you in this book, it will teach you more as you play and replay it over on your own board. You may even unravel some secrets no one else has found!

We'll use standard algebraic notation. The game began: **1. e4 c5 2. Nf3 d6 3. d4 cxd4 4. Nxd4 Nf6 5. Nc3 g6.**

Attacks on the Wings

- If 12. ... Bxb3, White should disregard the general middle game principle of capturing toward the center with pawns and play 13. cxb3, following up with Kb1, safe behind the pawns.

- **13. Kb1 b4 14. Nd5 Bxd5 15. Bxd5** (15. exd5 was stronger, switching from a flank attack to play down the king file.)

- **15. ... Rac8** (15. ... Nxd5!) **16. Bb3 Rc7** (To advance his a-pawn into the attack, Black must first protect that pawn so he can get his queen out of the way.) **17. h4.** (See next photo.)

Prying Open the File

- White threatens to pry open the h-file, yielding him a direct highway to the Black king for White's rook and queen.

- **17. ... Qb5** (Black is now ready for ... a5, but White is first!) **18. h5 Rfc8**

- If Black plays 18. ... Nxh5, White wins with 19. Bxg7 Kxg7 20. g4!. And if 18. ... gxh5, Fischer intends 19. g4 hxg4 20. fxg4! Nxe4 21. Qh2!, when White's attack is a steamroller.

- **19. hxg6 hxg6 20. g4 a5.** (See next spread, first photo.)

STILL A FIGHT

"Before the endgame," Siegbert Tarrasch wrote, "the gods have placed the middle game"

After twenty moves of Fischer vs. Larsen, Black is on the defensive but is not lost. In fact, the final third of the game contains ideas that are being debated to this day! Keep in mind that these two great players are not examining their moves in a laboratory atmosphere free of stress. They're in a mental battle that will determine who will go on to play

for the world championship! Their hearts pound, their concentration is intense, a crowd of spectators hangs on every move, and the players are, after all, human.

It's a very useful general rule that when Black plays the Sicilian Defense and reaches an endgame without suffering a serious setback, he is often better. But, as Dr. Tarrasch so

Delicate Balance

- **21. g5**

- Black's knight is one of his best kingside defenders. White's pawn-push chases the knight away from its ideal defensive square—f6, where it controls the center while guarding h7. Black moves the knight to block the dangerous h-file.

- **21. ... Nh5 22. Rxh5!**

- But White sacrifices the Exchange to shatter Black's defenses, reasoning that the game won't be decided by a material count or endgame, but by a decisive mating attack. (See next photo.)

Championship Disagreement

- **22. ... gxh5?** (This tips the balance strongly in White's favor. Instead, as Kasparov has shown (see sidebar, above), the *in-between move* 22. ... Bxd4! was better, keeping Black in the game.)

- **23. g6 e5 24. gxf7+ Kf8 25. Be3 d5!**

- This valiant try in a terrible position blocks the diagonal and sets a trap: If 26. Bxd5?, Black has 26. ... Rxc2!, when it's Black who has a bit of an advantage!.

- **26. exd5! Rxf7 27. d6 Rf6 28. Bg5.** (See next photo.)

memorably put it," Before the endgame, the gods have placed the middle game." And this middle game may cut short the need for an endgame, because both players attack.

When the kings are castled on opposite sides, normally the side whose attack breaks through first wins.

Although Black was the first to cross the center line with his pawn storm, his attack was slower than White's. Black has had to resort to slow maneuvers to advance his a-pawn. White's attack looks to be breaking through, but the situation on the board is not clear.

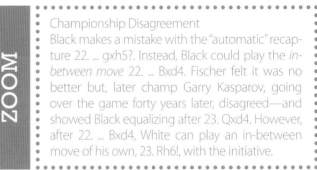
No Way Out

- **28. ... Qb7** (Fischer pointed out 28. ... Qd7 29. Qd5! Qf7—not 29. ... Rf7 30. Be7+!—30. Bxf6, winning material.)

- **29. Bxf6 Bxf6 30. d7 Rd8 31. Qd6+, Black resigns.**

- White forces mate in three: 31. ... Kg7 32. Rg1+ Kh8 33. Qxf6+ Kh7 34. Qg7#.

- But White had an even better move. See the photo in the next panel, which shows the position after 30. ... Rd8. Can you find the best move?

Quicker Mate

- The quicker mate is 31. Qh6+!. Now Black mates in only two. (Yes, mating one move earlier makes it a better move, but the result is the same—Fischer won.) 31. ... Ke7 (31. ... Bg7 is worse—32. Qd6#) 32. Qh7+ Kf8 33. Qf7#.

- A classic Bobby Fischer game from his teens. White was never in any trouble, and—even though he was playing one of the best players in the world—Fischer makes it all look easy and almost preordained.

KASPAROV ON THE ATTACK

Garry Kasparov is the most famous chess world champion since Bobby Fischer, and deservedly so

Garry Kasparov, the highest-rated chess player of all time, was born in the Soviet-controlled nation of Azerbaijan in 1963, and became the youngest-ever undisputed chess world champion by defeating Anatoly Karpov in 1985. Then in 1993, Kasparov broke with the world chess federation and for the first time since the initial official world championship

in 1886, established a rival championship crown. Kasparov continued to hold a world title until 2000.

Despite being one of a handful of players to be considered the best ever, he became the first world champion to lose a match (a series of games) to a computer when in 1997 IBM's "Deep Blue" beat him. That same year, Kasparov played the

Scotch Game

- In this position, play continued: **4. Nxd4 Nf6 5. Nxc6 bxc6 6. e5.**

- White's last pawn advance chases Black's knight away from his post in the center. With **6. ... Qe7,** Black pins and attacks White's e-pawn, but White's **7. Qe2** defends

while breaking the pin, so Black's knight has to move.

- After the moves **7. ... Nd5 8. c4 Ba6,** Black pins and attacks White's c-pawn, which now can't capture the knight without exposing the white queen. (See the next photo.)

Pins and Fianchettoes

- White calmly plays **9. b3,** protecting his pawn. Now when he moves his queen, the black knight will be threatened. Black replies **9. ... g5,** with two ideas in mind: He creates support for his knight to move to f4, and he makes g7 available for his bishop. But the pawn push weakens his kingside

squares—and can't be taken back!

- **10. g3.** White secures f4 and gives his light-square bishop some moves.

- **10. ... Bg7 11. Bb2.** Both sides have fianchettoed their dark-square bishops on the long diagonal.

white pieces in the game below in Linares, Spain, the annual site of one of the strongest chess tournaments in the world. Kasparov's opponent was the Bosnian superstar Predrag Nikolic.

Kasparov plays the first three moves we recommend in Chapter 9 as your opening for White against 1. ... e5. He varies from our repertoire on move four by playing the Scotch Game instead of gambiting a pawn. (If you like the feel of his preference, give it a try in your own games!)

Using standard (short-form) notation, the game began **1. e4 e5 2. Nf3 Nc6 3. d4 exd4.**

Castling into It

- Now Black tempts fate with **11. ... 0-0.** He should not rush into this, since White has the makings of an attack against Black's weakened kingside. Instead, Black should keep open his option to castle queenside.

- After **12. Nd2,** and Black responds with another questionable move, **12. ... f6.** White immediately plays **13. Qh5!,** bringing his most powerful piece to Black's weakened kingside. As Kasparov foresaw on move nine, he gains a tempo because Black must now see to his threatened knight. (See the next photo.)

Ignoring the Threat

- With **13. ... Nb4,** Black threatens to fork the white king and rook with ... Nc2+. But White ignores this threat, continuing his attack with **14. h4!.**

- Now Black can't follow through with the fork because of 14. ... Nc2+ 15. Kd1 Nxa1 16. hxg5!, when Black can't survive the open lines and White's pawn storm.

- **14. ... g4.** Instead, Black should consider 14. ... Qe8, trying to *trade off the attacker* to ease the pressure on his king. **15. Kd1!.** (See the next spread, first photo.)

225

SAFE IN THE CENTER

Kasparov sees that he can switch from a kingside attack to an easily won endgame

At the game's midpoint, White's king stands in the center, and Black is castled. Black, however, is the one in trouble. To begin with, his knight now has no safe moves, and White threatens 16. a3, attacking it. Although castled, Black's king is very unsafe behind his distorted line of kingside pawns.

White's bishop on b2, along with his pawn on e5, pressures the Black defenses on the long diagonal. White's queen attacks the unprotected pawn on g4. At the same time, White's queen pressures h7, which currently is defended only once. So if the queen gets help, it will be bad for the black king. That makes White's future Bd3 the elephant in the room. Once Black's knight no longer controls d3, White's

The Battle for d3

- Note that White guards c2, so the fork is no longer threatened, and Black is left with an even more porous kingside pawn cover.

- Black plays **15. ... c5** to give his knight a retreat square.

- After **16. a3 Nc6 17. Bd3,** White pushes back Black's

one aggressive piece and develops his own last undeveloped piece, his king's bishop, putting even more pressure on Black's kingside. Black is running out of defensive options.

- **17. f5 18. Bxf5 Bxe5 19. Re1.** (See next photo.)

Pinning and Simplifying

- Black captured White's advanced pawn, keeping material even, but White immediately pins the black bishop to its queen.

- **19. ... d6 20. Be4** (Now Black's knight, hoping to get to d4, is also pinned! White has a winning position. There is black material

lying around for him to pick up, allowing White to transition into a clearly won endgame.)

- **20. ... Bb7 21. Qxg4+ Qg7 22. Bd5+ Kh8 23. Bxe5** (White *simplifies* into a won ending. See next photo.)

bishop can occupy d3 to add another powerful attacker to the assault of h7, normally the weakest point in Black's camp when he castles kingside.

White's king, on the other hand, is not threatened. Indeed, if a transition is made from this complex middle game to an endgame, White's monarch is well positioned to step into the reduced fray.

This idea of a transition is important here in spite of the vicious attack in progress. A defender often tries to relieve the pressure on his position by trading off material. Indeed,

sometimes this important defensive technique is successful. But sometimes by reducing forces, the defender gives the attacker a chance to switch from a middle game attack to a winning endgame. If the attacker doesn't see a clear way to checkmate his opponent, this transition to a simpler winning position can be the best way to win.

Chess is a game that requires a player to have a plan, but also to be flexible and alert to changing opportunities!

Isolated Pawns

- **23. ... dxe5** (Now all of Black's pawns are isolated, and his c-pawns are doubled as well. But he had no choice. He can't recapture with his queen because then 24. Rxe5 would leave him hopelessly down in material.)

- **24. Qxg7+ Kxg7** (White has forced the queens off, removing chances for Black to complicate the game he's losing.)

- **25. Ne4.** (See next photo.)

Hopeless Endgame

- White attacks the c5-pawn, which can't be defended.

- **25. ... Rad8 26. Nxc5** (Black doesn't have time to play ... Rxf2 because his bishop is threatened. He has to retreat it or lose it next to Nxb7.) **26. ... Bc8 27. Ra2.**

- White defends his f2-pawn and will double his rooks on the d-file. Nikolic, himself a world-class player, has had enough. He's two pawns down, with weaknesses all over the board.

- Black resigns.

227

RESOURCES

One of the many great things about chess is that it can be played anywhere, by anyone, with minimal equipment. It's a game that can be played in your home with a cheap plastic set on a vinyl board, or with elegant wooden chessmen at a prestigious tournament in an exotic locale. No matter how you want to play chess, there are plenty of resources that both casual players and those who take chess more seriously can use to increase their enjoyment of the game.

Where to Play

The backbone of the chess community is the local chess club. These organizations give both casual and competitive players a place to meet, socialize, and play chess with fellow enthusiasts in the area. Most clubs offer tournaments officially sanctioned by the United States Chess Federation. Such tournaments give you the chance to get an official rating to see how you rank against all other competitive chess players in the U.S.! Some chess clubs sell equipment. They're also a great place to make contacts with your local chess community; it's always nice to have someone nearby whom you can call up when you feel like playing a game or two, or who might be willing to travel to a tournament with you.

Most countries also have a governing body for chess, usually known as a federation. For instance, the United States Chess Federation (USCF) is the governing body for chess in the United States. Like most national federations, the USCF sanctions tournaments, organizes national events, and sets the rules for chess throughout the country. Membership in the USCF is required to play in official tournaments. You are welcome to join. USCF benefits can include an official monthly magazine, the right to play in official tournaments and receive an official rating, and access to online news and information. From the USCF, online or by phone, you can also get the contact information for official chess clubs near you in the U.S. See the USCF's contact information on page 229.

The body responsible for international chess affairs is the World Chess Federation, also known by the French name Fédération Internationale des Échecs, or its acronym, FIDE. These federations can provide a wealth of information on how to become more involv[ed] the chess community. If you're outside the U.S., you can find in[formation on] most national chess federations from FIDE.

If you're a competitive person, or just want to play against the [best] players you can find, you'll eventually want to try participating [in a] chess tournament. Again, your local chess club is probably the [best] way to get started. Most clubs organize small tournaments w[ith a] friendly atmosphere. You might play one game at each meetin[g over] several weeks, or play a few rapid games in a single night. Club [tour]naments are a great way to get a feel for what tournament che[ss is] like, and playing in them will earn you a chess rating that will a[llow] you to play in larger events. The biggest chess tournaments at[tract] hundreds or even thousands of players and offer large cash p[rizes.]

and trophies to the winners of each section. Players of different ratings can play in different sections, allowing participants of many different skill levels the chance to win prizes.

Would you rather play chess from the comfort of your own home? You can still do more than just play with friends and family. Correspondence chess allows players from across the country and around the world to play against each other without ever meeting. Moves are sent using postcards or e-mail, and games can take months (or even years) to play. There are even national and international tournaments that take place entirely by correspondence.

Using Your Computer to Play Chess

Computers have become an important resource in modern chess. They help us analyze our games, improve our play, and find new opponents to match wits against. If you have a home computer, you'll undoubtedly find a chess-related use for it.

There are two ways to play chess on a computer. The first is to use the computer itself as an opponent. Computer programs are quite powerful. But don't let that scare you; there are dozens of computer programs designed for casual players. Many of these programs will allow you to customize your computer opponent to your ability level, so that you can find a virtual opponent that's right for you.

Of course, no computer program can replace the thrill of playing with another person. If you have an Internet connection, your computer offers you a world full of new opponents ready to play chess online at any of dozens of sites devoted to the game. Some places, like Yahoo! Chess, are designed with the casual player in mind, while others such as the Internet Chess Club cater to more experienced players. Other sites offer correspondence games. Some of the more serious sites charge fees for playing, but most will at least let you try a free trial first. If you're just interested in playing a fun game now and then, you may be better served by a free site rather than one that charges you for features you don't plan on using.

Sources of Information for Playing Chess

Your greatest resource for chess information will be a local chess club, if you have one. There will be experienced players who can answer all of your questions, help you decide what equipment or resources you'll need, and help you get more involved in the chess community. Even if you don't intend to become a member of the club or play competitively, it's worth making the occasional trip to keep in touch with fellow chess enthusiasts and find out if there are any local chess events you might want to participate in.

If you don't have a local club, or you'd like a more official answer to your questions, you should contact your regional or national chess federation. These groups will be happy to answer your questions, and can often provide you with additional resources and information that local clubs can't provide.

Chess Federations

United States Chess Federation (USCF), PO Box 3967, Crossville, TN 38557; (931) 787-1234. www.uschess.org.

Fédération Internationale des Échecs, www.fide.com.

Clubs and Tournaments

USCF Clubs & Tourneys, main.uschess.org/content/blogsection/18/95/. Search for clubs or tournaments by state.

Internet Chess Sites

Board Games on Yahoo! Games, games.yahoo.com/board-games. A site designed for casual chess players—a good place to start online play.

Internet Chess Club (ICC), www.chessclub.com. A dedicated chess server catering to strong tournament players. Watch out!

Improving Your Chess

If you want to become a stronger chess player, there are numerous resources that can help you get there. Studying chess is a challenging but rewarding journey. Not only will studying improve your play and your results, it leads to a greater understanding of chess that can help you better appreciate the battles waged by history's gre players.

Books and Software

The best single chess course available is the *Comprehensive C Course,* edited by three-time U.S. champion Lev Alburt. Alburt international grandmaster, world-famous for his teaching technic His course is available many places online and in large bookst Although his course is made up of a number of volumes, each b stands alone and will provide the best of chess instruction. Of co there are many other good books on chess. Your local club mem will be happy to offer opinions.

Computer software and instructional DVDs are also available. computer programs can also analyze your games for you, merci pointing out flaws in your play—humbling, but useful!

Grandmaster Lev Alburt's seven-volume
*Comprehensive Chess Course:
from Beginning to Master*

231

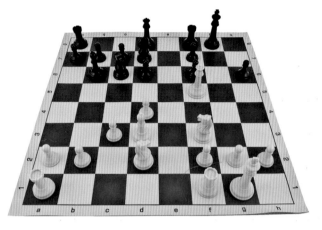

Finding an Instructor

Perhaps the most effective way to improve at chess is by taking lessons with a well-thought-of teacher. Taking lessons from a very accomplished teacher and player can save you years of study on your own and get you off to the right start. Two of the most renowned teachers in the U.S. are:

Grandmaster Lev Alburt, e-mail: GMLevAlburt@aol.com
Bruce Pandolfini, e-mail: chessiac2@aol.com

Your local club may be able to recommend someone as well. Of course, never miss a chance to go over your games with a stronger player. Many players at your local club will do this just to be helpful if you ask them.

Author Information

Please feel welcome to visit the author at www.allawrence.com

Sources of Information for Improving Your Chess

Instructional Web Sites

About Chess, chess.about.com

ChessCafe, www.chesscafe.com

Chess News

ChessBase, www.chessbase.com

The Week in Chess, www.chesscenter.com/twic/twic.html

Chess Publications

Chess Life, main.uschess.org/content/blogcategory/218/365/. The official magazine of the USCF.

New in Chess, www.newinchess.com

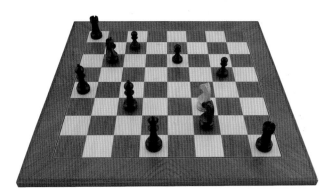

GLOSSARY

Backward Pawn: A pawn that lags behind its neighboring pawns so that they cannot defend it.

Bad Bishop: A B restricted by its own men, especially pawns.

Battery: Two or more long-range pieces lined up along one file, rank, or diagonal.

Bishop: Minor piece that moves diagonally; abbreviated "B," and worth approximately three pawns.

Bishop Pair: Ownership of the two Bs, rather than N and B or two Ns.

Bishops of Opposite Color: A situation where each player has one bishop, traveling on different color squares.

Black: Darker army that moves after White, can be any color.

Blitz Chess: Fast chess timed by a clock, frequently giving each player five minutes for the entire game.

Candidate Moves: the moves being seriously considered by a player on move.

Castling: One move that relocates both a player's K and R, bringing the K into safety and R into the action.

Center: The e4, d4, e5, and d5 squares, important to control.

Check: A move that attacks the K.

Checkmate: The goal and end of the game, when one side's king is in check and can't escape.

Chessboard: A checkered board, with 64 alternating light and dark squares, eight squares on a side.

Chess Clock: Really two timers connected to keep track of each player's elapsed time during a game.

Combination: A forced series of moves with a central idea intended to gain an advantage.

Correspondence Chess: Chess by mail or email, allowing lots time to think.

Development: Getting pieces off their original squares and rea for battle.

Diagonal: A slanted row of squares of the same color.

Doubled Pawns: Two friendly pawns on the same file, frequent weakness because they cannot defend each other.

Doubled Rooks: Two friendly rooks on the same file, making a powerful *battery.*

Draw: A tie game, scored 1/2-1/2.

Endgame: The third stage of a chess game, when few pieces remain and passed pawns take on great importance.

En Passant: French for "in passing," a special move capturing an enemy pawn that has just taken its initial two-move option.

En Prise: French for "in take," an attacked, undefended piece.

Exchange/exchange: Trading a minor piece for a more valuable R is "winning the Exchange"; an equal trade is an "exchange."

Fianchetto: Development of a B to g2, g7, b2, or b7.

Fifty-move rule: When there has been no capture or pawn move for fifty moves, a player can claim a draw.

Files: The eight vertical rows of squares.

Forfeit: Loss of a game by overstepping the time limit or some other rule violation.

Gambit: A *sacrifice* (normally a pawn in the opening) for some advantage, normally initiative.

Initiative: The ability to dictate play.

Isolated pawn: A pawn with no friendly pawn neighbors to protect it.

Kibitzer: An annoying person who comments on other people's games while in progress.

King: The most important chess piece, abbreviated "K."

King Safety: Crucial principle of sound play--keep your king safe!

Kingside: The half of the board from the e-file to the h-file.

Knight: A minor piece and the only leaping chessman, abbreviated "N."

Long Diagonal: The two eight-square diagonals, one dark and one light, that run from the corners through the center of the board.

Long-range Pieces: Qs, Rs, and Bs, which can travel an entire open line in one move.

Major Pieces: Qs and Rs, potentially controlling more squares than any other pieces.

Match: a series of games played between two players, as a opposed to a *tournament* of three or more players.

Middlegame: the second of three stages of a complete chess game, in which the real battle normally begins.

Minor Pieces: Bs and Ns.

Open File: A file with no pawns on it.

Opening: First of three stages of a complete chess game, when the pieces are developed to bear on the center.

OTB: Over-the-board play, when two players sit across from each other, as opposed to correspondence or online play.

Outpost: A piece in enemy territory that can't be attacked by a pawn.

Passed Pawn: A pawn with no enemy pawns on adjacent files to stop its advance.

Patzer: Polite slang for a weak player, also a "fish."

Pawn: The footsoldiers of chess, eight on each side; three equal approximately a minor piece.

Pawn Grabber: A player who snatches material with disregard for the consequences, a victim of many traps.

Pawn Storm: An attack on the enemy position spearheaded by two or more pawns.

Pawn Structure: The placement of the pawns, the backbone of a position.

Perpetual Check: An inescapable series of checks not leading to checkmate, making the game a draw.

Pieces: Ks, Qs, Bs, Ns, and Rs are pieces; pawns are not pieces.

Promotion: When a pawn reaches the opposite side of the board, it must be exchanged for any piece, normally a queen.

Queen: A major piece worth approximately rook, knight, and pawn; abbreviated "Q."

Queenside: The half of the board from the d-file to the a-file.

Rank: The horizontal rows of squares on the chessboard.

Rating: The numerical evaluation of a tournament player's results, the higher the better, earned by playing in USCF events.

Resignation: Giving up in the face of certain loss.

Rook: A major piece, generally worth a minor piece and two pawns, abbreviated "R."

Sacrifice: Giving up material in hopes of forcing an advantage.

Simul: Short for "simultaneous exhibition," in which a chess expert plays a number of opponents at the same time.

Smothered Mate: Checkmate by a knight against a king that is blocked in by his own men.

Stalemate: A drawn position resulting from the side on move having no legal move available but not being in check.

Staunton Design: The standard design of chess sets used in all official contests.

Strategy: Long-term planning in chess.

Tactics: A forced series of moves taking advantage of a short-term opportunity.

Touch Move: When you touch a chessman without first saying "Adjust" (or the French *"j'adoube"*), you must move it if it has a legal move.

USCF: United States Chess Federation, governing body of chess in the U.S. and the membership organization for chess players.

Variations: Possible lines of play in a chess game.

White: The chess army that moves first—it can be any color, but is always the lighter-colored army.

Woodpusher: A friendly term for a chess player, especially a non-expert.

INDEX

INDEX